EVIDENCE AND COMMENTARY
Historical Source Books

SERIES EDITORS:
C. M. D. Crowder, M.A., D.Phil.
L. Kochan, M.A., Ph.D.

THE REVOLUTIONS
OF 1848–49

The Revolutions
of 1848-49

EDITED BY

FRANK EYCK
University of Calgary

OLIVER & BOYD
EDINBURGH

Published 1972 by
OLIVER & BOYD,
Tweeddale Court,
14 High Street,
Edinburgh EH1 1YL
A division of Longman Group Limited

Introduction, text as printed, final comments, bibliography
© Frank Eyck

ISBN   0 05 002536 8 (Paperback)
          0 05 002537 6 (Hardback)

Printed in Great Britain by
Cox & Wyman Ltd, London, Fakenham and Reading

CONTENTS

CONTENTS

GENERAL EDITORS' PREFACE

HISTORICAL WRITING IS based on the control of evidence and commentary. Everything that has happened in the past is potentially historical evidence, and it therefore follows that the historian must apply rigorous selection if his story is to have intelligible form. The inroads of time and common sense greatly reduce the quantity of evidence that is effectively available; but what is left still demands discernment, if its presentation is not to be self-defeating in volume and variety. Even the residue left from this process of irrational and rational refinement does not tell its own story. Documents may speak for themselves, but they say different things to different listeners. The historian's second task is commentary, by means of which he completes the interpretation of the evidence which he has previously selected. Here he makes explicit the insights which have guided his choice of what to include and what to omit. Here he may go beyond what have hitherto been accepted as the common-sense limits of historical territory; the history of public events is extended to the history of private thoughts and beyond this to the historical analysis of instinctive, unreasoned attitudes, and to the gradations of man's experience between these extremes. By this extension of its range history as a discipline has moved some way to meet sociology, borrowing some of the sociologist's methods to do so.

As a result of the processes by which the historian has become increasingly self-conscious and self-critical students are introduced nowadays not only to the conclusions drawn from new historical exploration, but to the foundations on which these conclusions rest. This has led in turn to the proliferation of collections of historical evidence for senior students, mainly documentary evidence of a familiar kind rather than the visual and aural records which are made available to younger age-groups.

The question has already been asked whether any further series of this kind is needed. The volumes to be included in this series will effectively prompt an affirmative answer by their choice of significant subjects which, as they accumulate, will provide the basis for comparative study. Each title will authoritatively present sufficient material to excite but not exhaust the curiosity of the serious student. The passages chosen for inclusion must often abbreviate the original documents; but the aim has been to avoid a collection of unconnected snippets. The necessary framework of interpretation is provided, but the student still has the opportunity to form his own judgements and pursue his own insights. A modest critical apparatus and bibliography and an editorial conclusion will, we hope, direct readers beyond these selections to seek further evidence for use in constructing their own commentary.

CHRISTOPHER CROWDER
LIONEL KOCHAN

INTRODUCTION

No TWELVE-MONTH PERIOD between 1815 and 1914 in Europe can compete in intensity, variety, extent and lasting effect with that which began with the revolution in France at the end of February 1848. The revolutions of 1848–49 threatened not only the established national, but also the international order. This was due to their twin principles of representative government and nationalism. In Germany and Italy the demand was not only for increased popular participation in government but also for the right of the people to form a new state, the right of self-determination. Representative government and national self-determination were two sides of a coin. They were both combated by Metternich, the Austrian chancellor, whose ideas dominated the European continent between the Vienna settlement of 1815 and the revolutions of 1848. Metternich, who had witnessed the French revolutionary and Napoleonic wars, was determined to secure for Europe a period of peace, order and consolidation after all the turmoils of the previous age. This policy entailed not only the attempt to maintain the frontiers laid down at Vienna, but also a coordinated effort to prevent the spread of revolutionary movements and thus, if necessary, to intervene in the internal affairs of countries affected. As France did not pursue a consistent policy over the 1815–48 period as a whole, Britain, particularly under Palmerston, was the main country to be at times openly critical of the policy of the Eastern Powers, Austria, Russia and Prussia.

The reasons for the outbreak of the revolutions, in France, Germany, Austria, Italy and various parts of the Habsburg Monarchy, were mixed and varied and will never cease to give rise to debate among historians. On the whole, the controversy is mainly between those who emphasise economic, and those who stress other—principally political—aspects above all.

Generally it may be said that the Metternich system was rigid and did not provide the flexibility necessary for sufficient change, that it bought present stability at the risk of future explosion. With the historian's hindsight, the timing of the outbreak is not surprising. Something like a generation had been spanned since the end of the Napoleonic wars. Although the turmoil and the ravages of the 1789–1815 period left a deep impression on all those who passed through them, more

I

recent experiences were beginning to overshadow it and to many
Robespierre and Napoleon were merely names in history books. There
was a mounting feeling even in circles around courts and governments
that too high a price was being paid for peace and order under the
Metternich system. The Chancellor himself, who was in his mid-
seventies in 1848, was increasingly out of touch with what was going
on. A similar fate overtook Louis Philippe, the King of the French,
whose style and policies had broken new ground in the 1830's.
In Prussia, Frederick William IV had not fulfilled, and indeed
could not have fulfilled, more than a part of the often contradictory
hopes and expectations his accession to the throne in 1840 had aroused.

Not only at the highest political and diplomatic, but also at the social
level, the Governments of the three Eastern Powers and of France—the
four continental Great Powers—had not been able to react quickly
enough to new developments. With the construction and rapid development of railways and the spread of industrialisation, the rising class of
capitalist entrepreneurs was eager for a share of political power which
the social system, for instance in a country like Prussia, largely denied
them. In many ways, the base of the old order in Europe was becoming
too narrow. There were too many critics, from moderate to radical, too
many discontented. It is true that the opposition was heterogeneous,
that it consisted of elements whose interests and ideas were totally
opposed to each other, that many of its aims were vague. This was no
disadvantage when it came to mounting the barricades in February and
March, because the Governments were too stunned to attempt a political
dialogue there and then. But the heterogeneity of the opposition does
help to explain the apparent contradiction between the ease with which
the revolution succeeded in February and March, and the later dis-
appointments of the party of movement.

Barricades and revolutions, like international wars, generally lead to
polarisation. There appear to be only two sides. Yet this was less the
case after the revolution even than before, and the division into the forces
of conservatism and of movement was far less clear-cut before 1848
than was made to appear afterwards. For one thing, the Governments
had often acted as innovators, as the Prussian foundation of the
Zollverein shows. There was little the authorities of largely new states,
like Bavaria or Baden in Germany, could conserve; they had to build
up something new. Furthermore, there were varying opposing coalitions
on different issues. While in general the churches added their sanction
to the state, there were serious conflicts between state and church,
for instance both in Prussia and in Bavaria, which forced the Catholic
Church into the role of an opposition. And in Italy, the new Pope
elected in 1846, Pius IX, was considered by many as the potential
leader of an Italian national state. However much church dignitaries,

both Catholic and Protestant, in many parts of Europe may have supported the existing order, the Pope himself certainly did not begin his long reign as an ally of the established order. In Austria, many senior civil servants were disenchanted with the Metternich system. In view of the not very advanced state of political life, the opposition was partly found in the Government service. In the countries affected by the revolutions, there was as always a large body of public opinion which was neutral except where its own interests were affected. A strong conservatism was widespread among many sections of the population, for instance among craftsmen who wanted to maintain or reintroduce the guild system or to limit freedom of movement of persons to protect their own interests, as in Southern Germany. Nothing would be more misleading than to think uniformly of 'reactionary' governments and a 'progressive' public opinion. These two adjectives should be used only sparingly and with good reason. Those who opposed change were not necessarily wrong and those who advocated it not necessarily right. The road to a solution of the problems which vexed Europe in 1848, both internal and international, was not clearly marked beforehand. Indeed, many of the solutions then advocated, for resisting which many historians have castigated the statesmen of the time, were not found to be all that was expected of them, including German unification itself. Not all the remedies proposed by the radicals in 1848 were practicable, from 'the right to work' in France to the demand for a republic in Germany. However, many European regimes in the previous period must share in the responsibility for the immaturity of much radical thinking. The extremists could make any demands they liked because they hardly ran the risk of having their ideas put into practice. Where they did obtain power, as in parts of Italy and Germany, this was only temporary and over comparatively limited areas.

The radicals in Germany themselves believed that, even if their aims were partly or mainly economic, they had to begin by securing political power. Similarly, it cannot be inferred from the low place on the agenda which economic and social questions had for the middle party in Germany during 1848 that the moderate liberals were indifferent to these questions. Indeed, in Germany, the first national assembly—the Frankfurt Parliament—established an economic committee which played a considerable role and many of the decisions of the assembly, for instance on the Basic Rights, were of far-reaching social and economic significance. At a time of economic crisis and economic change, a great many problems arose, though their solution was not so easy as historians have sometimes claimed. In France, as in Germany, the movement of population from rural districts into towns led to poor housing conditions and to real distress. Many craftsmen found their traditional livelihood threatened. It would be harsh and uncharitable to deny the existence of

distress. However, the historian, in trying to explain the course of
events, must determine to what extent these particular conditions led to
revolution. As Crane Brinton pointed out many years ago in *The
Anatomy of Revolution* uprisings do not necessarily occur when conditions deteriorate or because they do so. However that may be, particularly in France, and also in some urban centres in Germany—for
instance in Berlin—there were always enough people to make up a
crowd and to demonstrate. But in most of the places affected by revolutions, the rallying cry was mainly political, rather than economic.
Although both in France and in Germany there is evidence of economic
risings and their suppression before 1848, the slogans of the revolution
were political. The principle of 'the right to work' became more
prominent after than during the February revolution. The reason for the
prevalence of political over economic slogans is that economic and
social issues tended to divide rather than to unite. There were clashes of
interest, particularly at a time of considerable economic change. The
time had not yet come for large working-class political movements. For
that the change in social structure resulting from the increase in the
number of factories employing large numbers of workers was not yet
sufficiently advanced.

We thus have to look elsewhere for the main motivation of the revolutions. In so far as vocal evidence is conclusive, the main demands made
were invariably political, whether in France, in Italy, in Germany, in
Austria or in Hungary. They were generally concerned with representative government in all its implications and with national unification
where this had not yet been achieved.

It is not surprising that the demand for representation had a wide
echo, although even here the clash of interests, to which reference has
already been made in connection with social and economic facts, was
present. In any case, the principle that government should be more
responsive to public opinion was bound to find a considerable following.
When it came to details, for instance to the extent of the franchise, there
was liable to be a divisive effect. Still, many months passed after the
revolutions before the various parliaments reached this item on their
agenda. In general, the moderate liberals, the grouping to which the
new capitalist entrepreneurial class found itself mainly attracted, did
not favour too wide an extension of the franchise, partly because of
their gradualist—British Whig—approach, partly because the bourgeoisie, about to succeed to a share of political power, was not yet ready
to share it with the population as a whole. Before 1848, the common
aversion to so much of the policy of the Governments had masked the
differences of opinion between various groups in the opposition. When
the former opposition began to take over government in 1848, when
practical decisions had to be taken, decisive differences of opinion soon

became apparent. While clear categorisation is not possible in each individual instance, in all the countries concerned there was a split between moderates and radicals. As moderate liberals—and generally not radicals—were entrusted by the princes with ministerial posts, the gap between the former allies grew. The pitfalls and limitations of the system of representative government were yet to be experienced. In March 1848, for instance in Germany and Austria, the appointment of ministers possessing the confidence of the people seemed to offer a solution even to princes who had previously strenuously opposed this solution. The citadels of power were rushed, even more in the realm of ideas than in that of the use of hard physical force. After the quick crumbling of the power of Louis Philippe at the end of February, the formation of a crowd demonstrating before a royal or ducal palace was sufficient to obtain the almost instantaneous granting of all demands in the medium-sized and smaller German states during the early days in March. The demands were monotonously the same, with small variations. They were for a constitution, if one did not already exist, for the establishment of a ministry possessing the confidence of the people, for a properly functioning state parliament, an independent judiciary with the introduction of a jury system in criminal and possibly in political cases, the abolition of censorship, and often also the need for a German national parliament. Not least to some of the German and Italian princes, representative government was an almost magic remedy. The vagueness of the new programme, an advantage in the short term, was bound to be a long-term disadvantage. The hopes placed in the new system, which was expected to operate efficiently at once in spite of its newness, were too great for their realisation.

In such countries as Germany and Italy, which had not yet achieved national unification, the demand for self-determination went closely together with that for representative government. Metternich had held that the implementation of the principle of self-determination in these two countries was not compatible with the maintenance of the Vienna settlement as he saw it, that it was bound to lead to war and to shatter the almost general peace of non-Ottoman Europe since Waterloo. He was fully aware of the threat the principle of self-determination presented to the Habsburg Empire, with its multi-national composition, its leading influence in Germany, its possessions in Northern Italy and its general position in the Apennine peninsula. Owing to the partition of Poland, all the three Eastern Powers had a vested interest in keeping self-determination in the background. Perhaps thinking on national unification was somewhat clearer in Italy than in Germany, possibly because the problems were not quite so complicated. In Italy, even before 1848, there were schools of thought favouring particular plans, for instance that the King of Sardinia, or the Pope, should lead the new

Italy. In Germany, however, very little practical attention was paid to the intricacies of the relationship with Austria before 1848, a question which had to be settled if any progress was to be made. It was perhaps inevitable that national movements need several decades at least to develop a practical programme. A national movement attempts to create a country based on nationality. Its main claim will rest on a historical basis, that the nationality concerned is an old-established one and is entitled to form a state of its own, or that its state was destroyed earlier—like that of the Poles. Historical reminiscence, a romantic delving into the past, is part of the process, but it does not make for a practical approach. Romanticism may easily lead to a lack of realism. A more practical approach is only adopted in the second stage.

The confusion of the period over the nature of nationalism perhaps comes out most clearly in the relationship between the Italian national movement and Pope Pius IX. As in Germany, where the unification movement was still strongly affected by the cosmopolitan aspirations derived from the period of the Holy Roman Empire, the Italian national movement sought to reconcile national and international elements. The Pope, then still in his 'liberal' phase, had some sympathy with the national aspirations of the Italian people from which he came. But it soon became clear that the ruler of the Papal state was primarily head of the Catholic Church and was therefore not as free to send his soldiers into battle against the Catholic Emperor of Austria as other Italian rulers. This is not to deny that a common religion can be a great support to a national movement, as the Catholic Church has been to the Poles, although this is easier when the foreign ruler belongs to another church.

In their preoccupation with political and economic factors, many historians have tended to neglect the religious aspect. Religion was an important issue, both to the believer and to the unbeliever. In spite of the influence of rationalism and the enlightenment in the past, the strongest conviction of the greatest number of people in the countries affected by revolution may well still have been religious rather than political, at any rate up to the spring of 1848. Religious education is likely to have been more widespread than its political counterpart. Eighteen forty-eight offered the religious groups in Germany for the first time the opportunity of utilising the media of public opinion and of politics for the realisation of their demands. In Germany it marked the entry of the churches into the struggle of the political parties. There the Roman Catholics particularly—rather than the Protestants—took full advantage of this. In the German unification debate, for instance in the question of the relationship with Austria, religious allegiance was an important factor. At the same time, those who rejected religious beliefs, or wished to see the power of the churches curbed, also had their chance in 1848. The relations between church and state occupied considerable attention. Although religious issues were important and often turned the scale, they were not the cause of the outbreak of the revolutions or the primary ones on which matters turned in 1848–49.

The year 1848 began with the Sicilian rising, but the rebellion there was too peripheral to Europe and too much of its own kind to set Europe alight. The decisive moment came with the overthrow of Louis Philippe at the end of February. France had been quickly received back into grace in the legitimist period after 1815, and following the 1830 revolution had played a considerable part in European and Mediterranean affairs, fully committed neither to the Eastern Powers nor to Britain, co-operating with the former or the latter as it suited her. With the abolition of the monarchy in France in February 1848, for the first time in the restoration period a major European country had a republican government. Once more, as frequently in the period from 1789 to the advent of Napoleon, and again in 1830, France had changed her government by violence, arousing, as on previous occasions, fears of the spread of instability in Europe. These fears were twofold, that France would act as a revolutionary centre and that she would rediscover her territorial ambitions of the era before 1815.

For the forces of movement, the Paris revolution was a signal. Metternich had been both right and wrong; right in holding that peace and order in non-Ottoman Europe was indivisible, wrong in believing that repression was the only policy to maintain it. The hour of reckoning for many of the existing regimes was all the more terrible because of the attempt to stifle change in the past. During March, two of the strongest pillars of the old order, the Habsburg Empire and the Prussian monarchy, were severely shaken. The change of regime in Vienna and Berlin required a greater show of force than in the smaller German states. The Hohenzollern regime would not give up any of its powers without a severe struggle. The resignation of Metternich in Vienna on 13th March was a historical turning point, but the much more severe street fighting in Berlin on 18th March—though not quite so important internationally—left behind a greater legacy of bitterness. Of the three Eastern Powers, only the third, Tsarist Russia, escaped the contagion and was preserved under Nicholas I as the policeman of Europe, to return to active duty in this role during 1849.

It was perhaps no coincidence that matters came to a head in Vienna a few days before they did at Berlin. The Habsburg Empire, more than Prussia or any other state, faced to the greatest extent the dual challenge of 1848, of constitutionalism and nationalism. Prussia and Russia, too, ruled over other nationalities, but one national group predominated in each country. In the Habsburg Empire, no one national group had a majority, although the Germans played the leading part outside the

Kingdom of Hungary and the Magyars within it. The demand for self-determination was liable to exclude the Habsburgs from Germany and Italy and to weaken their position in Hungary. The Habsburg Empire was the supreme example of an accumulation of mainly territorial states not necessarily corresponding to ethnic units, which had come under the rule of the dynasty for a number of reasons, some quite fortuitous, such as dynastic marriages. Generally, the conversion of old territorial states and of more recent institutions like the German Confederation—including many non-Germans—into national states was far more difficult than the liberals of 1848 allowed. They compounded the problem even further by thinking more in terms of French centralism than American or Swiss federalism. Furthermore, as always, nationalities viewed problems only from their own point of view. To begin with, the definition of nationality was a matter of considerable difficulty, as the Slavs found at their Congress in Prague in June 1848. Historic kingdoms, former or existing, whether that of Poland or that of Hungary, did not usually neatly coincide with ethnic units, as France largely did (leaving aside the complex problem of Alsace-Lorraine). There was the criterion of a common language and culture; sometimes religious allegiance could also be an important touchstone. Finally, there were natural frontiers and economic viability to be considered. In the case of the Italian national movement, the main long-term aim was the unification of the whole of the Apennine peninsula, including Sicily, i.e. the realisation of natural frontiers. There was, however, also some concern for Italians living elsewhere, for instance on the Adriatic coast, in particular those in Trieste, a concern which was to become increasingly strong during the late nineteenth and early twentieth centuries. No more than the Italians did the Germans base their national aims on a single concept. The principle of natural frontiers was hardly convenient to them. In the West it would have meant excluding considerable German populations, but it was used to some extent in the East and the South to justify German claims. In 1848, a considerable part of the German programme, when analysed carefully, was supported by historical and territorial arguments. Naturally the new state was to be based primarily on German language and German culture. But in several cases territories were to be included which had considerable non-German populations, such as the Eastern provinces of the Kingdom of Prussia with their Polish inhabitants. In 1848 the Schleswig-Holstein question was not finally settled, but in general the German national movement demanded the incorporation of the whole of the Elbe Duchies, in spite of the fact that the North of Schleswig was inhabited by Danes. The reason for this attitude was that history had, in the German view, established the two duchies as an indivisible entity. As the majority of the population consisted of ethnic Germans, the whole of the Duchies therefore had to go to Germany. Except for a brief moment at the beginning of the rising in the Duchies in March, there was no willingness to concede the principle of self-determination to the Danes. However, most members of the Frankfurt Parliament were not seriously interested in forcing the non-Germans in territories of the Habsburg Empire belonging to the German Confederation—such as Bohemia—into a German national state. And, as distinct for instance from the aims of National Socialists, there was no systematic attempt to establish links with German groups outside the proposed state, with the eventual aim of bringing them in some way into the Fatherland. At any rate, in each particular question, the Germans, like all the other nationalities, carefully chose the appropriate line of argument.

It is curious that nationalism should come into its own in the post-1815 period at a time of the greatest internal bitterness, for instance in Germany. This bitterness prevailed not only in the relations between some rulers and ruled up to the moment in March when changes were made, but even more so, as the year progressed, between the moderate liberals and the radicals, formerly in alliance. The Left, the radicals, the republicans, often felt cheated. They had gone on the barricades, but the moderate liberals, who had been absent from them, reaped the benefit. As government became more responsive to public opinion, groupings tended to be more sophisticated. Any two-fold division—into government and opposition—which there might have been before 1848, became at least threefold. There was now a Right, which wanted to go back as far as possible to the situation before concessions were made in the spring of 1848, as well as moderate liberal governments and, finally, oppositions.

Some historians, who see the struggles of 1848 as purely bilateral between 'reaction' and 'progress' have suspected the princes in Germany and Austria of making concessions only with the set purpose of revoking them as soon as possible. This can hardly be supported generally and on the whole the new 'March' ministers had little to complain about regarding the loyalty of their monarchs, except for instance in Prussia, where Frederick William IV had his 'ministers behind the curtain', the *Camarilla*, including General Leopold von Gerlach. The moderate liberals had their opportunity and the problem for the historian is to explain why they failed to seize it fully. Their eventual failure can be attributed either to their own limitations, or to the difficulties they encountered from Left and Right, or both. The crucial problem for them was not their relations with the rulers, but with their former left-wing allies. As early as the beginning of April, the extreme wing of the Left in Germany under Friedrich Hecker and Gustav von Struve made up their minds that the only way to achieve their aims was by a further —a second—revolution. This group was not prepared to await the results of the elections for the German national assembly to be held a few weeks later. The main body of the Left, however, decided to utilise the elections and to accept seats in the parliamentary bodies. The rising in Baden led by Hecker and Struve in April 1848, was a disastrous failure, initiating a series of 'second revolutions' in Europe during 1848 and 1849, all equally doomed to failure. In general, the Left did not do well in parliamentary elections and was driven to extra-parliamentary courses when it did not win sufficient votes. Even in France the Left failed to dominate parliament and government. The June rising in Paris crushed by General Cavaignac marked the beginning of the recovery of the forces of order which eventually outflanked the moderate liberals and led to the appointment of more right-wing ministers. France shows perhaps most clearly that the threat to the moderate liberal position and the trend to the Right is explicable without blaming the princes for their intrigues, for the Second Republic did not have this particular problem. In December, the French electorate put Prince Louis Napoleon into presidential office, ending the 1848 revolutions, but paving the way for a regime completely different from that of Louis Philippe, or indeed from that of the new Prussian and Austrian Governments which came into office at about the same time.

The recovery of the Prussian and Austrian monarchies in the second half of 1848 was a gradual process, helped by the divisions in the ranks of the moderate liberals and the radicals, as well as by the differing interests of the various nationalities. During the summer, the Frankfurt Parliament dominated the scene in Germany. At the end of June, at about the time that the Paris rising was crushed, the German constituent national assembly asserted its authority by itself electing a vicar of the empire and setting up a provisional central power to take the place of the Diet of the German Confederation. The Archduke John, an uncle of the Austrian Emperor Ferdinand, who was particularly popular in Germany, was elected Vicar and accepted the office. In theory, all this was meant to pave the way for German unification. In practice, however, the cavalier disbandment of the Diet of the German Confederation, which represented—however imperfectly—the only effective institution for the states belonging to it, proved a severe handicap when it came to the implementation of policies approved by the Frankfurt Parliament. The Provisional Government found itself in the unenviable position of being accountable to the National Assembly without having any effective authority in relation to the state governments. This situation had tragic effects in September, after the Prussian Government had concluded an armistice with Denmark at Malmö at the end of the previous month. Prussia, which had borne the brunt of the war effort, realised that the Schleswig-Holstein conflict was not to be won. The naval superiority of the Danes, so much resented by the German national movement which demanded the creation of a strong fleet, played havoc with German shipping and trade. The North of Germany suffered particularly. The Left in the Frankfurt Parliament, however, supported by the Schleswig-Holstein group in the assembly, resisted the treaty. After an initial suspension of approval and the resignation of the Reich Government, the assembly passed the treaty. The Left inveighed against the 'betrayal' of the German cause and feelings got so heated that street fighting broke out on 18th September. Troops were called in and suppressed the rising, but only after two members of the Assembly, Felix, Prince Lichnowsky, and General Hans von Auerswald had been murdered. There were many casualties among the insurgents whose idealism and integrity cannot be doubted. However, whatever the motives of the insurgents, they did poor service to the cause of German unity in which they believed. The divisions became so bitter that the real basis for a coming together of Germans in one state was lost.

In the meantime, the Habsburg Empire was, if only slowly, on the way to recovery. The victories of Field-Marshal Radetzky in Northern Italy began to restore the self-confidence of the authorities and the end of the fighting with Sardinia in August allowed the Habsburg Monarchy to concentrate on its many other problems. Hungary proved intractable as yet, but the courage was at least found to give—albeit hidden—support to the great anti-Magyar, the Ban of Croatia, Jelačič. The main problem was to restore Vienna to obedience. Field-Marshal Windischgrätz, who had already crushed the Prague rising in June, was given the task of dealing with Vienna. The October rising in the Austrian capital was doomed from the beginning, as the Hungarians under Kossuth were either not serious about coming to the aid of Vienna or were unable to save the city. Fundamentally, the opponents of the Habsburg Monarchy were divided among themselves. Once more in Vienna during October, as at Frankfurt in the previous month, radicals and extremists who had very little popular following in their countries as a whole, challenged governments with superior armaments and professional soldiers, refusing to accept a deferment of their reform plans. The bravery shown in Vienna was exceptional, but at the same time the insurgents could not fail to be brutal, as the conquering troops were later. Each side was bound to commit inhuman acts in pursuance of the logic of its cause. The Vienna rising had a sequel for Germany. The Left in the Frankfurt Parliament had sent a deputation to Vienna during the uprising to express its solidarity with the revolt. The leader of the Left at Frankfurt, Robert Blum, and a member of the Extreme Left there, Julius Fröbel, took part in the fighting in Vienna. They were both sentenced to death; Blum was executed, but Fröbel reprieved. Fröbel's account to the Frankfurt Parliament on his return is a notable document illuminating those terrible days.

It was perhaps only to be expected that the forces of the Right would eventually triumph in Austria once more, though the historian is not equipped to prove or disprove this theory. However, it does seem likely that the particular personality called to power in November, Felix, Prince Schwarzenberg, owed his appointment to the need felt for a strong leader after the October struggle in Vienna. Schwarzenberg was to be Austrian Prime Minister until his death in 1852. He was a new type of conservative leader, possessing a much stronger determination than Metternich, as well as a ruthlessness alien to the former chancellor. He had great ability and the recovery of the Habsburg Empire, also marked by the abdication of the Emperor Ferdinand and his succession by his nephew Francis Joseph, owed much to Schwarzenberg. Not only radicalism, but also moderate liberalism had received a severe check, although Schwarzenberg retained some previous ministers in his government. The new Prime Minister gave warning that Austria was resuming her rightful place in Germany. She insisted on being consulted about any reorganisation there. Schwarzenberg's appointment also spelt the eventual end of plans for Italian unification.

In Italy, too, the Habsburgs benefited from the divisions among their opponents. In spite of the greater willingness of the leading state, Sardinia, to take the lead in the national cause, than was the case in Germany, a real cooperation between all concerned, including King Charles Albert, and the republican leaders like Garibaldi, Mazzini and Manin was lacking. After the withdrawal of Sardinia from the war in August 1848, the struggle was carried on by the republicans, in Rome, in Venice, and elsewhere. The outbreak of violence perpetrated by extremists increasingly forced the Pope into the arms of the hyper-conservative forces. He had finally to seek asylum in the Kingdom of Naples. The short re-entry of Sardinia into the war in March 1849, did not change the picture and one after another the old regimes in Italy were restored. In spite of failure, the Italian unification movement had staked a claim which was not to be ignored in the future.

German national unification and with it moderate liberalism also ended on a sombre note. Both movements were in 1848 and 1849 closely bound up with each other, because the moderate liberals—the Right Centre of the Frankfurt Parliament—had taken the lead in the unification question. The radicals did not have a sufficiently strong position in either parliaments or governments to obtain their ends. In spite of the moderate liberal dominance of many governments and parliaments in Germany, in the end the base of their support proved too narrow, perhaps because they were mainly the party of the capitalist entrepreneur and of the educated classes generally. Furthermore, prominent moderate liberals in various part of the country were not agreed on the policy to be followed, in many cases because of divergent political, religious and economic interests. Undoubtedly, the net effect of radical opposition to the moderate liberals was to weaken the latter and to undermine their influence with the princes. It may, however, be argued contrariwise that fear of the radicals made the princes cling to their moderate liberal ministers. But soon the point was reached—in Prussia and Austria by November—at which the princes regarded law and order as so threatened by the radicals that they lost faith in the so much praised liberal remedy of the parliamentary safety-valve, decided that it was merely a matter of crushing insubordination, and felt that this was better done by men who had gained experience in army and officialdom before 1848 than by the new men. Like the appointment of Schwarzenberg in Austria, that of the less ruthless Count Brandenburg as Prime Minister of Prussia in November 1848 would be due to this kind of reasoning. While the moderate liberals gradually lost some of their ministerial positions, they continued to support the maintenance of law and order against radical disturbance. The moderates were frightened by the appalling possibilities of anarchy which runaway revolutions were liable to bring with them. This can be interpreted in terms of economic materialism. According to this version, the bourgeois class— like the peasants—had achieved all it wanted. The bourgeoisie had taken over at least some of the power formerly exercised by the aristocracy. But this is only one aspect. It is all too easy to criticise the bourgeois for fearing for his property.

The recovery of Austria and the deep divisions in Germany hardly made the imperial crown offered by the Frankfurt Parliament to King Frederick William IV of Prussia at the beginning of April 1849 very attractive. The refusal of the crown led to a gradual disintegration of the Frankfurt Parliament and to the final series of 'second revolutions' in May 1849, in Saxony, the Palatinate and Baden. None of these ever had a permanent chance and they were all crushed. For a time the Prussian Government took the initiative in unifying at least part of Germany under its leadership, but the Prussian scheme of union only had a limited success. Like the Italian, the Hungarian war dragged on into 1849. The Hungarian rising still offers difficulties of interpretation after the lapse of more than a century. It can be seen positively as a liberal national movement, but also criticised as narrow both in its social and national base. The Magyar rulers of the Kingdom of Hungary were certainly heartily disliked by many of their subject peoples. With the considerable autonomy granted to or taken by the Kingdom of Hungary in 1848, the Magyars under their radical and liberal leaders exercised the greatest power of any of the 'peoples of state' in the Habsburg Monarchy. The defeat of the radical Kossuth and his followers by the Austrians with Russian help in 1849, though regretted by liberals in England, was a relief to many non-Magyars in the kingdom. Looking to the future—for example to the state of Czechoslovakia in the 1919–38 period—the failure of Kossuth showed that parliamentary government and constitutionalism do not in themselves give a fair deal to all sections of the population, particularly when a centralist form of government favours one of the nationalities in the state. It was only very slowly and incompletely that the European liberals moved away somewhat from the pure centralist concept on which so much of their thinking was based. The radicals, too, tended towards a centralist form of government. In any case, the whole history of the 1848–49 period shows that the responsiveness of the radicals to public opinion and to elections was severely limited. They persevered in their plans for a take-over, although they had no mandate from the people. They could, however, claim in many cases that the franchise was so limited as to make the elections unrepresentative. There was something Messianic about the radicals and a certain attachment to Rousseau's concept of the general will. Any idea that the radicals had pacifist leanings must be dispelled by their conduct in 1848 and 1849. They abhorred neither civil nor international war. It was mainly the German radicals in September 1848 who wanted to prolong the Schleswig-Holstein war, even against hopeless diplomatic and military odds.

By 1850, Austria and Russia between them were so strong as to be able to frustrate Prussian plans for changes in Germany. At Olmütz in November 1850, Prussia finally agreed to give in and to work together with Austria once more in the German Confederation. The Schleswig-Holstein conflict, too, was terminated. Prince Christian of Glücksburg was designated by the European powers as eventual heir to Denmark and the Elbe Duchies on the extinction of the male line of the royal house. In Germany, the years from 1851 to 1858 were regarded as a period of reaction by the liberals and radicals.

Although the Italian princes were restored, although the Habsburg Empire survived the troubles of the revolutionary period without any loss of territory, although liberal and radical politicians were without influence and often persecuted, Europe was never the same again. Too many questions had been asked in 1848 to permit a return to the *status quo ante*, to legitimism and to the pattern of the pre-1848 society. Not all reforms were undone and one of the most lasting ones was the abolition of the remains of serfdom, particularly in Austria, Moreover, the economic forces which had stagnated in the economic crisis of 1847 and in the political troubles of the revolutionary period resumed their march and in the long run contributed to ensuring further social and political change.

In spite of the help given by Nicholas I to Francis Joseph in Hungary and of the restoration of the German Confederation, of the installation of 'conservative' governments in the German states and in Austria, the age of legitimism and of an ideological alliance of the three Eastern powers was over. This was realised by Schwarzenberg in Austria and by Count Brandenburg's successor Otto v. Manteuffel in Prussia, and perhaps even dimly by Nicholas I. Not the least convert to the necessity of change, to an abandonment of some long-cherished principles and to their replacement by *Realpolitik* was Otto von Bismarck, Prussian delegate to the Diet in Frankfurt in the 1850's, a man who was not prepared to accept a junior role in a dualism in which Austria predominated. From 1853 onwards, the policy of Nicholas I, which resulted in the Crimean War, shattered the understanding between the three Eastern courts. In the changed diplomatic situation which for a time offered great opportunities to the Emperor Napoleon III, 1848 proved to be a forerunner to Italian and German unification between 1859 and 1871.

The revolutions of 1848 have always attracted the particular attention of the historian. The raw material on which the historian has been able to draw has been rich, from autobiographies and letters to parliamentary debates and eye-witness descriptions of particular events. There have been many historical accounts of the revolutionary periods in the various countries. For details the reader is referred to the bibliography.[1] Here a few particularly important accounts will be singled out and briefly described.

For Germany the standard account of the revolutions of 1848 and 1849 is still the monumental work by Veit Valentin, *Geschichte der deutschen Revolution von 1848–49*, published in two volumes in 1930 and 1931 by the Ullstein publishing house in Berlin. Valentin, soor afterwards to flee from Germany under the Nazis, tried to emphasise the good points of both radicals and moderate liberals in 1848. A more recent work on a smaller—but still considerable—scale is by Jacques Droz, *Les Revolutions allemandes de 1848* (Paris, 1957), which is based partly on a manuscript by the late E. Tonnelat. The book is good on the pre-1848 intellectual background and on radical movements in the revolutionary period. The centenary of the revolution yielded a crop of interesting surveys. The most notable was Rudolf Stadelmann's *Soziale und Politische Geschichte der Revolution von 1848* (Munich, 1948). In a careful analysis Stadelmann found that social factors were important, but not overriding. *1848. Werk and Erbe* (Stuttgart, 1848), is a fine and objective interpretation by the cultured and fair-minded first President of the Federal Republic, Theodor Heuss.

On Italy, G. F. H. and J. Berkeley, *Italy in the making*, 3 vols., 1932–40, is a fascinating account of the period from 1815 up to and including 1848. The author's considerable detail never wearies the reader. The work is particularly good on religious questions and the role

[1] See below, p. 185 ff.

of the papacy. G. M. Trevelyan's classics *Garibaldi's defence of the Roman Republic, 1848–9* (London, 1907) and *Manin and the Venetian Revolution of 1848* (London, 1923), hardly need any recommendation.

There is an ample literature on France. C. Seignobos, *La Revolution de 1848 et l'Empire* (Paris, 1921) is still the standard work. A more recent account is *1848: The making of a revolution*, by Georges Duveau (New York, 1968), which contains a detailed description of the revolutionary days in February and pays particular attention to social groupings. Frederick de Luna in *The Republic under Cavaignac, 1848* (Princeton, 1969) argues that the National Assembly elected in April did not have a republican majority and that therefore one cannot speak of a 'betrayal' of republican ideals after the June rising crushed by Cavaignac. This thesis is interesting because it would tend to show that as in Germany the radicals did not yet possess a majority. Donald Cope McKay in *The National Workshops. A Study in the French Revolution of 1848* (Cambridge, Mass., 1933) held that social and economic questions played a greater part in the events of the period from February to June 1848, than has usually been allowed.

For the Habsburg Monarchy, the massive works by Anton Springer, *Geschichte Österreichs* (2 vols., Leipzig, 1865) and by Heinrich Friedjung, *Österreich von 1848 bis 1860* (vol. I, Stuttgart, 1908) are still useful and deal intensively with the various nationalities in the Empire. On Hungary a detailed work is M. Horvath's *Geschichte des Unabhängigkeitskrieges 1848–1849* (3 vol., Budapest, 1872). On Bohemia, Stanley Z. Pech provides a careful study in *The Czech Revolution of 1848* (North Carolina, 1969).

One of the most stimulating essays on the period of the revolutions generally is '1848: The Revolution of the Intellectuals', by Sir Lewis Namier, in *Proceedings of the British Academy* 30 (1944). However, the present author cannot share some of Namier's anti-liberal and anti-German conclusions. Useful published papers of congresses on 1848 held on the occasion of the centenary are Comité Français des Sciences Historiques, *Actes du Congrès Historique du centenaire de la revolution de 1848* (Paris, 1948) and *Convegno di Scienze Morali Storiche e Filologiche* (Rome: Accademia Nazionale dei Lincei, 1949), the latter in the language of the participants. *The opening of an era, 1848*, edited by F. Fejtö (London, 1948) is also useful.

For the documentary section, extracts from the London *Times* and the *Annual Register* (published in London) have been utilised. These provide contemporary accounts, in the case of the *Times* within a few days of the happenings, in that of the *Annual Register* within a year or eighteen months. The reports of the debates of the Frankfurt Parliament based on short-hand transcripts, *Stenographischer Bericht über die Verhandlungen der deutschen constituirenden Nationalversammlung zu Frankfurt am Main* (9 vol., Frankfurt/Main, 1848-9), edited by F. Wigard, were used as a source for a number of important speeches.[2] Extracts were reproduced from two articles in the contemporary encyclopaedia published in Leipzig by F. A. Brockhaus, *Die Gegenwart. Eine encyklopädische Darstellung der neuesten Zeitgeschichte für alle Stände* (vol. I, 1848, vol. II, 1849). The articles are anonymous and generally try to be fair both to the moderate liberals and to the Right wing of the radicals. One of them deals with the social question[3] and the other[4] balances the account of the events in Berlin on 18th March 1848 given by General Leopold von Gerlach,[5] a member of the right-wing Camarilla at the court of Frederick William IV in *Denkwürdigkeiten aus dem Leben Leopold von Gerlachs*, vol. I, Berlin, 1891) edited by his daughter. Two extracts[6] come from *Clotilde Koch-Gontard an ihre Freunde. Briefe und Erinnerungen aus der Zeit der deutschen Einheitsbewegung 1843–1869* edited by Wolfgang Klötzer (Frankfurt/Main, 1969). The writer of the letters and diaries was a well-known Frankfurt hostess at whose *salon* Heinrich von Gagern, perhaps the most distinguished member of the Frankfurt Parliament, was a frequent visitor. The famous work by Louis Blanc on the organisation of labour, *Organisation du Travail*[7] originally published in Paris in 1839, and the history of the national workshops, *Histoire des Ateliers Nationaux* (Paris, 1848) by their director Emile Thomas are reprinted with an introduction in *The French Revolution in its economic aspect* edited by J. A. R. Marriott (2 vol., Oxford, 1913).[8] Some of the interpretations put forward in Marriott's introduction are corrected in McKay's book, *The National Workshops* mentioned earlier in this introduction.[9] E. Ashley in *The Life of Henry John Temple, Viscount Palmerston, 1846–1865* (vol. I, London, 1876) quotes from the Foreign Secretary's letters and dispatches in this period.[10] *The Life and Writings of Joseph Mazzini* (vol. V, London, 1869) contain much interesting material on the Roman republic. Similarly, P. C. Headley, *Life of Kossuth* (Auburn, 1852) is a plentiful source, in this case on the Hungarian rising.[11]

Use is also made of a number of documentary collections. These are

[2] Documents IV. 1. D, IV. 1. G, IV. 4. D, V. 2. A.
[3] Document II. 10. A.
[4] Document II. 6. B.
[5] Document II. 6. A.
[6] Documents III. 1. G. and IV. 1. F.
[7] Document I. 6. A.
[8] Documents II. 3. G. and III. 4. A.
[9] See above p. 16.
[10] Documents III. 6. A, V. 5. A, V. 5. B.
[11] Documents IV. 3. C, IV. 3. D, V. 4. A.

The Map of Europe by Treaty (vol. II, London, 1875), edited by E. Hertslet; F.-A. Hélie, *Les Constitutions de la France* (Paris, 1880); *Deutsche Parteiprogramme* edited by W. Mommsen (Munich, 1960); and *Dokumente zur deutschen Verfassungsgeschichte* edited by E. R. Huber (vol. I, Stuttgart, 1961).

Comments on the other books used are made in the introductions to documents. All extracts are in English. The translations from the German and the French have been made by the editor, unless otherwise indicated. The advice on the French extracts given by Professor Peter Fothergill-Payne of the Department of Romance Studies in the University of Calgary was much appreciated by the editor.

I

PRELUDE

THE DOCUMENTS IN this chapter reflect some of the problems already evident before 1848 which were to contribute to the revolutionary outbreak and to become central themes in the following months. Social and economic questions were attracting increasing attention, for instance in Germany and France. The election of a new pope in 1846 gave rise to liberal and national hopes. The Austrian annexation of Cracow in the same year kept the Polish question before the eyes of Europe. The summoning of the United Diet in Prussia in 1847 by King Frederick William IV aroused hope and disappointment. Prussia's attitude to constitutional reform was not yet clearly delineated. The last pre-revolutionary year ended with a civil war in Switzerland, which was a trial of strength in miniature between the conservative and radical forces. The conservatives lost.

I.1 THE WEAVERS' RISING IN SILESIA, 1844

Increasing industrialisation and outside competition proved a dire threat to traditional methods of production, such as manufacture carried on in homes. The tragic situation of groups unable or unwilling to accept change is illustrated by the weavers' rising during June 1844 in Silesia, one of the provinces of the Prussian monarchy. There is no reason to question the desperate financial straits and incredibly low standard of living of the Silesian weavers.

I.1.A   The following description of the rising and its suppression was written by Wilhelm Wolff and published in the same month as the rising. Wolff, an extremist who had already spent several years in prison for political offences, lived in Breslau, the capital of Silesia, teaching languages and writing. He later fled to London, where he belonged to the circle of Karl Marx, became a member of the Frankfurt Parliament (Extreme Left) and died in exile in Manchester, England, in 1864. The playwright Gerhart Hauptmann used Wolff's essay for his famous play 'Die Weber' (The Weavers). Extract, translated from German, from *Das Elend und der Aufruhr in Schlesien*, originally published June 1844, reprinted Berlin, 1909, pp. 23 ff.

Here in the great villages Langenbielau (13,000 inhabitants) and Peterswaldau (5,000 inhabitants) and in the other villages such as Arnsdorf, Peilau, etc., cotton weaving particularly is done at home. The distress of the workers was and is here not less important, perhaps even more so than in other areas, although one might think that misery could not reach a higher degree than can be found in the Landshut, Hirschberg, Bolkenhain and other districts. In the winter already, at the beginning of February, a small rising took place in Bielau. A crowd used signals to call together the weavers of the village. A comrade who had been arrested was freed. The crowd was appeased by some gifts. An inquiry into the incident followed but owing to the secrecy of our procedure this event remained almost unknown even in Breslau, that is among the non-governmental public. In the meantime the distress and the urge to obtain work was used by the individual manufacturers to the greatest possible extent in order to obtain a great quantity of goods for little pay. Among these the brothers Zwanziger in Peterswaldau were preeminent. For a web of cotton of 140 ells, on which a weaver had to work for nine days and for which other employers paid 32 silver groschen[1] they paid only 15. For 160 ells of fustian which required eight full days of strenuous work, they paid a wage of $12\frac{1}{2}$ and 12 silver groschen. Indeed, they declared themselves ready to give work to another three hundred weavers prepared to work as much for 10 silver groschen. Bitter misery forced the poor to work even under these conditions. From his 12 or 10 silver groschen respectively the weaver had to give up $2\frac{1}{2}$ to 3 silver groschen to the bobbin winder, bear all state, communal and seignorial dues and—live. Oh! If only someone would explain to me why . . . the major, colonel, general . . . retires after a bloodless game of war during a long period of peace with a pension of 1,000, 1,500, 2,000 taler[2] and the industrial worker becomes brutalised and grows dull, deprived of all moral and intellectual development, [and] gains for his daily laborious work of 14 to 16 hours not even so much that he can satisfy at least the needs of an animal, the demands of the stomach! . . .

The fortune of the Zwanzigers, which was not initially too large, had in a short time grown into great wealth. . . . I can guarantee the following short report which I repeat from the accounts of eye witnesses, and indeed trustworthy men. A poem composed to the popular melody 'There is a Castle in Austria' [Es liegt ein Schloss in Österreich] and sung by the weavers was, as it were, the Marseillaise of the needy. They sang it several times particularly in front of the house of the Zwanzigers. One of them was seized, taken into the house, flogged and handed over

---

[1] One silver groschen was one thirteenth of a taler.
[2] During the early years of the German Reich, the Prussian taler was worth three marks.

to the local police. Finally, at two o'clock in the afternoon of 4th June, the stream overflowed its banks. A crowd of weavers appeared in Nieder-Peterswaldau and on its march attracted all weavers from their dwellings on the left and right. Then they went to the not far distant Kapellenberg and formed up into pairs and moved towards the new residence of the Zwanzigers. They demanded higher pay and—a present! With ridicule and threats this was refused to them. Now it was not long before the crowd stormed into the house, broke into all chambers, vaults, lofts and cellars and smashed everything, from splendid mirror windows, trumeaus, chandeliers, tiled stoves, porcelain, furniture, to the staircases, tore up the books, bills of exchange and papers, penetrated into the second residence, into the coach houses, into the drying house, to the mangling machine, into the baggage warehouse and threw the goods and stock out of the windows where they were torn up, cut into little pieces and trodden under foot, or—in imitation of the Leipzig mess business—distributed to those standing around. In fear of death Zwanziger fled with his family to Reichenbach. The citizens there, who did not want to tolerate a guest like that who could draw the weavers towards them, made him travel on to Schweidnitz. But there, too, the authorities signified to him that he should leave the city because they could become exposed to danger by his presence; and so he finally found safety here in Breslau.

The police official Christ and a policeman carried out an arrest in Peterswaldau, but the weavers soon freed the prisoner. The manufacturer Wagenknecht lived next to Zwanziger. He had treated the weavers more humanely, he was spared. As he also gave them a small present, they cheered him. Soon weavers from Arnsdorf and Bielau arrived. Whatever had been left at the Zwanzigers was now finally smashed. Night interrupted the work of revenge. I may not omit—because it is too characteristic—the proposal of some weavers to set fire to the houses and its rejection for the reason that those thus damaged would then receive fire insurance money [Brandgelder] and that the main thing was for once to make them poor so that they would experience the effect of hunger. On the following day, the 5th of June, was the third turn for the establishments of the Zwanzigers. A stock of yarn in the loft of the house had not been discovered on 4th June; therefore it was destroyed today. In the end even the roofs were partially destroyed. After all this had been completed, the mob went to the manufacturer F. W. Fellman Jun. Fellman appeased the men by paying them 5 groschen each and gave them bread and butter as well as some sides of bacon. A piece of bread and a coin of 5 groschen sufficed to keep in check the fury of men driven by hunger and revenge! Then they went on to E. G. Hofrichters Witwe und Söhne. The weavers now already numbered nearly 3,000. Hofrichter, too, paid a present of 5 groschen to each individual but only the first ones received this, the last ones less.

From here the crowd moved to the 'Sechsgröschel Hilbert'. Hilbert and Andretzky live in Bielau. The destruction in this place began with their house. At first it was the turn of the Gebrüder Dierig. The pastor Seiffert, son-in-law of Dierig, to whom his wife had brought a dowry of 20,000 taler, and who now, comfortable in the calm resignation of the true Christian in his fate, wanted to speak of the joys which beckon to the sufferer on this earth, up there, and admonish the crowd to calm and peace, is reported to have been thrown into the water. In the meantime the clerks had assembled the factory servants and other people, armed them with clubs and whatever else came to hand, and now attacked the weavers under the leadership of the farmer Werner. After a heavy battle the weavers fled out of the building with battered heads and leaving behind manifold traces of blood. However, those who had escaped turned up with new arrivals in front of the second house of Dierig. These included in particular many weavers who worked for Dierig. The latter had promised all who protected his property—and thus preserved their opportunity of continuing to work—a present of 5 silver groschen. Several strangers who wanted to break in were re- pelled by those ready to provide this protection. In the meantime the military who had already been requisitioned twenty-four hours before from Schweidnitz, moved into Bielau.

I do not guarantee that Pastor Seiffert said to his father-in-law that now he need not have to pay any more, as the military were there! Suffice it to say that this has been almost universally reported. What is certain is that the crowd had just arranged itself in an orderly fashion in order to accept the 5 silver groschen promised by Dierig on a piece of paper which had been pasted on to the house, when the military arrived. The troops secured themselves some space by moving back; weavers spoke to them close by and the commander may rightly have considered such conversation dangerous. Therefore the major moved from his first place in order to choose a more advantageous position behind the house and on either side. A lieutenant with ten men was ordered into the garden in front of the house. The weavers formed two rows so that each could receive his 5 silver groschen. The distribution was supposed to take place by Dierig's house and everybody was to retire into the open through the house soon after receiving it. The entries and exits were occupied by soldiers. But it took so long and the payment was delayed so much that the crowd became impatient and, furthermore, nervous at the sight of soldiers, roughly called to order by some non-commissioned officers and soon convinced that they would receive no money, it pressed increasingly against the troops. The major,

who saw Dierig's house and his troops increasingly threatened, ordered
his men to open fire.

As a consequence of three rifle volleys, eleven people were killed
instantly. Blood and brains gushed forth all over the place. The brain
of one man protruded above his eye. A woman who stood two hundred
steps away at the door of her house sank down motionless. One side of a
man's head was torn away. The bloody brain and skull was at some
distance from him. A mother of six children died on the same evening
of several shot wounds. A girl who was going to her knitting lesson sank
to the ground, hit by bullets. A woman who saw her husband fall went
to the loft of her home and hanged herself. A boy of eight years was
shot through the knee. So far it has become known that twenty-four
people were severely or mortally wounded in addition to the eleven dead
mentioned above. Perhaps one may learn later how many kept their
wounds secret. After the first volleys there was for a few seconds a
mortal silence. But the sight of blood around and next to them, the
sighs . . . of the dying, the moaning of the wounded, drove the most
courageous among the weavers to resistance. They replied with stones
which they snatched up from the stone heaps in the streets. When some
more shots had been fired and some weavers were again wounded by
them, while the weavers escaped on the one side and returned from the
other and continued under the most terrible oaths and curses to throw
stones, and advanced with clubs and axes, etc., Major von Rosenberger
effected his retreat. If he had delayed any longer it might have been too
late for ever. At ten o'clock in the evening Major von Schlichting arrived
in Peterswaldau with four companies. Four guns also arrived from
Schweidnitz.

On 6th June, early in the morning, this infantry and artillery moved
to Bielau, but one company remained in Peterswaldau which yet on the
same day, because there was again a violent ferment, received support
from a second. The guns drove up into Bielau, the artillerymen with
burning slow matches marching beside them. On the night of the 5th
and 6th June, after the departure of von Rosenberger's troops, one of
Dierig's houses, as well as an annexe, had been demolished. A part of
his soldiers was posted by Major von Schlichting near Dierig's houses,
the others at the manor house. It is true that on this morning clusters of
people were to be seen moving up and down the alleys; it is true that the
blood which had congealed thickly in front of Dierig's house, mixed on
posts, planks and steps with parts of brains, attracted the fixed gaze of
the crowds of weavers standing about, and that all this seemed bound to
unleash once more the inwardly raging fury of revenge. It was solely
the strength of the military power, of the infantry and artillery and later
even of the cavalry that prevented the weavers from trying any further
resistance.

I.2 THE ELECTION OF POPE PIUS IX, JUNE 1846

The election of Cardinal Mastai-Ferretti as successor to Pope Gregory
XVI in June 1846, under the name of Pius IX, was widely interpreted
as a defeat for the anti-liberal and anti-national policy of the aging
Austrian Chancellor, Prince Metternich. In 1848 the feasibility of
combining the roles of a patriotic Italian with that of a supreme pontiff
was to be put to a severe test. Pius IX, in a long papal reign, died in
1878, severely criticised by many 'liberal' Catholics.

I.2.A   This document is taken from *The Times* of 3rd July 1846, p. 4,
         Col. 5.

We received last night letters of the 22nd ult. from our correspondent
in the city of Rome. The coronation of Pope Pius IX had taken place on
the preceding day, and a grand display of fireworks was given at night
in the Piazza de Popolo in honour of the event. The elevation of
Cardinal Mastai Ferreti appeared to afford general satisfaction, as he is
of a good family, a Roman by birth, and of political opinions sufficiently
liberal to give hopes of a change of system, though not violent enough
to create alarm from the fear of too rapid a change. The selection is
purely national, made by a secret understanding among the body of the
Cardinals, who on this occasion were determined to resist foreign influence; and if the new Cabinet be wisely chosen, great hopes are enter-
tained of a gradual improvement being introduced into the Roman
States.

I.3 ANNEXATION OF CRACOW BY AUSTRIA,
     NOVEMBER 1846

The Treaty of Vienna of 1815 established, as a pale shadow of the
former Polish state, the Free City of Cracow. In view of continued
plotting by Polish groups to regain their independence and to overthrow
the conservative order, the Eastern Powers decided to end the special
position of the remnant of Poland and to have it annexed by Austria.

I.3.A   Austria, Prussia and Russia signed a convention at Cracow on
         6th November 1846, uniting the Free City of Cracow to the
         Austrian Monarchy. Extract from Hertslet (ed.), *The Map of
         Europe by Treaty*, II, 1875, pp. 1061 ff.

The Lieutenant Field-Marshal Count Castiglione, President of the
Provisional Government of the Free City of Cracow, in the name of the
3 Protecting Powers Austria, Prussia, and Russia, causes it to be known

. . . that they have concluded and signed at Vienna, the 6th of the present month, a Convention, of which the following is the tenor:

The 3 Courts of Austria, Prussia, and Russia,

Considering, that the Conspiracy which in the month of February, 1846, produced the well-known events in the Grand Duchy of Posen, in Cracow, and in Gallicia, was organised in places at a distance from the Country in which it was supported by numerous accomplices; . . .

Considering, that Cracow became the seat of a central authority calling itself the *Revolutionary Government*, and that the acts which emanated from that authority were intended to direct the insurrection; . . .

. . . Considering, moreover, that by the Treaty concluded between them, the 3rd May 1815, the City of Cracow, with its Territory, was declared a Free and Independent and strictly Neutral City under the Protection of the 3 High Contracting Parties;

Considering, that by this Stipulation the 3 Courts were desirous of giving effect to the Article relating to the City of Cracow, in their respective Treaties concluded the 3rd May 1815 . . .

Considering, that the existence of the Free City of Cracow, far from being in conformity with their intentions, has on the contrary been a source of disturbance and disorders, which during nearly twenty years not only compromised the peace and prosperity of this Free City, and the security of the adjoining Provinces, but, moreover, tended to overthrow the order of things established by the Treaties of 1815;

Considering, that numerous facts of this nature, the notoriety of which renders enumeration superfluous, have completely altered the nature of the existence of the Free City of Cracow; that by acts contrary to the tenor of Treaties, Cracow has on several occasions freed herself from the obligations which the condition of strict Neutrality imposed upon her; that these acts have on several occasions led to the Armed Intervention of the 3 Powers; that all the modifications introduced into the internal Constitution for the purpose of giving to its Government more power, have not sufficed to prevent the recurrence of these deplorable facts; . . .

. . . Considering that the City of Cracow has proved that it was a political body evidently too weak to resist the unceasing machinations of the Polish Emigration, who held it morally subjected; that accordingly that City no longer presents any guarantee to the Powers against the recurrence of attempts already repeated at various times; . . .

Considering, that the stipulations relative to Cracow resolved upon by the 3 Courts have only been repeated in Articles VI, VII, VIII, IX, and X of the General Act of the Congress of Vienna, of the 9th of June 1815, for the purpose of including in that Act the several results of their individual negotiations;

B

Considering, that the 3 Courts, in now changing a state of things which had spontaneously been created by them in 1815, with regard to Cracow, only re-enter into the exercise of an incontestable right; ...

Have agreed upon the following resolutions:

1. The 3 Courts of Austria, Prussia, and Russia, revoke the Articles relative to the City of Cracow, of the Treaties which they respectively concluded, the one between His Majesty the Emperor of Austria, and His Majesty the Emperor of All the Russias, and His Majesty the King of Prussia, signed by them the 3rd May 1815, as well as the Additional Treaty between Austria, Prussia and Russia of the same date.

2. In consequence of this resolution, the City of Cracow and its Territory shall be restored to the Court of Austria for the purpose of being re-united to the Austrian Monarchy, and of being possessed by His Imperial and Royal Apostolic Majesty in the same manner as he possessed them before the year 1809. ....

I.3.B   Britain protested to the three Eastern Powers against the incorporation of the Free City of Cracow in the dominions of the Emperor of Austria. Extract from the instructions of the Foreign Secretary, Viscount Palmerston, to the British Minister in Vienna, Viscount Ponsonby, of 23rd November 1846, from Hertslet (ed.), *The Map of Europe by Treaty*, II, pp. 1069 ff. Similar instructions were sent to Berlin and St Petersburg.

... Her Majesty's Government have received this communication[3] with deep regret and with much surprise. The communications which of late have been had with the Representatives of the 3 Powers at this Court had led Her Majesty's Government to expect that some proposal would be made by the 3 Powers for some modification of the Political Condition in which the Treaty of Vienna has placed the Free State of Cracow, with a view the better to secure the Territories of the 3 Powers from risk of disturbance by plots which might be formed in Cracow; but Her Majesty's Government were not prepared for such a communication as that which they have now received; and Her Majesty's Government feel themselves bound to Protest against the execution of the intention which has thus been announced. ...

After the events of 1830 and 1836, it is to be remarked that the 3 Powers had recourse to measures which they thought sufficient for the security of their respective Dominions, and those events can scarcely be quoted now as affording grounds for fresh measures of severity against Cracow; and with respect to the inroad made by the people of Cracow into the Gallician Territory about a twelvemonth ago, and the alleged

[3] About the annexation of Cracow.

dissolution of the Government of Cracow by its own act, Her Majesty's Government would observe, that if General Collin, who was invited into Cracow by the Government of that State for the maintenance of order, had not suddenly withdrawn his troops, it is probable that no inroad would have been made by the people of Cracow into Gallicia; and as that General carried away with him all the constituted authorities of the City, and left the City and State in a condition of administrative anarchy, it can hardly be said that the dissolution of the Government was the act of the people of Cracow themselves.

But it is alleged that Cracow has long been, and if it remains Independent, will still continue to be the centre of intrigues; . . .

. . . But no stranger can reach Cracow except by traversing a vast extent of Territory belonging to one or other of the 3 Powers; . . .

. . . if the laws of Cracow do not give the Government power to prevent . . . abuse of the shelter of the Free State, those police regulations might be improved and those laws might be altered; . . .

. . . But Her Majesty's Government must at all events deny the competency of the 3 Powers to decide upon and to execute such a measure, of their own separate authority, and without the concurrence of the other Powers who were parties to the Treaty of Vienna of June 1815.

There is no doubt that the erection of Cracow and its Territory into a Free and Independent State, together with many of the details of its organisation, are matters which were first recorded by the Treaty of the 3rd of May 1815. But that Treaty merely recorded one part of the various arrangements made by the General Congress of Vienna; and it was by Article CXVIII of the General Treaty declared to be an integral part of the arrangements of the Congress of the European Powers, and to have everywhere the same force and value as if it had been inserted word for word in the General Treaty.

But besides this the leading stipulations about Cracow which are contained in the Separate Treaty of the 3rd of May, concluded between the 3 Powers, are inserted word for word in the General Treaty to which all the Powers are parties, and those stipulations constitute the Articles VI, VII, VIII, IX, X, of that General Treaty.

It is demonstrable, therefore, that with whomsoever may have originated the plan of erecting Cracow and its Territory into a Free and Independent State, that plan was carried into effect by stipulations to which all the Powers were equally parties; and consequently it is not competent for three of those Powers by their own separate authority to undo that which was established by the common engagements of the whole; and it is manifest that the special duty which the 3 Powers undertook, of protecting the Independence of the State, cannot invest them with any right to overthrow that Independence and to destroy it.

For these reasons Her Majesty's Government are of opinion that the

execution of the intentions which the 3 Powers have announced, would
be a measure justified by no adequate necessity, and would involve a
violation of positive stipulations contained in the General Treaty of
Vienna; and Her Majesty's Government, deeply impressed with the
conviction that it is above all things important that the engagements of
Treaties should at all times be faithfully observed, most earnestly hope
that means may be devised for guarding the Territories of the 3 Powers
against the dangers adverted to in their identic communications, without
any breach of the Treaty of 1815 . . .

I.4   THE PRUSSIAN UNITED DIET, 1847

There were great hopes when Frederick William IV ascended the
Prussian throne in 1840, that Prussia would advance on the road to
constitutional reform. The new king certainly succeeded in liquidating
some of the problems left by his predecessor, particularly in the religious sphere. He waited until 1847 before he took his first major constitutional step, the calling of the United Diet.

I.4.A   The patent of King Frederick William IV of Prussia of 3rd
February 1847, concerning the establishment—for the first time—
of a United Diet for the whole of the Prussian Monarchy, translated from the German text in *Leben und Wirken Sr. Majestät
Friedrich Wilhelm des Vierten, Königes von Preussen*, I, Leipzig,
1855, pp. 38 ff.

. . . We Frederick William by the Grace of God, King of Prussia . . .
declare:

. . . Since the beginning of Our reign We have always devoted special
attention to the development of the estates of Our realm. We recognise
in this matter one of the most important tasks of Our Royal calling
which has been entrusted to Us by God, in which We aim at a dual
goal: to preserve intact for Our successors the rights, dignity and power
of the Crown which has been passed on to Us by Our ancestors of
glorious memory, at the same time, however, to entrust to the faithful
estates of Our monarchy that activity which is, in consonance with those
rights and the peculiar position of Our monarchy, able to secure to the
Fatherland a prosperous future. With regard to that We have decreed
as follows, on the basis of the laws given by Our Father's Majesty resting
in God, namely the ordinance on state debts of 17th January 1820 and
the law regulating the provincial estates of 8th June 1823:

1. Whenever the needs of the state require either new loans, or the
introduction of new or the raising of existing taxes, We will
assemble the provincial estates of the Monarchy around us in a

united diet in order firstly to claim the co-operation of the estates provided by the ordinance about state debts, and secondly to assure Ourselves of their approval.

2. We shall henceforth call together the united committee of the estates periodically.

3. We entrust to the united diet, and on its behalf to the united committee of estates:

(a) in relation to the advice of the estates in legislation that collaboration which was given to the provincial estates by the law of 5th June 1823 . . . as long as no general assemblies of the estates take place;

(b) the collaboration of the estates provided by the law of 17th January 1820 in connection with the paying of interest and amortisation of state debts, in so far as this is not transferred to the deputation of the estates for state debts;

(c) the right of petition about internal, not merely provincial, affairs.

All this according to the more detailed regulations of today's decree about the formation of the united diet, about the periodic calling together of the united committee of estates, its powers, and about the formation of a deputation of the estates for state debts.

Inasmuch as We have, going beyond the promise of Our Father's Majesty of blessed memory, made the levying of new as well as the increasing of existing taxes dependent on the consent of the estates, as lies in the nature of the German constitution, and have thus given to our subjects a special proof of Our royal confidence, We expect, with the same trust in the often proved faithfulness and honesty, with which We have ascended the throne of Our Fathers, that they will faithfully assist Us in this important steep, and will support Our strivings for the welfare of the Fatherland according to their strength, so that they may not lack success under the gracious assistance of God. . . .

I.4.B   The patent did not go far enough for the Prussian liberals. One of their leaders, Ludolf Camphausen, Prime Minister of Prussia in 1848, explains why. Extract translated from the German text of the speech to the diet on 1st June 1847 in R. Haym, *Reden und Redner des ersten Preussischen Vereinigten Landtags*, Berlin, 1847, pp. 332 f.

. . . The struggle we wage, Gentlemen, centres around two points. The first point is that the legislator is, after the issue of a law, committed to the law, thus any law which has been promulgated [and] which has not been amended [or] repealed obliges the legislator himself just as it does every citizen in the state. That this limitation of the highest power, this dividing line which distinguishes authority from arbitrariness be recognised, that each certain or hesitating promise which has not yet been fulfilled be brought to conclusion by way of law, that any contradiction between existing laws and reality be removed, that is the first point for which we fight. The second point is that participation in the power of the Government which should be granted to the people through its elected representatives in relation to the affairs of the community, whether this participation be great or small, whether it consists of advice or approval, should form, within the limits fixed by law, a uniform, indivisible and independent right: uniform, that is to say not to be exercised by provincial estates, but by Reich [i.e. Prussian] estates; indivisible, therefore not belonging partly to a small assembly, partly to a greater assembly; independent, thus in relation to the date of participation not dependent on the pleasure of the Government or on its judgement about need, but fixed in advance by the law. In this struggle we shall remain victors, that is my firm conviction; how long it will take, that I do not undertake to foresee or to predict. Yesterday a member who is accustomed to sit opposite spoke words of warning. I do not share the fear he entertains but I will say on my part, may it not happen as it did with the sibylline books whose number decreased the longer their acquisition was delayed . . .

I.5 THE SONDERBUND WAR IN SWITZERLAND, 1847

The Swiss Republic, which combined so many different elements in national culture, politics and religion, reflected, on a small scale, many of the tensions in the years before 1848. In 1847, the conflict between the Protestant, mainly radical, and the Catholic, mainly conservative, cantons erupted into a civil war which might have become international if the Eastern Powers had made good their intention to intervene on the side of the Catholic *Sonderbund* which wanted to secede from the Swiss Confederation. But the quick victory of the Protestant and radical defenders of Confederation in November 1847, followed a few months later by the revolutionary changes in Europe, saved the leading democratic republic on the continent in the pre-1848 era from a contest with the conservative monarchical forces.

I.5.A On 20th July 1847, the Diet voted that the *Sonderbund* of the seven Roman Catholic cantons was illegal. The Catholic cantons protested against this declaration. Extract from *Annual Register*, 1847, pp. 367.

1. The alliance of the seven Cantons of Lucerne, Uri, Schwytz, Unterwalden, Zug, Friburg, and Valais is incompatible with the essential dispositions of the Compact of the 7th of August 1815, and is declared to be dissolved.

2. The above-mentioned Cantons are to be held responsible for the execution of this decree.

3. The Diet reserves to itself, should circumstances require, to adopt ulterior measures to enforce obedience to its decree. . . .

I.5.B   On 3rd September 1847, the Protestant cantons in the Diet adopted the following resolutions on the Jesuits. Extract from *Annual Register*, 1847, pp. 367 f.

. . . In conformity with articles 1 and 18 of the Compact, the Diet is bound to watch over the maintenance of order and the internal security of the Confederation.

Considering that the existence and the secret practices of the Jesuits are incompatible with the order and peace of Switzerland, and seeing, in fine, their presence, particularly in Lucerne, one of the Cantons of the Directory – decree,

1. The question of the Jesuits is within the competency of the high Diet.

2. The Cantons of Lucerne, Schwytz, Friburg, and Valais, in which the Jesuits are established, are invited to expel them from their territories.

3. The admission in future of Jesuits into any one of the Cantons of Switzerland is interdicted.

I.5.C   Following the departure of the deputations of the *Sonderbund* cantons on 29th October 1847, the Federal Diet, on 4th November, issued the following decree. Extract from *Annual Register*, 1847, p. 371.

Article 1. The decree of the Diet, dated July 20 of the present year, respecting the dissolution of the separate league, concluded between the Cantons of Lucerne, Uri, Schwytz, Unterwalden, Zug, Friburg, and Valais, shall be carried into execution by force of arms.
Article 2. The General-in-Chief of the Federal troops is charged with the execution of the said decree.
Article 3. The Diet will adopt all ulterior measures necessary.
Article 4. The Federal Directory is requested to communicate, without delay, the present decree to the General-in-Chief of the Federal troops to the Federal council of war, and to all the Cantonal Governments.

I.6 LOUIS BLANC AND THE RIGHT TO WORK

The social and economic consequences of the upheavals caused directly and indirectly by increasing industrialisation led to the rise of many theories aimed at the creation of greater stability, particularly in France, where the discontent aroused by poverty increased the strains on the regime of Louis Philippe. In his famous treatise on the organisation of work, first published in 1839, Louis Blanc, a member of the Provisional Government in 1848, advocated the entry of the state into the competitive arena of production, by creating social workshops.

I.6.A   The extract is a translation from the French of an appendix of the 5th edition of Louis Blanc, *Organisation du Travail*, Paris, 1848 (with introduction dated July 1847), pp. 274 ff., reprinted by J. A. R. Marriott (ed.), *The French Revolution of 1848 in its Economic Aspect*, I, Oxford, 1913.

CONTRACT

Article 1. The associated workers shall be distributed in two families, each composed of an equal number of members. As the number of workers increases, so the number of families shall be increased in proportion. So far as possible the members will be chosen according to their place of domicile in order to form a family.

Article 2. The general assembly of workers shall appoint a recallable central administrative council whose special functions shall be to look for work, to deal with third parties, to distribute between the councils of the families . . . the work to be done and the price to be divided up in such a manner that each family receives in proportion [to its numbers] the same number of hours of work and the same remuneration.

Article 3. There shall be in each family a council designated by the name of family council, composed of the members who shall be elected by the family and recallable if necessary.

Article 4. Each family shall elect one of its members in order to take special charge of the examination of the books and the verification of work done. . . .

Article 5. Each worker shall receive pay, on the price of the job, at the rate of five francs per eight hours of work.

The benefits thus obtained over and above this sum shall form part of a common fund. . . .

Article 6. At the end of the year, an exact balance sheet of the position of the society will be drawn up. . . . If there is a favourable balance, it shall be divided into two parts, of which one shall be divided among the participants in equal proportions, and of which the other shall constitute an inalienable collective capital, destined for the growth of the association by successive additions. . . .

Article 7. Each member who has become infirm or sick and who can prove it, shall be entitled to the same wage, to the same advantages as if he had remained in good health.

Article 8. There shall be due to the worker who leaves voluntarily or as a result of misconduct only the wage of his work which has not already been paid to him.

Article 9. Recognising that the right to work belongs to every man and that any association invested with an exclusive character violates the doctrine of fraternity, the parties to the contract undertake in the most formal manner to admit among them on the basis of perfect equality any worker who shall present himself adhering to the statutes, provided that he shall be of the trade, that he proves himself, and that the situation of the society does not render his admission absolutely impossible.

Article 10. In order to decide that, there shall be formed a jury composed of seven members and elected by the whole membership.

Article 11. Those contracting recognise that it is worth more to gain less than to prevent a brother from living. The workers' jury shall therefore be bound to decide cases of admission according to this principle, that to monopolise work is to commit a crime of high treason against humanity.

Article 12. The parties to the contract are divided, from the present onward, . . . into two families. They shall be able to grow by successive additions up to a figure of one hundred members each, and shall then be declared full. Any new members shall be distributed, in equal numbers, among the two existing families, until they attain the number of one hundred. . . .

Article 13. The jury of workers shall be chosen, by the members, as an arbitration tribunal, and it shall judge, in this capacity, the disputes which could ensue among the parties to the contract. It shall decide on the legitimacy of causes of resignation or the facts of illness; it will also declare, on the report of the inspectors, the exclusion of workers convicted of laziness. It shall finally be able to declare, after public debate, the recall of those members of the councils who shall deserve to be recalled; and this in the form followed by the arbitration tribunal for its judgements.

Article 14. Elections to the councils and to the jury shall take place each year [members shall be re-eligible].

II

REVOLUTION
(JANUARY TO MARCH 1848)

THE DOCUMENTS CONTAINED in this chapter illustrate the rapid spread of the revolutionary movement over wide parts of the continent of Europe during the first quarter of 1848. The dramatic year opened with the Sicilian rising in mid-January on the periphery of Europe. Italy was now beginning to be affected, as is seen in the granting of the Sardinian constitution early in February. The pace quickened with the overthrow of Louis Philippe and the establishment of the republic in France at the end of February. This in turn affected Germany and Austria. Metternich was overthrown and constitutional regimes installed. Both the German and the Italian national movement asserted themselves. Sardinia challenged Austria in Northern Italy and the Schleswig-Holstein question led to war between Germany and Denmark, with the risk of further international complications.

II.1 THE SICILIAN RISING, JANUARY 1848

The Sicilians were not satisfied with being ruled from the mainland as part of the Kingdom of Naples, and matters were not made better by the refusal of King Ferdinand II to grant reforms. The Sicilian revolt in January 1848 was inspired, like the other revolutions of the year, by a mixture of motives, political, economic and social, often contradictory. The movement in Sicily was essentially somewhat different from that on the Italian mainland, where the preoccupation was with Italian unification and with the establishment of constitutionalism.

II.1.A The extract gives the text of the proclamation issued to the inhabitants of Sicily from Palermo on the eve of the revolt of 12th January, from *Annual Register*, 1848, p. 332.

'Sicilians! the time for prayers is passed; pacific protestations, supplications, and demonstrations—all have remained ineffectual. Ferdinand has treated them all with contempt; and we, a people born freemen, and now loaded with chains and reduced to misery, shall we still delay to claim our legitimate rights? To arms! sons of Sicily: our

34

united force will be invincible. At the break of day of January 12 shall be the signal for the glorious era of our universal regeneration. Palermo will receive with transport every Sicilian who shall come armed to sustain the common cause, and establish reformed institutions in conformity with the progress and will of Europe, of Italy, and of Pius IX. Union, order, obedience to chiefs, respect to property. Robbery is declared a crime of high treason against the country, and shall be punished as such. Whoever may be in want of resources shall be supplied at the common charge. Heaven will not fail to second our just under-taking. Sicilians, to arms!'

II.1.B   Lord Minto, a member of the British Government, was already on a special mission to Italy when the Sicilian revolt broke out. He proceeded to Sicily to use his good offices for some kind of a peaceful settlement which would at the same time lead to reform. The pace of events, soon, however, quickened too much for any mediation of this kind. Extract from a letter of Lord Minto to his son-in-law, Lord John Russell, the Prime Minister, dated Rome, February 3, 1848, from G. P. Gooch (ed.). *The Later Corres-pondence of Lord John Russell 1840–1878*, I, London, 1925, p. 321.

. . . I am within a quarter of an hour of starting for Naples and can-not write you more than a line. Sicily at present appears to be the only hitch in the way of a speedy settlement of affairs there, and I rather dread that the King may not easily be brought to consent to the only terms likely to go down with the Sicilians, a separate Parliament of their own. There is a notion that he will make an attempt to obtain an Euro-pean mediation in the affairs of the two Sicilies. This would never do, and we should insist upon having the Italians left to manage their own matters for themselves. My sympathies are so strongly with the Sicilians, whose conduct has been very noble, that I hardly trust my judgement in their cause, and the conduct of the Neapolitan troops has been so atrocious that one can only feel them to be worthy of their Bourbon King. Pray let me know your views as to the degree of protection we should give the Sicilians, and what to say if Austria advances to Naples. . . .

II.2   SARDINIA'S ROLE IN ITALY

The evidence of a wind of change gradually being felt in Europe was not lost on King Charles Albert of Sardinia, forever watchful for any oppor-tunity which might enhance the role of his kingdom and of his dynasty, that of Savoy. As in Germany, it was believed in Italy that the develop-ment of constitutional regimes was a prerequisite to national unity.

II.2.A On 8th February 1848, Charles Albert issued the following manifesto, on which the Sardinian and later the Italian constitutional
monarchy was based. Extract from *Annual Register*, 1848, pp.
317 f.

. . . 'Now, therefore, that the times are ripe for greater things, and, in
the midst of the changes which have occurred in Italy, we hesitate no
longer to give our people the most solemn proof that we are able to give
of the faith which we continue to repose in their devotion and dis-
cretion. . . .

. . . for the present we have much pleasure in declaring that, with the
advice and approval of our Ministers and the principal advisers of our
Crown, we have resolved and determined to adopt the following bases
of a fundamental statute for the establishment in our states of a complete system of representative Government.

Article 1. The Catholic, apostolic, and Roman religion is the sole
religion of the state.

The other forms of public worship at present existing are tolerated
in conformity with the laws.

Article 2. The person of the Sovereign is sacred and inviolable. His
ministers are responsible.

Article 3. To the King alone appertains the executive power. He is the
supreme head of the State. He commands all the forces, both naval and
military; declares war, concludes treaties of peace, alliance, and commerce; nominates to all offices, and gives all the necessary orders for the
execution of the laws without suspending or dispensing with the
observance thereof.

Article 4. The King alone sanctions and promulgates the laws.

Article 5. All justice emanates from the King, and is administered in
his name. He may grant mercy and commute punishment.

Article 6. The legislative power will be collectively exercised by the
King and by two Chambers.

Article 7. The first of these Chambers will be composed of Members
nominated by the King for life; the second will be elective, on the basis
of the census to be determined.

Article 8. The proposal of laws will appertain to the King and to each
of the Chambers, but with the distinct understanding that all laws im-
posing taxes must originate in the elective Chamber.

Article 9. The King convokes the two Chambers annually, prorogues
their sessions, and may dissolve the elective one; but in this case he will
convoke a new assembly at the expiration of four months.

Article 10. No tax may be imposed or levied if not assented to by the
Chambers and sanctioned by the King.

Article 11. The press will be free, but subject to restraining laws.

Article 12. Individual liberty will be guaranteed.

Article 13. The judges, . . . will be irremovable, after having exercised their functions for a certain space of time, to be hereafter determined.

Article 14. We reserve to ourselves the power of establishing a district militia . . . composed of persons who may pay a rate, which will be fixed upon hereafter. This militia will be placed under the command of the administrative authority, and in dependence on the Minister of the Interior.

The King will have the power of suspending or dissolving it in places where he may deem it opportune so to do.' . . .

II.3 FEBRUARY REVOLUTION AND SECOND FRENCH REPUBLIC

By the beginning of 1848, the regime of Louis Philippe in France was coming under increasing internal criticism. The movement for parliamentary and electoral reform was gradually taken over by radicals no longer content with a constitutional monarchy. Processions in connection with banquets to promote the cause of reform led to disorders and by the morning of the 24th of February Paris was in revolt. The King abdicated and fled to England, the first of a series of prominent refugees to arrive there. The republic was proclaimed. The following documents illustrate the policy of the new regime and some of its difficulties.

II.3.A The King's hope of saving the Orleans dynasty was not to be fulfilled. Declaration dated 24th February, translated from the French text in F.-A. Hélie, *Les Constitutions de la France*, Paris, 1880, p. 1067.

. . . I abdicate this Crown which the voice of the Nation has called me to wear in favour of my grandson, the Count of Paris. May he succeed in the great task which falls to him today! . . .

II.3.B Under the pressure of popular turmoil, Louis Blanc, a member of the Provisional Government, drafted the following decree on 25th February. From Marriott (ed.), *The French Revolution of 1848*, I, pp. lx f.

. . . The Provisional Government engage themselves to guarantee the existence of the workmen by means of labour.

They engage themselves to guarantee labour to every citizen.

They take it to be necessary for the workmen to associate with one another, in order to reap the legitimate reward of their toil.

The Provisional Government restore to the workmen, who are its real owners, the million belonging to the late Civil List, which will soon be due.

II.3.c   The decree of the Provisional Government proclaiming the Second
Republic is translated from the French text in Hélie, *Les Constitutions de la France*, Paris, 1880, p. 1080.

. . . Citizens, Royalty under whatever form is abolished. No more
legitimism, no more Bonapartism, no regency. The Provisional Government has taken all the measures necessary to render impossible the
return of the former dynasty, and the accession of a new one. The
republic is proclaimed. The people are united. All the forts surrounding
the capital are ours. The brave garrison of Vincennes is a garrison of
brothers.

Let us preserve with respect this old republican flag whose three
colours have made with our fathers the round of the world. Let us show
that the symbol of equality, of liberty and of fraternity is at the same
time the symbol of order and of the most real, the most lasting order,
because justice is its basis and the entire people its instrument.

The people have already understood that the provisioning of Paris
has required a freer circulation in the streets of Paris, and the hands
which erected the barricades have in several places made in them an
opening sufficiently large for the free passage of vehicles of transport.
May this example be followed everywhere; that Paris may resume its
accustomed look, commerce its activity and confidence, and that the
people may at the same time watch over the maintenance of its rights
and may continue to assure—as it has done hitherto—calm and public
security. . . .

II.3.d   An attempt to implement the right to work was made on 27th
February, in the following decree, taken from Marriott (ed.), *The
French Revolution of 1848*, I, p. lxi.

. . . The Provisional Government decrees the establishment of
National Workshops. The Minister of Public Works is charged with the
execution of the present decree. . . .

II.3.e   Partly to neutralise Louis Blanc, the Provisional Government set
up a Labour Commission on 28th February. Extract from Marriott (ed.), *The French Revolution of 1848*, I, pp. lxii f.

. . . Considering that the Revolution made by the people ought to be
made *for* them;

That it is high time to put an end to the iniquitous and protracted
sufferings of workmen;

That the labour question is one of supreme importance;

That there is no problem more worthy of the attention of a Republican
Government;

That it is a duty more especially incumbent on France to study and to endeavour to solve a problem submitted at present to all the industrial nations of Europe;

That it is advisable to think, without delay, of making him that works enjoy the legitimate reward of his labour;

The Provisional Government decree:

A permanent Commission shall be formed for the express purpose of inquiring into the social condition of the operatives;

In order to show how great is the importance which the Provisional Government attach to the solution of such a problem, they place at the head of the 'Government Labour Commission' two of their colleagues, MM. Louis Blanc and Albert, the former in capacity of president, the latter, a workman himself,[1] in that of vice-president. Workmen will be called upon to be members of the said Commission, the seat of which will be the Luxembourg. . . .

II.3.F Though welcomed by radicals throughout Europe, the establishment of another French republic was bound to arouse many fears, not only among the legitimists, but also among the moderate liberals. In his 'Manifesto to Europe' the Foreign Minister, Lamartine, attempted to reassure foreign countries. Extract from Alphonse de Lamartine, *History of the French Revolution of 1848*, II, translated from the French, London, 1849, pp. 3 ff.

You know the events of Paris—the victory of the people; their heroism, moderation, and tranquillity; the re-establishment of order by the co-operation of the citizens at large, as if, during this interregnum of the visible powers, public reason was, of itself alone, the Government of France.

The French revolution has thus entered upon its definitive period. France is a republic. The French republic does not require to be acknowledged in order to exist. It is based alike on natural and national law. It is the will of a great people, who demand the privilege only for themselves. But the French republic, being desirous of entering into the family of established governments, as a regular power, and not as a phenomenon destructive of European order, it is expedient that you should promptly make known to the Government to which you are accredited, the principles and tendencies which will henceforth guide the foreign policy of the French Government.

The proclamation of the French republic is not an act of aggression against any form of government in the world. Forms of government have diversities as legitimate as the diversities of character—of geographical situation—of intellectual, moral, and material development among nations. Nations, like individuals, have different ages; and the

---

[1] Note in Marriott, an inaccuracy. See also D. C. McKay, *The National Workshops*, p. xxii.

principles which rule them have successive phases. The monarchical, the aristocratic, the constitutional, and the republican forms of government, are the expression of the different degrees of maturity in the genius of nations. They require more liberty in proportion as they feel equality, and democracy in proportion as they are inspired with a greater share of justice and love for the people over whom they rule. It is merely a question of time. A nation ruins itself by anticipating the hour of that maturity; as it dishonours itself by allowing it to pass away without seizing it. Monarchy and republicanism are not, in the eyes of wise statesmen, absolute principles, arrayed in deadly conflict against each other; they are facts which contrast one with another, and, which may exist face to face by mutually understanding and respecting each other.

War, therefore, is not now the principle of the French republic, as it was the fatal and glorious necessity of the republic of 1792. Half a century separates 1792 from 1848. To return, after the lapse of half a century, to the principle of 1792, or to the principle of conquest pursued during the empire, would not be to advance, but to regress. The revolution of yesterday is a step forward, not backward. The world and ourselves are desirous of advancing to fraternity and peace.

If the situation of the French republic in 1792 explained the necessity of war, the differences existing between that period of our history and the present time explain the necessity of peace. Endeavour to understand these differences and to make them understood by those around you.

In 1792 the nation was not united. It may be said that two nations existed on the same soil. A terrible conflict was kept up between the classes who were deprived of their privileges and the classes who had just conquered equality and liberty. The dispossessed classes coalesced with captive royalty and jealous foreign powers, to deny France her right to revolution, and by invasion to force back upon her monarchy, aristocracy, and theocracy. At the present time, there are no distinct and unequal classes. Liberty has enfranchised all. Equality in the eye of the law has levelled all; fraternity, whose implementation we proclaim, and whose blessings the National Assembly will administer, will unite all. There is not a single citizen in France, whatsoever may be his opinion, who does not rally round the principle of the Fatherland before every other consideration, and by that very unity France is rendered invulnerable to attempts and alarms of invasion.

In 1792 it was not the whole body of the people who made themselves masters of the Government; it was the middle class alone that wished to exercise liberty, and to enjoy it. The triumph of the middle class was therefore selfish, like the triumph of every oligarchy. The middle class wished to secure to itself alone the privileges acquired by all. Accordingly it was found necessary to create a powerful diversion against the advent of popular supremacy, by urging the people to the field of battle, and hereby preventing them from taking part in their own government. This diversion was war. War was the ardent wish of the monarchists and the Girondins; but it was not desired by the more enlightened democrats, who, like ourselves, were anxious for the genuine, complete, and regular reign of the people themselves; comprising under that denomination all classes, without exclusion or preference, which compose the nation.

In 1792 the people were made the instrument of the revolution, but they were not its beneficiaries. The present revolution has been achieved by them and for them. The people and the revolution are one and the same. When they entered upon the revolution, the people brought with them their new wants of labour, industry, instruction, agriculture, commerce, morality, welfare, property, cheap living, navigation, and civilisation. All these are the wants of peace. The people and peace are but one word.

In 1792 the ideas of France and Europe were not prepared to conceive and to accept the great harmony of nations among themselves for the benefit of the human race. The views of the century, then drawing to its close, were confined to the heads of a few philosophers. But at the present day philosophy is popular. Fifty years of the freedom of thought, speech, and writing, have produced their results. Books, journals, and tribunes, have accomplished the apostolic mission of European intelligence. Reason, dawning everywhere over the frontiers of nations, has given birth to that great intellectual commonwealth, which will be the achievement of the French revolution, and the constitution of international fraternity throughout the globe.

Finally, in 1792, liberty was a novelty, equality a scandal, and the republic a problem. The very name of the people, only just then revived by Fénelon, Montesquieu, and Rousseau, had been so far forgotten, buried, profaned by old feudal, dynastic, and ecclesiastical traditions, that even the most lawful intervention of the people in their own affairs appeared a monstrosity in the eyes of statesmen of the old school. Democracy at once spread terror among thrones, and shook the foundation of society. But now, on the contrary, both kings and people are accustomed to the name, to the forms, and to the regular agitations of that freedom which exists in various degrees in almost all states, even those subject to monarchical rule. They will become accustomed to republicanism, which is public liberty in its most perfect form, among the more mature nations. They will acknowledge that there is a conservative freedom; they will acknowledge that there may exist in a republic not only greater order, but that there may even be a more genuine order in the government of all for the sake of all, than in the government of the few for the sake of the few.

But independently of these disinterested considerations, interest alone for the consolidation and duration of the republic would inspire the statesmen of France with a desire for peace. It is not the country, but liberty, which is exposed to the greatest danger in time of war. War is almost invariably a dictatorship. Soldiers pay more regard to men than to institutions. Thrones tempt the ambitious; glory dazzles patriotism. The prestige of a victorious name veils the design against national sovereignty. The republic doubtless desires glory, but she desires it for herself, and not for Caesars and Napoleons.

But let no misapprehension exist. These ideas, which the Provisional Government charges you to convey to the powers as the pledge of European security, must not be understood as suing for pardon to the republic for having presumed to rise into being; still less must they be regarded as humbly soliciting that a great right and a great people may hold their place in Europe. They have a more noble object in view, which is to make sovereigns and people reflect, and to prevent them from being deceived respecting the character of our revolution; to place the event in its true light, and in its proper character; finally, to give pledges to humanity before giving them to our rights and our honour, should they be disavowed or menaced.

The French republic, therefore, will not commence war against any state; it is unnecessary to add, that it will accept war should conditions incompatible with peace be offered to the French people. The conviction of the men who govern France at the present moment is this: it will be fortunate for France should war be declared against her and should she be thus constrained to augment her power and her glory, in spite of her moderation; but terrible will be the responsibility of France should the republic itself declare war without being provoked thereto! In the first case, the martial genius of France, her impatience for action, her strength accumulated during many years of peace, would render her invincible on her own territory, and perhaps redoubtable beyond her frontiers: in the second case she would turn to her own disadvantage the recollections of her former conquests, which give offence to the national feelings of other countries; and she would compromise herself with her first and most universal allies, the good-will of nations and the genius of civilisation.

According to these principles, Sir, which are the principles coolly and deliberately adopted by France and which she avows without fear and without defiance, to her friends and to her enemies, you will impress upon your mind the following declarations.

The treaties of 1815 have no longer any lawful existence in the eyes of the French republic; nevertheless, the territorial limits circumscribed by those treaties are facts which the republic admits as a basis, and as a starting-point, in her relations with foreign nations.

But if the treaties of 1815 have no existence—save as facts to be modified by common consent—and if the republic openly declares that her right and mission are to arrive regularly and pacifically at those modifications—the good sense, the moderation, the conscience, the prudence of the republic do exist, and they afford Europe a surer and more honourable guarantee than the words of those treaties, which have so frequently been violated or modified by Europe itself.

Endeavour, Sir, to make this emancipation of the republic from the treaties of 1815, understood and honestly admitted, and to show that such an admission is in no way irreconcilable with the repose of Europe.

Thus we declare without reserve, that if the hour for the reconstruction of any of the oppressed nations of Europe, or other parts of the world, should seem to have arrived, according to the decrees of Providence; if Switzerland, our faithful ally from the time of Francis I, should be restrained or menaced in the progressive movement she is carrying out, and which will impart new strength to the fasces of democratic governments; if the independent states of Italy should be invaded; if limits or obstacles should be imposed on their internal changes; if there should be any armed interference with their right of allying themselves together for the purpose of consolidating an Italian nation,—the French republic would think itself entitled to take up arms in defence of these legitimate movements towards the improvement and nationhood of states.

The republic, as you perceive, has passed over at one step the era of proscriptions and dictatorship. It is determined never to veil liberty at home; and it is equally determined never to veil its democratic principle abroad. It will not suffer anything to intervene between the peaceful dawn of its own liberty and the eyes of nations. It proclaims itself the intellectual and cordial ally of popular rights and progress, and of every legitimate development of institutions among nations who may be desirous of maintaining the same principles as her own. It will not pursue underhand or incendiary propagandism among neighbouring states. It is aware that there is no real liberty for nations except that which springs from themselves, and takes its birth on their own soil. But by the light of its intelligence, and the spectacle of order and peace which it hopes to present to the world, the republic will exercise the only honourable proselytism, the proselytism of esteem and sympathy. This is not war, it is nature; it is not the agitation of Europe, it is the life of nations; it is not kindling a conflagration in the world, it is shining in our own place on the horizon of nations, and is at once to anticipate and to direct them.

We wish, for the sake of humanity, that peace may be preserved; we also expect that it will. There was a war agitation a year ago between France and England; the agitation did not come from republican France, but from the dynasty. The dynasty has carried away with it that danger of war which it created for Europe by the exclusively personal ambition of its family alliances in Spain. That domestic policy of the fallen dynasty, which for the space of seventeen years has been a dead weight on our national dignity, has also, by its pretensions to a crown in Madrid, operated as an obstacle to our liberal alliances, and to peace. The republic has no ambition; the republic has no nepotism, and it inherits no family pretensions. Let Spain govern herself; let Spain be independent and free. For the consolidation of this natural alliance, France relies more on conformity of principles than on the succession of the house of Bourbon.

Such, Sir, is the spirit of the councils of the republic; such will invariably be the character of the frank, firm, and moderate policy which you will have to represent.

The republic pronounced at its birth, and in the midst of a conflict not provoked by the people, three words, which have revealed its soul, and which will call down on its cradle the blessing of God and man: *liberty, equality, fraternity.* It gave on the following day, in the abolition of the punishment of death for political offences, the true commentary on those three words, as far as regards the domestic policy of France; it is for you to give them their true commentary abroad. The meaning of these three words, as applied to our foreign policy, is this: the emancipation of France from the chains which have fettered her principles and her dignity; her reinstatement in the rank she is entitled to occupy among the great powers of Europe; in short, the declaration of alliance and friendship to all nations. If France be conscious of the part she has to perform in the liberal and civilising mission of the age, there is not one of those words which signifies *war.* If Europe be prudent and just, there is not one of those words which does not signify *peace.*

II.3.G   The problems created by the national workshops are illustrated in the following account by Emile Thomas of his proposals to the Provisional Government on 5th March 1848. Extracts translated from the French in Emile Thomas, 'Histoire des Ateliers Nationaux' (Paris, 1848), reprinted in Marriott, *The French Revolution of 1848,* II, pp. 48 ff.

. . . I do not know exactly, gentlemen, the difficulties . . . of the situation, but as far as I can see it seems to me that they consist above all in the impossibility which most of the mayoralties of the arrondissement find themselves in, of carrying out the new service for workmen, without hindering the functions of the municipal department, which is already overburdened by enrolments in the mobile guard, the extension of the work of welfare agencies, the census and growth of the National Guard, and also its armament and equipment, by the making-up of electoral rolls for general elections as well as for the National Guard, and finally by the immoderate activity which necessarily falls to each part of the service, for which the personnel of the offices, although perhaps doubled, hardly suffices.

It is not in doubt that if the municipalities could attend to those under their administration from the new point of view under discussion; if unity of action and organisation could be brought to bear, there would be no need to seek for anything better than the normal authority with which they are invested and which depends directly and naturally on each of the citizens making up the commune.

But, unfortunately, gentlemen, it is not like that and grave abuses, terrible occasions of disorder and anarchy, come about in following this path which, in ordinary times, would be preferable to any other. Most of the workmen you receive occupy furnished lodgings whose not very scrupulous masters accord them lodging certificates in advance—sometimes even false ones—with deplorable ease. The days of police commissioners are hardly sufficient to check these certificates whose validity there is nothing to confirm. Your employees who receive them thus have no other means of control over them; hence there occur inevitably double and triple and even fraudulent inscriptions obtained by men who have no need of them, for they know that the open workshops have a surplus of hands and that the certificates of admission, which they obtain in their mayoralty in order to go there, entitles them to a purely notional visa and is, for them, as good as 30 sous per day in cash which they only have to draw at your offices.

On the other hand the good workmen are irritated because the guarantee of labour which was given to them ends up only in humiliating relief; all those who have claims are impatient and grumble because they have to wait in the rain and in the cold for long hours until their turn to draw this relief; the paternal authority of the mayoralties is not acknowledged because it is impossible for them to keep an eye on the unquiet and turbulent spirits within them; they lack all means of pressure and of effective repression against the discontent which shows itself in threats, sometimes in violence, and becomes more dangerous every day.

Finally, I do not speak of the confusion and disorder caused in the courtyards in front of the town halls and in their neighbourhood for quite some distance by tumultuous meetings of workmen which begin early in the day and often do not disperse until the night, and whose most appreciable effect is to hinder movement, almost to destroy the working of each municipality.

Such a state of affairs, gentlemen, cannot last any longer without danger to public security; and here, therefore, is what I am going to propose to you in order to lessen the evil as far as possible, if not to make it disappear altogether.

The means of repression are lacking, it is true; there is not and perhaps there may not be for a long time in Paris the military body which has the physical power to achieve maintenance of order. But one of the most energetic means which can lead to the same goal is at your disposal—I want to speak of moral influence.

You know, gentlemen, how much the people love young folk, above all the pupils of the schools; with what ease they allow themselves to be guided by them. This is natural, the people resembles nothing so much as a child. Open to bad influences, it is still more easily open to good ones, to generous thoughts. The germ of all that which has something beautiful, noble, great, and virtuous in it is in its heart, and only needs to be developed. One must follow it step by step, talk to it, advise ceaselessly, arouse its emulation, hold it in its joys, calm it in its hatreds, console it in its sorrows. To come to it without mistrust, and without weapons, with open arms, not to impose upon it, but to make it accept gently a superiority which it will appreciate quickly and which it will soon cherish.

This, gentlemen, is the useful role which I dare hope to play and which I want to share with all my comrades of the École Centrale [d'Arts et Manufactures]. Their education destines them to guide in the factories, in the art workshops, the workmen who form the principal element there; indeed, a great number of them were brought up in similar conditions; our former comrades, the civil engineers, have, furthermore, a practical habit of efforts of the same kind.

I therefore propose to you, gentlemen, to establish in a quarter sufficiently far from the great centres of population—so that there may be nothing to fear for our projects—an administration whose purpose will be to centralise the action of a dozen mayoralties in all matters concerning workmen. Each of the municipalities, on a day fixed in advance, will send us their workmen, furnished with their papers, certificates, etc., which are a unique but indispensable condition of admission. While registering their names, occupations, and lodgings, we will hand to them a workman's certificate designed for various controls which we will exercise over them and which they will not be able to evade. We will form them into brigades of a fixed number of men each; these brigades will form companies, of which each will be directed by one of our young comrades; a system . . . based on these principles and recognising the brigade as a unit will permit payment to be made regularly, be it of relief or of wages, at fixed hours, under a proper system of inspection and by means of marginal endorsements being made [on the record of] each worker.

Furthermore the Minister of Public Works, as also the Division of Public Works of the City, will let us know day by day the number of workers of each category who can be applied to the new open sites, on the orders made by the Government; and day by day, equally, we will direct to these works, whether in Paris or in the Departments, the workers for which we have been asked; our young men will accompany them. For the works of the Department of Highways they will leave the direction of the execution to the engineers of the Corps and will content themselves with the modest but useful position of officers charged with the maintenance of order and good discipline; those who do not come into this category will resume at the same time their profession as engineers.

Finally, the industrialists, the manufacturers, the contractors, who have need of workmen, will address themselves to us and will deal in each case with workmen received from our hands, instead of seeking them out where they are idle.

In a word, the scheme I propose is the opening of a Labour Exchange [Bureau de Placement], free and open to all, which during this special crisis shall perform the additional duty of centralising the distribution of doles at present in the hands of the mayors. This Bureau will first register the workmen according to their trades, and will then rearrange them according to their arrondissements, with a view to avoiding contact and union between men of the same trade, such as might—at any rate, in some trades—lead to grave inconvenience, if not danger.

In closing, gentlemen, I must not hide from you the fears which an organisation of this kind must inspire; mighty for the good, it can do harm for it is not that different in its form of organisation . . . from the cells of secret societies. If sufficient work does not turn up each day to allow us to distribute to the different sites the majority of the idle workmen, the [task of] direction will become extremely painful, if not dangerous, and incalculable disasters could arise. It will furthermore be impossible to prevent the existence of abuses—which I have had the honour of indicating to you today—in such a state of affairs. But with work all will turn out for the good; only real workers will come to us, and with pay being effected day by day on the site, in the presence of all, double employment will no longer be possible. . . .

. . . I retired . . . soon I was recalled.

Sir, the Chairman said to me, your project is adopted, you will put it into operation at once. . . .

The following day I received a communication about the decree which instituted the service; it was drawn up in these terms:

THE FRENCH REPUBLIC
LIBERTY EQUALITY FRATERNITY

The member of the Provisional Government, the Minister of Public Works, with reference to the Decree of the Provisional Government dated 27th February last, which orders the establishment of national workshops, decrees as follows:

Article 1. There will be established in Paris a central office for the organisation of the national workshops of the Department of the Seine.

This office will be put under the direction of M. Emile Thomas, appointed for this purpose Commissioner of the Republic.

Article 2. The works to be carried out in the interior of the city are exclusively reserved to the workers domiciled in the area of the twelve mayoralties. Workers residing outside the city can only be received in the workshops which have been opened in the suburbs.

Article 3. The workers domiciled in Paris or in the suburbs will have to have their property and their place of residence confirmed by the mayoralties of their communes.

After having sight of the certificates delivered by the mayors, the Director of the Central Office will proceed to the brigading and classification of the workers, in order to direct them successively to the places where it will be possible to establish workshops, up to the number indicated by the Chiefs of Service.

No worker who is not domiciled in the Department of the Seine may be included in this category.

Article 4. As the workshops will be established on the roads of communication which are maintained by the Minister of Public Works, the agents of all grades put in charge by the Minister or by the Director of the Central Office will have to conform, in the execution of the works, to the instructions which may be given to them by the engineers.

Article 5. The Director of the Central Office will publish, after an interval of two days, regulations for the carrying out of the present decree. These regulations will be submitted for approval to the Minister for Public Works.

The Minister of Public Works,
Member of the Provisional Government,
Mairie,
Paris, 6th March 1848.

II.4 DECLARATION OF THE HEIDELBERG ASSEMBLY

The February Revolution in France at once had an effect on Germany. The calling of a German national parliament was strongly demanded.

II.4.A   The fifty-one men who issued the Heidelberg declaration on 5th March 1848, were drawn from the two groups which were soon to fight each other bitterly, the moderate liberals and the radicals. Representation was mainly from the west and south-west of Germany. Extract translated from the German text in E. K. Huber (ed.), *Dokumente zur deutschen Verfassungsgeschichte*, I, Stuttgart, 1961, pp. 264 f.

Heidelberg, 5th March. Today fifty-one men were assembled here, from Prussia, Bavaria, Wurtemberg, Baden, Nassau and Frankfurt, almost all members of state assemblies, in order to discuss the most urgent measures for the Fatherland in this moment of decision.

Unanimously resolved in their devotion to the freedom, unity, independence and honour of the German nation, they all express their conviction that the establishment and defence of these highest blessings must be attempted by co-operation of all the German peoples with their governments, so long as delivery is still possible in this manner.

No less unanimous was the deep expression of sorrow that sad experience of the effectiveness of the German Confederation authorities has shaken confidence in them so much, that an address of the citizens to them would evoke the worst discord. This is deeply grievous at a moment when these authorities appeal to the tragic experiences of history and speak with pretty words of the high position to which the Nation is called among the peoples, in which they ask every German to co-operate in confidence [with them]—deeply grievous at this moment is the memory that they have themselves forbidden Germans to address petitions to them.

The assembled unanimously expressed their conviction of what the Fatherland urgently needs as follows:

'Germany must not be involved in war through intervention in the affairs of the neighbouring country or through non-recognition of the changes in the state made there.

Germans must not be caused to diminish or rob from other nations the freedom and independence which they themselves ask as their right.

The defence of the Germans and of their princes may be sought in the main only in the faithfulness and the proven military courage of the nation, never in a Russian alliance.

The meeting of a national representation elected in all the German lands according to the number of the people must not be postponed, both for the removal of imminent internal and external dangers, and for the development of the strength and flowering of German national life!'

In order to contribute to the representation of the nation as speedily and as completely as possible, those assembled have resolved: 'to urge the governments concerned most pressingly, as soon and as completely as possible, to surround the whole German Fatherland and the thrones with this mighty protective rampart'.

At the same time they have agreed to concentrate their efforts so that as soon as possible a more complete assembly of men of trust from all German peoples should come together in order to continue deliberation of this most important matter and to offer its co-operation to the Fatherland as well as to the Governments.

To this end seven members were requested to prepare proposals concerning the election and the establishment of an appropriate national
representation and speedily to take care of the invitations to an assembly
of German men.[2]

A main task of the national representation will in any case be common
defence . . . and external representation, whereby great sums of money
will be saved for other important needs, while at the same time the
identity and suitable self-administration of the different states remains
in existence.

With the prudent, faithful and manly co-operation of all Germans,
the Fatherland may hope to achieve and to maintain freedom, unity
and order in the most difficult situations, and joyfully to greet the
advent of a hardly expected strength and flowering . . .

II.5 VIENNA REVOLUTION AND OVERTHROW
OF METTERNICH

Nobody had realised better than the Austrian Chancellor that the
political stability of Europe was indivisible. Events in France and Germany were bound to shake the Metternich regime in Austria. Demands
for constitutional reform, so long silenced, were heard in Vienna early
in March. A rising took place on 13th March, followed by the resignation of Metternich.

II.5.A The following extract gives the imperial proclamation of 15th
    March, one of many constitutional concessions to follow. From
    Annual Register, 1848, p. 404.

By virtue of our declaration abolishing the censorship, liberty of the
press is allowed in the form under which it exists in those countries
which have hitherto enjoyed it. A National Guard, established on the
basis of property and intelligence, already performs the most beneficial
service.

The necessary steps have been taken for convoking, with the least
possible loss of time, the Deputies from all our provincial States, and
from the Central Congregations of the Lombardo-Venetian kingdom
(the representation of the class of burghers being strengthened, and due
regard being paid to the existing provincial constitutions), in order that
they may deliberate on the constitution which we have resolved to grant
to our people.

We therefore confidently expect that excited tempers will become
composed, that study will resume its wonted course, and that industry
and peaceful intercourse will spring into new life.

[2] The Pre-parliament, see III, 1. A and C.

II.6   THE BERLIN REVOLUTION

The regime in Berlin was weakened by the overthrow of Metternich and by many other concessions made by governments in Germany. The reasons for the collapse of the old order in Prussia are seen from inside and outside the royal palace in the following two documents.

II.6.A   General Leopold von Gerlach, Adjutant-General of King Frederick William IV and his close confidant, belonged to the legitimist, Protestant pietistical circle with which Bismarck was associated during the earlier part of his political career. In the following extract, written soon afterwards, the events of the 18th March in Berlin are described by an advocate of resistance to the revolution. Extract translated from the German of *Denkwürdigkeiten aus dem Leben Leopold von Gerlachs*, I, Berlin, 1891, pp. 131 ff.

. . . Sunday, 12th [March 1848] at eight o'clock in the morning the lame Arnim[3] came to me. . . . He disclosed his political views to me, his joy at the overthrow of Louis Philippe and of Guizot, the necessity and justice of the French Republic. I opposed him directly and sharply, but naturally without success. He adjured me not to hinder the calling together of the [Prussian] Diet. The following day it was already announced in the newspapers. Thus we had arrived on the broad path of concession which leads downhill with constantly increasing speed . . .

. . . Monday [13th March] . . . the garrison first marched out . . . On the Stechbahn the dragoons and the garde du corps dispersed the mob with rifles at the ready. In the *Zelten* there were meetings, speeches were made there which were quietly tolerated. On Wednesday [15th March] Pfuel as Governor [of Berlin] distributed the troops in such a way that the Schloss [Royal Palace] was occupied by two battalions, the Zeughaus [arsenal] by one battalion. The squadron garde du corps and the Ulanen [lancers] stopped in the courtyard of the Academy. The Schlossplatz [Palace Square] was absolutely full of people who then insulted the troops barring the palace portals in the most insolent manner and finally even threw stones at them. Pfuel stationed himself in front of the infantry in full uniform, but forbade any retaliation, which angered the Prince of Prussia,[4] who spoke violently of a demoralisation of the troops and the like. Finally, when the situation was constantly getting more grave, General Prittwitz received the command to advance from Unter den Linden with the cavalry. As soon as the latter

[3] Alexander Heinrich von Arnim-Suckow, Prussian minister to France, who was to become Foreign Minister soon afterwards.

[4] The oldest brother of the King and heir to the throne, William, later himself King and also German Emperor.

arrived at the corner of the Palace, the infantry was to stream out of the portal . . . and at the first shot all battalions still assigned to their barracks were to march to the Palace. At this time, it being already dark, about seven o'clock, I rode with Prittwitz to the Town Commandant's office, the regiment of Ulanen came towards us; I joined it . . . I rode quickly through the Palace and saw how the infantry advanced, arrested a lot of people and delivered them to the cellar under the Palace guard-room. As the Ulanen arrived in the Palace Square, the trumpet was sounded, they advanced and in the shortest time the Square was as if it had been swept. I rode with the Ulanen into the Breite Strasse where we discovered an unfinished or destroyed barricade which proved no obstacle. When, however, we wanted to get from the Gertraudten Strasse to the Brüderstrasse, we found a second barricade which could not be passed. The Ulanen turned about, rode back along the Breite Strasse, then to the Brüderstrasse. In the Brüderstrasse the cavalry encountered a barricade from which stones were thrown violently. The cavalry fell back in order to wait for the infantry, which soon came and after a few shots climbed over the barricade. Everybody ran away from it, the street was cleared, the barricades in the Gertraudten Strasse as well as the one on the Jungfern-Brücke were also taken after a few shots. These skirmishes were the cause of our taking little care on Saturday [18th March]. There was an argument whether shots had been fired from a house in the Neumannsgasse or not. It did not occur to anybody to occupy the houses militarily, which would have been so useful on Saturday. The whole fight had a fresh character, everything worked smoothly. In the morning, to my indignation, the Paris Arnim had said that today the position could not be held any longer. I did not yet see the situation in these dark colours. On the afternoon of Thursday [16th March] I was at the Commandantur when some shots were fired and the Square in front of the Zeughaus was suddenly cleared. Women fled into the Commandantur and begged for help. I went to the guard-room where I was told about what had happened. A troop of infantry which marched from the Palace of the Prince of Prussia to the Wache [guard-house] was enveloped by the crowd. Captain Cosel faced the Brandenburg Gate, everybody withdrew after the drums had been beaten three times, while stones were thrown from the direction of the Palace. He turned about and when the crowd did not give way after the drums had been beaten four times, he had six shots fired, of which at least two hit. Everybody ran away and in a few minutes the whole Square was as if it had been swept. In the evening I was with the King; around the Palace everything was quiet, only in the Brüderstrasse could a crowd of people show itself. The Grand Duke [of Mecklenburg] Strelitz was with His Majesty. The King went with me to the corner room of the Palace; I went down, there were not many people there. The Prince of Prussia expressed the opinion that the shooting in a densely populated district had made an impression. I still did not view the situation so gravely and ridiculed Arnim, but yet with bitterness in my heart about his Cassandra-prophecies, which he—differently from the old Cassandra—has helped to fulfil. On this evening and before on that of Wednesday, the King declared—he told me himself in Potsdam—that he wanted to leave Berlin and go to Potsdam in order, so he said, to deprive the rising of its object. Everybody pressed arguments on him in order to make him change this resolution, they even spoke of fear. He answers correctly: 'But what reason is there of fear?' The Queen was ill and could not stand the journey; 'so I could not,' said the King, 'leave my wife alone in Berlin; but I had to pay dearly for that.' The King was right, but I, too, would not then have advised him to leave Berlin, so little dangerous did the risings appear to me. The old Wellington said of Prittwitz, when the events of March were related to him, 'mais pourquois ce brave général, dont vous me dites tant de bien, n'a pas commencé ses opérations par éloigner le roi' [but why did this brave general of whom you have told me so much good not begin his operations by removing the King]. Friday, the 17th, passed quietly . . . Bodelschwingh [the virtual Prime Minister] said on this day to Meyendorff [the Russian Minister] that now everything was over [i.e. the crisis had passed] . . . Bodelschwingh later denied this . . . Minutoli [the Chief-of-Police in Berlin] said to the King about the very evening the Rhenish deputation arrived, led by the Ober-Präsident a revolution. At the same time he advised against the use of force; thus we governed alongside and at loggerheads with each other. On this very evening the Rhenish deputation arrived, led by the Ober-Präsident [Chief Administrator of the Province] Eichmann. The unfortunate edicts about Germany and about the freedom of the press were considered in Eichmann's presence and settled. He is believed to have already sung the old song of the secession of the Rhineland if one did not put oneself at the head of Germany. According to the account of Canitz [the Foreign Minister], Thile [another Minister] spoke decidedly against constitutionalism, he [Canitz] against the federal state. Bodelschwingh who had drafted the edicts would not accept any changes. I told him on Saturday . . . I had rather have had a hand chopped off than have signed these edicts . . . If only the old Ministers had left the signing of the edicts to the new ones, the latter would have had an easier game and probably would have made fewer concessions. The King, influenced by Radowitz, signed and later told me in Potsdam that the granting of constitutionalism had been necessary because of Germany.

18th March. On Saturday morning the town was in a terrible excitement. I went to the Commandantur and to the Palace. The deputations here succeeded each other quickly, representatives of the Town Council, and of the City Government, and when the Rhinelanders with Eichmann came down the steps, I was down below with the troops. While this was taking place Count Arnim[5] negotiated with the King about his ministry. He had been summoned that morning to Bodelschwingh . . . and there he read the edict of the 18th written in Bodelschwingh's own hand. Wussow [one of the royal adjutants] appealed to His Majesty in an emphatic speech to put himself at the head of Germany. Already he had explained the necessity of concessions which the Prince of Prussia would have to take to Cologne [where he was supposed to take up his Command], and Major Schöler was of the same opinion. I went home very sad and said, today everything would probably be quiet, for now truly misfortune had befallen us. The King had made concessions in everything, yesterday I had still been of good courage, but no longer today. In the meantime the King, after the edicts had been announced to the deputies and had thus become known, had appeared twice on the balcony and been cheered. Bodelschwingh had in vain tried through speeches to send away the crowd. Seditious cries of 'back with the military!' had already been heard. The continued news of disorders in the town urged me again to the Palace. The Palace Square was full of people, the shots lyingly called 'fatal' had taken place, the dragoons had made their 'murderous attack'. At the suggestion of Alvensleben [a former minister] the King had relieved General Pfuel of the command of the troops, and between one o'clock and two o'clock, had handed it over entirely to General Prittwitz. The latter at the same time received from the King, who became uneasy owing to the sinister-looking crowd of people and the seditious cries in front of the Palace, the command to move it from there. Prittwitz himself called the dragoons and rode with them . . . to the Palace Square. Here he wheeled around, and had the Square cleared in ordinary time. Then the crowd rushed towards the dragoons and fell on to their reins, so that the latter retreated. A corporal was jostled and an attempt was made to pull him down from his horse. Then at this place the soldiers took up their rifles and some blows fell, but without causing injury. The infantry posted in the Palace broke forth from the portal . . . when it saw the fighting of the dragoons. General Prittwitz commanded it to fall back, and the mob cheered him. Thereupon a line of skirmishers advanced from the portal nearest to the Long Bridge and here the so-called fatal shots were fired. Observers from the balcony of the Palace believed that they noticed clearly how after these shots the crowd dispersed in various directions, probably in order to take up their posts; for now already the real rioters were on the

[5] Adolf von Arnim-Boitzenburg.

stage. The sight of the masses was horrible. Speakers on the carriages which had been stopped, Heinrich Arnim with his nephew and the Minister Count Arnim on horseback, Lichnowsky,[6] Wussow, already in mufti, a board with the loathsome inscription, 'it is a misunderstanding, the King wishes the best'. The hall of the King looked like a guard-room. Everywhere was full of people, the Queen passing through, the Princess of Prussia, several deputations, amongst others also one of the city representatives ... The King replied very well and with dignity to the latter, retorting to the princes who were interfering, 'when I speak, nobody else may continue speaking', then 'I know where you want to drive me', etc. In the meantime, everywhere in the town barricades were built and were rising even ... in sight of the Palace. Count Arnim was summoned to the King in order to form a new Ministry; he asked for time for reflection until the following day. The terrible embitter-ment can only be explained by the different strata which succeeded one another. The first in its majority may have cheered sincerely in stupid liberalism about the wretched edicts, the other following it consisted however mainly of strangers, Poles, Frenchmen, and a crowd of partly misguided, partly malevolent persons. In the *Augsburger Zeitung* an eye-witness reports that four Poles on horseback had carried out all the incitement, and in Posen in April the Poles bragged quite publicly that they had originated and carried out the whole Berlin revolution. What a state of affairs that something like this has even been possible; in that the Liberals are right, our police state was not adequate. Probably the shots were signals. The guard in front of the bank is reported to have been murdered beforehand. It is certain, according to a great number of testimonies, that building the barricades had already begun earlier and everyone who was capable of a judgement was convinced that on this day and *only* on this day a battle prepared according to plan took place. How unimportant were the skirmishes on Wednesday when there was still argument whether shots had been fired from a house.

The first conflict with the troops was at the Zeitungshalle [newspaper hall] where a barricade had been erected in front of the Government House. Here shots were fired and similarly at a barricade in the Jerusalemer Strasse. ... The second outbreak of fighting took place at a barricade in the Charlottenstrasse which the second regiment of guard conquered, the third in the Mauerstrasse. Naturally, the mob nowhere stood firm. Against a barricade at the Friedrich- and Tauben-Strasse and against the one in the Charlottenstrasse two guns were employed. Near the Palace we stood for a long time opposite the barricades in the Königs- and Breiten-Strasse before the King allowed the attack; these are the only places where I was present. It may have been about six

---

[6] Felix, Prince Lichnowsky, killed in the September massacres in Frankfurt where he was serving in the German Parliament.

o'clock when the attack on the Königsstrasse was commenced. Two guns were driven up on the Long Bridge and the cannonballs ricocheted along the street. One could discern three, maybe four barricades, one behind the other, on which construction had taken place continually in our presence. At the artillery fire everybody ran from the first . . . and also from the second barricade, but when the troops advanced towards the following barricade, they were met with violent rifle fire and with many stones thrown from the houses, particularly from those at the corner. The marksmen of the fusilier battalion concentrated on the houses and the corporals with their barrels shot so that they often silenced the fire. The battalion had tools with them and so the houses were soon forced open and captured. While penetrating into the houses . . . the soldiers were shot at, but a real defence did not take place. However, in them [the houses] many were slain and stabbed, and many prisoners were made, too, who were often maltreated by the embittered soldiers. The Guards battalion easily took all the barricades and advanced up to the Alexander-Platz where it combined with the Leibregiment, which had broken into the Frankfurt Gate, which it had found closed. This regiment had surmounted at least ten barricades and apparently had some wounded, but no dead. Continuous building took place at the barricade at end of the Breitenstrasse; the attack, however, was constantly postponed because deputation after deputation came to the King to ask that they should be spared and to assure him that work on the destruction of the barricades had begun. . . . We were at that time all so inexperienced in this kind of warfare that we did not consider how every postponement only made matters worse. We should have replied to the deputations with the occupation of the Köllnische Rathaus [the Town Hall of a part of Berlin] the prevention of which would have been an obvious act of hostility. None of all this happened. The insurgents took up an increasingly firmer position in the houses, dragged stones up to them, uncovered the roofs and fortified the barricades increasingly. We stood on the Palace Square until a quarter-to-nine. At the chandelier, I finally spoke to the Prince of Prussia. I told him that I was glad that it had come to fighting once more, for we now again had our enemies opposite us and not, as this morning, among us. He expressed the opinion that the King was now entitled to revoke all his concessions. He enjoined the troops not to fire a shot before a quarter-to-nine. I had at this time on one occasion gone up to the Neumannsgasse and believed that it had been abandoned because I saw so few people next to and behind the barricade. I reported this to General Prittwitz; the latter sent me to the King who now finally gave the command to attack. It began with artillery fire, then the fusilier battalion of the Regiment Franz advanced. The latter met such heavy fire from the houses, particularly from corner houses and the Köllnische Rathaus, that it twice turned about. Finally, after prolonged operations, the houses were forced open and in no time the grenadiers were at the windows of all floors. At the same time, the fifth company of the first Guards Regiment took the barricade. In the Rathaus there were ferocious scenes and many people were killed and captured there; a great number fled through the door to the Gertraudtenstrasse. When the outcome of the fighting was in the balance, I was worried and said to Beyer, 'this could get bad'. But soon my courage returned. The artillery had not done very much damage because the barricade had been left at once. In addition to the cases which have been mentioned, use of artillery was only made at the artillery barracks at the Oranienburg Gate. A line of wagons was supposed to move ammunition from there to the troops. It was held up by the mob, thereupon one gun turned about after being charged with grape shot, drove out by the back door . . . and charged the mob once. The Friedrichstrasse up to the Linden was cleared completely in this way. No house was attacked by artillery. The small loss of troops, 18 dead, 26 missing, 204 wounded, is explained by the fact that stones are only a dangerous weapon if thrown with particular care; that roofing slates almost never cause injuries, that the insurgents shot badly from cowardice, that they stopped firing in the Königstrasse, for instance, as soon as one of them had been wounded, and that houses were defended mainly at the entrances and only occasionally from desperation on the highest loft.

In the evening, when it was all over, I went to the hall [in the Palace], where I found the well-known Landtag deputy Vincke waiting for the King in travelling clothes. General Thile had introduced him and had said, things must be going well because they send orators instead of continuing to fight! I saw Vincke here for the first time. When the King came he addressed him in a well-composed speech. Conditions in the town were terrible, the troops exhausted, discouraged, etc. The shooting had made an unpleasant impression on him. I and some officers laughed about the speech. Enraged about this Vincke turned to us and said we would not laugh the following day. Unfortunately he proved to be right because his bad advice was followed. The King took him to one side and asked him what would happen if the troops were withdrawn. Whereupon Vincke with his miserable controversialist dialectic, well-known from the United Diet, replied: but what will happen when the people are victorious? The King denies Vincke's influence on the proclamation, 'To my dear Berliners'. After Vincke arrived . . . the King no longer spoke to anybody but to Prittwitz, apparently just before he came out in order to listen to Vincke's speech. In the evening I went home late from the Palace. Everywhere troops stood about; . . . General Prittwitz ordered his generals in the evening quietly to remain in their positions; it was not his intention to continue advancing. Then he

c

reported to the King. Today and tomorrow and even for another day he believed he could contain the situation very well; should the riot continue any longer, he advocated leaving the city with the King and the troops, and posting himself outside in a blockading position. This view of the situation General Prittwitz still expressed on Sunday [19th March] morning to Minutoli. . . . Part of the cavalry received the order to leave the city at daybreak and to take up a position which would make a possible siege feasible. The King had been terribly pressed by deputations and bad advice. The Queen remained quite firm and said: 'If only the King does not give in.' I then regarded yielding as impossible. In the night, at three o'clock, the King wrote the proclamation, 'To my dear Berliners'.

The scenes on Sunday [19th March] and the history of this day are difficult to describe. Fighting had ceased, the troops stood at the barricades; we only heard single shots . . . I returned to the Palace and saw how all the troops moved towards it. They had just received the order to do so which to me who inferred a concentration, did not yet appear as yielding, although things already made me somewhat uneasy. In the early morning General Prittwitz had reconnoitred the position of his troops. He found the streets quite empty. The first person he met was a servant girl fetching pastries, but then the streets filled very rapidly with unarmed yet suspicious looking masses of people. An attempt was made to block some streets, when this did not help the general wanted to let cavalry advance or to fire a few blind cannon shots. But before this could be carried out, a copy of the royal proclamation was handed to him, of which he had hitherto heard nothing at all. Now no steps were taken. It was still night when the King sent the proclamation he had himself drafted to the minister Bodelschwingh with a request to examine whether it should be retained, changed or printed. Bodelschwingh, without consulting anybody, had it printed unchanged. . . .

At the Palace several deputations appeared again . . . from the city government, the town councillors, etc. . . . Mayor Naunyn . . . had previously turned to General Prittwitz and adjured him, in view of the great danger for the city, the country and the King, to come to the Palace with him. First in the Queen's Chamber, then in the red corner room a kind of council of war was held in which it was decided—as the Prince of Prussia relates—that the proclamation should be carried out on the understanding that, where a barricade was levelled by the citizens, the troops opposite would be withdrawn. With this reply the deputations appeared content and for the most part left. Hereupon another deputation entered with the report that on the other side of the Königstrasse three barricades were being levelled by the people. (This report, which was received as a kind of triumph by the peace-loving, later proved completely untrue.) The Prince of Prussia proposed having this report confirmed by officers but this was rejected by those who wished to yield. . . . Suddenly the Minister Bodelschwingh entered the room where everyone was assembled and the last deputation was waiting. He declared in a loud voice: 'As the barricades are disappearing so His Majesty commands that the troops should be withdrawn from all streets and squares.' In vain General Prittwitz declared that such a disappearance of the troops from the streets and squares was not feasible, because then the only remaining way was to let the troops from outside move off to their cantonments, the local ones to the barracks—but then communications between the various units would at once be lost, the garrison at the Palace and at the arsenal could no longer be supported and the troops would see themselves surrendered to the enemy with tied hands. The minister once more thundered out to the Prince and to the General, 'Nothing must be turned and twisted in the words of the King.' Once more the Prince asked if by all squares the Palace Squares also were to be understood, because these were the only ones where the returning troops could take up positions. The minister thundered to him once more the same words. Even a member of the deputation remarked, 'it is naturally understood that the Palace Square is excepted', whereupon Mayor Naunyn replied, 'all'. The minister now turned to the officers present and said, 'now run and ride, gentlemen, to hand over the commands of the King. The troops are to march off with drums beating and trumpets sounding.' The Aide-de-Camp Brauchitsch refused to undertake this task and General Prittwitz took over the further commissions and left with the deputation, after a further council held in the reception room of the Queen ended without success. The King took no part in this council, as General Prittwitz narrates: *The Prince of Prussia had at once sought out the King in his cabinet and not found him. They met in the red room. The King saw the general consternation. The Prince told him about the scene with Bodelschwingh whereupon the King declared he had given no other instruction, no other command than that which was contained in the proclamation, and it would at once have to be changed.* Major Count Röder of the Regiment Alexander, who accompanied Mayor Naunyn to the barricades, now received the command to let the departure of the troops begin, but only to continue it if the barricades opposite were cleared and levelled. Count Röder was insulted most grossly and only protected from maltreatment by his calm and by the vicious striking out of his horse. The freeing of the Spandau prisoners, etc., was demanded. A change was impossible, the troops being already fully engaged in marching off, for the people rushed after them everywhere. The order of the King to occupy the Long Bridge could no longer be executed. . . .

II.6.B   The following account of the same events seen by an anonymous
          sympathiser with the revolution is translated from the German of
          the encyclopaedia published by Brockhaus, *Die Gegenwart*, II,
          Leipzig, 1849, pp. 549 ff.

. . . There was the most cheerful and sunny spring weather [on 18th
March 1848] and the crowd of people on the Palace Square and in
Unter den Linden were already growing again to significant masses
which moved about in an uncertain mood. Then suddenly towards two
o'clock in the afternoon came a report that the expected proclamations
of the King had been carried out and would be distributed in a special
edition of the *Allgemeine Preussische Zeitung* which was just ready.
Soon one saw the paper in everybody's hands in the street; it was read
out aloud amongst several groups of people and its contents broadcast
further with jubilation. Joy, astonishment, doubt appeared in turn on
all faces. But on a closer look, the stipulations of the two patents which
had been issued, contained nothing further than a law about the press,
which—it is true—abolished censorship but fettered the newspaper
press with deposits [Cautionen], and a patent concerning the speedier
summoning of the 'United Diet'. . . . Those who soon sought together
to deny the fact of a Berlin revolution and to represent the 'achievements' springing from the March struggle as a concession of the Crown
already granted before the fighting, have always wanted to base this
assertion on the patent of the morning of 18th March. . . .

It was, however, not to be denied that at mid-day on the 18th March
a glad and somewhat satisfied feeling spread through the masses, who
betook themselves at one o'clock in great crowds to the Palace Square
and wanted to express their thanks to the King in a vivat. . . . The King
himself twice appeared on the balcony of the Palace where he was
greeted in a thousand voices from below by the jubilation of the citizens.
. . . Citizen marksmen hoisted the Prussian flag on the opposite balcony
of the Palace Square, which on the one hand was applauded while on the
other the national flag in black-red-gold was demanded. Suddenly in the
middle of the cheering the persistent call was heard: Away with the
military! Back with the military! Others cried: the King ought to
entrust himself to his citizens! The entries to the Palace were, indeed,
partly occupied by units of the Potsdam Guards. . . . Count Arnim, who
was in the entourage of the King, reported to the latter the wishes of
the people. The King replied: they could not demand a dishonourable
retreat of the troops! Now began an unprecedented confusion which
will always retain something mysterious and inexplicable about it. The
rumour that the King did not wish to withdraw the military spread like
lightning among the masses. This was combined with a sinister notion
that a new attack by the soldiers on the people was intended. Thus began

a pressing and pushing of the crowd which found the most varying expressions in its fear and rage. Several town councillors rushed out of their session to the Palace Square in order to ask the people to remain calm, hoping to achieve this by the public reading of the royal patent. While on the one side of the Square this placard was read aloud accompanied by waving of hats and the cheering of the crowd, on the other side of the Stechbahn appeared the regiment of dragoons, which was received with the call, 'Away with the military!' When the regiment thereupon wheeled several times, there was loud cheering by the mass, because it was believed the troops now actually wanted to march off. This seemed to embitter the commander of the regiment; he let the troops face [the crowd], and the cavalry went towards the crowd at a trot and with blank weapons. At the same moment a battalion of the Regiment Kaiser Franz emerged from the middle portal of the Palace and marched up to the middle of the Palace Square, whereupon it turned off to the Long Bridge with fixed bayonets, while it drove the already retreating crowd in front of it with the sound of drums. At this moment, from the ranks of the soldiers, two shots were heard about whose origin there was much argument afterwards, and which—as was later asserted—were due to the accidental discharge of two rifles. With horror and cries of revenge the people dispersed and went into the adjoining streets. Matters had suddenly turned to incalculable disaster.

In the interior of the Palace, matters looked strange at this time. The King, surrounded by the ministers, all the princes, many generals and high state officials, as well as other important personalities who had rushed along under the pressure of the moment, kept to his rooms. The fatal crisis which had suddenly come about was still discussed with great optimism; it was believed that it would pass like all the earlier ones. After the catastrophe on the Palace Square had occurred, the ministers descended a little while into the palace yard, where several town councillors moved up and down with a view to gaining audience of the King. These town councillors still believed they could make an attempt at mediation, and they negotiated with the ministers Count Arnim, Bodelschwingh and Rohr, who had come down to them, about the withdrawal of the military. The ministers replied that nobody could take responsibility for a measure like that, and referred the petitioners to General Prittwitz. . . . Here it was above all that strange phenomenon of the special military honour on which any attempts at possible mediation and prevention of an extreme conflict foundered. The town councillors, as well as several citizens and state officials who had the same outlook, were told that it would be acting against the honour of the Prussian troops if one were now to withdraw them! At this moment the princes, too, descended into the courtyard and were assailed tempest-uously with these petitions. Prince Charles accepted them most frankly and left with a promise that he would attempt mediation with the King.

Some events around mid-day of the 18th March inside the Palace already pointed to division and wavering here, between a readiness to make constantly broader concessions to the popular will, and a resolu-tion to pursue a decisive struggle. The former intention expressed itself in an alteration of the ministry which was already in fact decided by the King at mid-day on the 18th March. Between one and two o'clock the rumour spread through the whole town that the King had, in order to signify his complete breach with the old system, dismissed the former ministers, and was resolved on the formation of a new cabinet whose members were named as the heroes of the United Diet, Schwerin, Auerswald, Camphausen, Beckerath. Another circumstance at this time . . . did not correspond with this intention in pointing to a peaceful compromise. This was the sudden dismissal of General Pfuel from his post as Governor of Berlin. This general, earlier especially known through his position in Neufchatel and shortly before called to Berlin as Governor, had in the latter capacity acted with special circumspection and moderation. . . .

The news of what had happened on the Palace Square spread like wildfire through the whole town. The crowds running back from there rushed away with the general cry, 'to arms!' There were loud complaints about the treason which had been committed, some cried that no under-standing was possible any more, that at last an open struggle had to be begun! Expressions of rage at military barbarism were combined with the most determined political utterances. Everywhere there was the call to break up the old military state of Prussia in order to arrive at a new state and freedom! It remained doubtful whether the shots which had been fired on the Palace Square had killed anybody; the lack of evidence for this assertion only became clear later. From other sides the word 'misunderstanding' was voiced to calm and to deter, but it could not effect any cooling or any check to the overflowing popular rage. The area of the Palace was suddenly empty of people, the great squares looked as though swept, and only from time to time did an orderly ride past to deliver orders to the troops in the barracks. But soon the first crashes were heard from the construction of the barricades, and isolated shots which proclaimed the attack against them were let off. At the moment when the fighting was about to start the minister Count Arnim appeared on the balcony of the Palace with a white flag, which signified an appeal for peace; . . . during the late afternoon a flag was suspended from a window of the Palace on which could be read in large letters the word 'misunderstanding'. But these conciliations were no longer noticed, and what had long been ripe had to be finally harvested. . . . The fighting began soon after three o'clock at the corner of the Oberwall- and Jägerstrasse where the first barricade was erected at the corner house . . . two cabs, one coach, the guard-room of the bank building, the gutter bridges and some barrels served quickly for its construction—which was achieved as elsewhere in the town with astonishing virtuosity, as if the population had never had any other business. The military posts in the neighbourhood were disarmed, during which a guard at the bank was killed, apparently during a struggle for his rifle. The second barricade was put up at the corner of the Werderstrasse opposite the Government House. On the roofs of the houses people armed themselves with stones. These first barricades were hardly complete when already a unit of dragoons and a battalion of infantry advanced against them. . . . By five o'clock in the afternoon the whole town, even in its most distant parts, was covered with barricades, which in some streets reached into the first floors. The students armed themselves and fixed the black-red-gold cockade on their caps and hats. Everywhere citizens, artisans, students and working men rushed into the streets, supplied themselves as best they could with weapons, with some ammunition, with axes and iron bars, and rushed in various directions in order to seek out a place of fighting or to help to defend a barricade. The arms shops were every-where deprived of their stock, with a promise, which was afterwards kept almost completely, that the weapons would be returned honestly after the fighting. The weapon supplies of the Royal Königstädt-ische Theatre, too, were fetched by crowds eager for fighting. The armed crowds everywhere furnished themselves with the black-red-gold flag, which was declared and treated by the people as the 'flag of free-dom', and which soon flew from every barricade. Some students who had swung themselves on to horses galloped out through the Oranien-burg gate, stopped in front of the machine construction workshops and encouraged the workers fervently to come to the city and to participate in a struggle which—with freedom for all—would also lead to the fate of the workers taking a more favourable turn. The workers of the Borsig factory in particular responded to this invitation in great numbers, and by six o'clock in the evening probably something like 900 of them had moved into the town. It was above all due to their heroic courage and endurance behind the barricades on the night of the 18th March that a battle was fought which allowed the cause of the people to appear with an importance which could no longer be denied, and which, even if a material victory remained doubtful after the cessation of the struggle could, however, claim a spiritual victory, the maintenance of the rights irrefutably belonging to the people in the state.

Towards five o'clock the first shot was heard which grazed . . . the Königstrasse, where, up to the Alexander Square, one barricade after another rose at short intervals, firm and high. These barricades were made of cabs, omnibuses, a post wagon which had been stopped, wool sacks, beams, overturned well-enclosures. The armament of the fighters standing behind them—it is true—looked a poor sight, for there was a lack of rifles from the beginning, with the exception of a few pistols and carbines, and the other weapons often consisted of a plank which had been torn loose, a pitch-fork, an old rusty sword and similar weapons. The corner houses which surrounded a barricade were usually uncovered and their roofs arranged for defence, to which boys and girls carried baskets filled with stones. The greatest movement was on the Königstrasse down to the Alexander Square. In a work-house situated at the latter, the so-called 'Ox Head', the prisoners were freed and allocated to the revolutionary crowds forming there. The debtors, too, were freed. A peculiar free corps [Freischar] formed itself here at the Alexander Square under the leadership of a young Pole, who, clothed like a lancer and wearing the Polish cap, came marching along at the head of a train of around 200 people. He swung a curved sabre in his hand and cried aloud, 'may freedom live!' A drummer followed him, then several flag-bearers with red and yellow flags, and after that his men, armed in the most varied manner. This may be almost the only outstanding case to prove that the Poles took part in the management of the Berlin March struggle. Here and there Poles fought behind the barricades, but the widespread assumption that the outbreak and leadership of the Berlin revolution were to be ascribed mainly to their influence was not only erroneous, but sprang at the same time from the reactionary intention to deny the popular origin of the Berlin movement and to trace it back to foreign influences, instead of to the original desire for freedom that was at last aroused in the people itself.

Between six and seven o'clock the most terrible barricade fighting broke out along the whole Königstrasse. The thunder of cannons resounded in increasingly quick succession, individual barricades already began to collapse in the street, and the more and more embittered and enraged advancing soldiers began a frightful hand-to-hand fighting. Where a barricade was taken by soldiers, they penetrated at once into the houses from which shots had come, fired into the rooms, killed and pursued all who allowed themselves to be encountered with a rifle, with their bayonets stabbed the beds, where even children were victims of the murderous steel, and rushed up to the roofs from which all who were found there were fetched down with the greatest maltreatment. By seven o'clock the greatest part of the Königstrasse had been taken by the soldiers. The whole street swam with blood, the houses were overcrowded with dead and wounded. At the corner of the Spandauerstrasse cannons were driven up whose shots were intended to clear the streets completely. The houses themselves were hit again and again and damaged by rifle shots. Throughout the city there began at this time a frightful sounding of the alarm bells which was kept up through the whole night by armed artisans who had climbed the church towers.

It was only several hours afterwards that the fighting started on the other side of the Royal Palace, where the Brüderstrasse, Breitestrasse and Rosstrasse formed a populous district. Here at first attempts at mediation were still regarded possible, and several inhabitants formed a deputation which went to the King at the Palace, led by Bishop Neander. This deputation did, indeed, get to the King but found him little inclined to pay attention to the request for an immediate withdrawal of the military. The King already regarded himself as victor in the struggle which had begun, and pointed with his hand out of the window to the Königstrasse saying, 'this street is already mine and the others I will take, too!' The King further remarked that it was only the 'crapule' of the population which had begun this fight. Then he suddenly pointed to the black-red-gold flag which fluttered in the air on the high house of the d'Heureuse Confectioner's Shop . . . and which must have attracted the King's attention like a ghost. 'Get that flag out of my sight!' said the King when he dismissed the deputation. . . . The Senate of the University of Berlin, too, at this time sent a deputation from its midst which came to the Palace in their robes of office and similarly approached the King about the withdrawal of the military. They, too, received an unqualified 'no'. . . . When news reached the Palace that it was mainly students who commanded on the barricades, the King violently reprimanded the professors about this. People in the Palace were absolutely confused and prejudiced about all that was really happening in Berlin. That public opinion in the capital did not agree with the intervention of the military and that therefore the cause at stake could not simply be a matter of the rabble, could undoubtedly have been gathered from the deputations which had been sent from such respectable quarters. But the court circle persisted in the view that they were only concerned with a mob made fanatical by foreign agitators! Furthermore one report of victory after another on the part of the military was brought to the Palace.

. . . In the various parts of the town in which there was fighting before and behind the barricades, only quite isolated battle scenes took place, for there was no question of any cohesion among the fighters in the various parts of the town, and they did not know in one end of the town what was happening in the other. . . . A strange way of life prevailed behind these barricades, behind which men of all estates, understanding each other without any arrangement, and pledging each other a fraternal solidarity to the last, carried on the struggle with gigantic exertions. Artisans, workers and casual labourers undoubtedly formed the main component of those who were fighting, amongst which, however, there may have been some suspect members of society. But this circumstance was afterwards exploited too much by the reaction, which, in order to represent the March struggle as an event foreign to the actual nation, wanted to find the heroes of the Berlin barricades preferably among the ranks of criminals and thieves. If the latter have, as in all revolutions, fought courageously with the others, they did it in no way in their capacity as criminals. For property was regarded by them during this night as in the following period, as sacred, in a manner which deserves the greatest admiration.

. . . The brutality and inhumanity of the soldiery appeared in a frightful and indeed incredible manner, particularly during arrests which they carried out during this night. During house searches not only everybody who allowed himself to be encountered with a weapon, but also anybody who was suspected in any way of participation in the events and who attracted the attention of the soldiers, was arrested by the latter, bound with the most terrible maltreatment and dragged away under constant blows with the rifle butt and the flat of the sabre, even officers stooping to this. To be arrested and dragged away, it was often sufficient just to meet a group of prisoners, to which anybody who in some way did not please the soldiers would be added with kicks and beatings. The prisoners were first led into the Palace Yard, where the units stationed there received them with ridicule and insults of all kinds and maltreated them anew with sabre and bayonet. After a short interrogation by two police commissioners, they were imprisoned in the Palace cellar, where eventually several hundreds of companions in misfortune from all estates found themselves.

. . . On the morning of 19th March at about seven o'clock, the last explosions of cannon had died away and the parties involved in the fight seemed to give themselves up to a momentary armistice . . . the military found themselves in the morning in possession of the main streets and squares of the city, had cleared away the barricades which had been found there, and had pushed back their defenders into the more distant parts of the city. But the people could be regarded as defeated as little as could the troops, for they stood ready in the suburbs and in the more distant streets to assemble again at any time and to begin the struggle anew. Even in the streets and squares occupied by the soldiers, groups of the people were formed, which spoke openly and aloud of the necessary continuation of the struggle. It was in these groups that the proclamation of the King 'To my dear Berliners', which had just appeared, was read, and which was distributed around seven o'clock in the morning in all the streets . . . the people everywhere shook their heads critically over this proclamation; here and there it was received with loud scorn and curses. . . .

... Some rifle and cannon shots could, however, still be heard. ... In the meantime the tolling of the alarm bells continued throughout the city, the reinforcement of armed citizens in the remaining barracks increased once more, in the houses and on the streets bullets were being cast, and the main aim to which the attack of the people would now have been directed would undoubtedly have been the Palace. It will not be so easy to judge with certainty how it was that the resolution suddenly matured in the King to recall the troops, and precisely at the very moment when the latter had taken up new positions from which they could recommence fighting, and when guns had been put in position on all the bridges. Mayor Naunyn had on that morning again come to the Palace where he explained to the minister Bodelschwingh the calamitous situation of the city and the necessity for the withdrawal of the troops, and received admittance to the King through the minister. The King now granted the request made to him, and General von Prittwitz received the command to attach adjutants to the Mayor and to some other citizens who had come to the Palace, who were to take this order to the troops through all parts of the town. The immense emotion of the King was betrayed in his whole appearance, in every expression of his face and figure. He could not have hidden from himself the doubtful position of things on the morning of the 19th, although he was in possession of a faithful and courageous army which stood there in a compact mass. But these troops were exhausted to death by the fighting of the night, and when one saw them stretched out on straw in the palace yards and resting, one had to recognise their weakness and to realise that they would not be able to stand such a night of horror a second time. The struggle of the soldier against his own fraternal people, too, only has a chance of success in the first moment of stormy fanaticism. The longer this fight is continued, the less secure and certain become the forces which have to wage it.

The news of the withdrawal of the soldiers spread like a fairy tale throughout the town. It was not yet known whether their total removal from Berlin was meant, and even in the council of the King there was some vacillation about this. Several persons close to the King were apparently of the opposite opinion and sought to influence the King in this direction. The King, who could not bear the thought of continued civil war and bloodshed, finally signalled his determination by giving an assurance of the complete departure of the troops, of whom only a small part was to remain in the barracks, to the renewed requests and wishes which were directed to him by citizens' deputations. At the same time the King declared that he would undertake a complete change of the ministry and would in this respond to the wishes of the people. The King promised the release of the prisoners, too, with the special addition, 'if these please you'. The departure of the troops from the streets was carried out with drums beating and trumpets sounding and with an air of festivity, which was reminiscent of a time of parades and suddenly provided a most penetrating and astringent contrast to the terrible night of blood. It appeared to be a tacit condition that the soldiers would have to march off in the guise of victors, or at least in a posture which left no doubt about the power of the crown having remained intact. . . . The appearance of the soldiers, however, was by no means a haughty one. In many one saw the . . . joy of having been relieved from the frightful service of the past night, others moved along downcast and in the deepest exhaustion. At the head of the soldiers and batteries withdrawing from the Palace, however, appeared the Prince of Prussia on horseback. . . . It was the last time that he was seen in public in Berlin during this period; his appearance was earnest and he summoned up all his strength, in his face now a dark redness blazed, now it became discoloured to the most extreme paleness. From the mass of the people which regarded him in silence he constantly turned somewhat away to the side. . . .

II.6.c   In this proclamation of 21st March 1848, Frederick William IV, under the pressure of events, turned to a policy of German unification and liberal constitutionalism. Document translated from the German of Huber, *Dokumente*, I, pp. 365 f.

To My People and to the German Nation

With confidence the King spoke to his people thirty-five years ago in the days of great danger, and his confidence was not put to shame; the King, united with his people, saved Prussia and Germany from disgrace and humiliation.

With confidence I speak to-day, when the Fatherland is in the greatest danger, to the German nation, among whose noblest tribes My people may proudly count itself. Germany is in a state of internal ferment and can be threatened by external danger from more than one side. It can be saved from this double, urgent danger only by the most intimate unity of the German princes and peoples under one leadership.

Today I take over this leadership for the days of danger. My people, which does not shirk danger, will not desert me, and Germany will follow me with confidence. I have today taken the old German colours and have put Myself and My people under the venerable banner of the German Reich. Prussia henceforth merges in Germany. The diet already called for 2nd April offers itself as a means and as a lawful organ with which to proceed in conjunction with my people to the rescue and calming of Germany. I intend to invite the princes and estates of Germany, in a form to be considered at once, to meet with organs of this diet in a common assembly. The thus-formed temporary assembly of the German estates will, in common free deliberation, take without delay the necessary precautions regarding the common internal and external danger.

What is needed above all today is:

1. The formation of a common German national federal army [Bundesheer];
2. The declaration of armed neutrality.

This arming and declaration of the Fatherland will inspire Europe with respect for the sanctity and inviolability of the area of the German tongue and the German name. Only unity and strength will today be able to preserve peace in our beautiful common Fatherland, with its flourishing trade and crafts.

Together with the measures for averting the momentary danger, the assembly of the German estates will deliberate about the rebirth and foundation of a new Germany, of a united, not uniform, Germany, of a unity in diversity, of a unity with freedom.

The general introduction of a truly constitutional constitution with ministerial responsibility, in all the states, public and oral administration of justice in criminal causes based on courts with juries, equal political and civic rights for all religious confessions, and a truly popular liberal administration, will alone be able to create and to strengthen such a higher and inner unity.

> Frederick William,
> Count Arnim, v. Rohr, Count Schwerin
> Bornemann. Arnim. Kühne.

II.6.D Unlike her husband William (the later German Emperor), Augusta, a Princess of Weimar, had already been well inclined towards German national unification and constitutionalism before 1848. William, who as heir to the throne had the title of Prince of Prussia, was obliged to flee from Berlin after the revolution because of his extreme conservative views. In England he was welcomed by Queen Victoria and Prince Albert. Bunsen, the Prussian minister to Britain, was—like Princess Augusta—an advocate of constitutionalism and unification. The extract is translated from a letter written by the Princess to Bunsen from Potsdam on 26th March 1848, found in P. Bailleu and G. Schuster (eds.), *Aus dem literarischen Nachlass der Kaiserin Augusta*, I, Berlin, 1912, p. 488.

. . . In our great misfortune I turn confidently to you, because I know your sentiments and am convinced that you will assist *my poor prince* with advice and action as a faithful servant. God has willed it so! He will help, too; I am resigned and calm, although the serious present only conceals an even more serious future, and I am not deceived for one moment about our situation! The Prince is an innocent victim; but as such he must not appear in England! Please see to it that the newspapers speak about him in a dignified manner and that he himself does not express himself too freely about his own impressions, which are only too true, so that one does not regard our revolution straightway as the downfall of Prussia. If I had been able to be useful to the Prince in England, how much would I have liked to have accompanied him, but my duty commanded me to stay with the children and I will be faithful to my duty until my end! . . . May God bless and protect the beloved Prince and the Fatherland!

Oh, the time weighs heavily upon us. . . .

II.7   THE SCHLESWIG-HOLSTEIN RISING

One of the leading objectives of the German national movement was to assert the right of Germany to the Elbe duchies. Both were ruled by the King of Denmark as Duke, but only Holstein belonged to the German Confederation. Following the various German revolutions, the Germans in the Duchies established a provisional government independent of Denmark on 24th March. These events led to the intervention of the German Confederation in the Duchies and to armed conflict with Denmark.

II.7.A   The proclamation of the Provisional Government at Kiel is taken from *Annual Register*, 1848, p. 345.

Fellow Citizens!

Our Duke has been compelled by a popular insurrection in Copenhagen to dismiss his late advisers, and to assume a hostile attitude with regard to the Duchies.

The will of the Sovereign is no longer free, and the country is without a Government. We will not tolerate the sacrifice of German territory as a prey to the Danes! Great dangers require great resolutions, and leading authorities are required for the defence of the frontiers, and the maintenance of order. In accordance with the demands of urgent necessity, and relying upon the confidence hitherto reposed in us, we have, in compliance with the cry which has been raised by the people, provisionally undertaken the conduct of the Government, which we will carry on for the maintenance of the rights of the country, and those of our native Duke, and in his name.

We will forthwith convene the united assembly of the States, and lay down the power which we have assumed as soon as the Sovereign is restored to freedom, or as soon as other persons are entrusted with the management of public affairs.

II.7.B   The reply of the King of Denmark, Frederick VII, is taken from *Annual Register*, 1848, pp. 345 f.

To you, men of Schleswig, I have declared, and hereby again declare, that in union with Denmark you shall now obtain a free and popular constitution. Your independence as Schleswigers shall, conjointly with your common constitution with Denmark, be secured by a Diet of your own, an administration of your own, and courts of your own; by a like share in the burdens of the State in proportion to your population, a just application of the surplus revenue, and an equal right of using either the German or Danish language, whether in the great Assembly of the whole realm or in your own Diet.

Men of Holstein,

My heart clings to you. You will not destroy the holiest inheritance from your fathers—the fame of Holstein for fidelity. Your Duke cannot abandon the hope that you will return to him. You have been seduced by faithless leaders, who do not think of your weal, but only of their own ambitious plans. Under my name they lead you into ruin;—only by pretending that I was not free, they have induced you to follow them.

II.7.C   On 4th April 1848, the German Federal Assembly decided to ask Prussia to intervene in the Duchy of Holstein which belonged to the German Confederation. This was the beginning of a war between parts of Germany and Denmark. Extract from Huber, *Dokumente*, I, pp. 458 f. (translated from the German).

1. The Federal Assembly declares in accordance with Article 38 of the [Vienna] Final Acts that the danger of an attack exists for the German federal territory of Holstein and declares its full acceptance of the preparations made by Prussia and the states of the 10th Federal Army Corps in a federal national sense for the protection of the federal frontier in Holstein.

2. The Federal Assembly, in order to achieve a unified leadership for the measures which may further be necessary for this purpose, requests Prussia to come to an understanding on this issue with the states of the 10th Army Corps.

3. The Federal Assembly is ready to take over mediation in order to avoid the shedding of blood and to achieve a friendly settlement and requests Prussia to take over this mediation in the name of the German Confederation on the basis of the undiminished rights of Holstein, particularly also with regard to its constitutional connection with Schleswig.

It is assumed as self-evident by the Confederation that hostilities will be terminated at once and the status quo ante restored.

II.8 THE MILAN RISING AND THE INTERVENTION OF SARDINIA AGAINST AUSTRIA

The 18th March proved a turning point in Milan as in Berlin. For on that day a rising against Austrian rule broke out there which resulted in the withdrawal of the Austrian troops under Field-Marshal Radetzky a few days later. Now Italy was alight. Sardinia intervened in Lombardy.

II.8.A The proclamation by King Charles Albert of Sardinia on 23rd March is taken from *Annual Register*, 1848, p. 321.

. . . For the purpose of more fully showing by exterior signs the sentiments of Italian unity, we wish that our troops should enter the territory of Lombardy and Venice, bearing the arms of Savoy above the Italian tricoloured flag. . . .

II.8.B The proclamation of the Provisional Government at Milan of 26th March is taken from *Annual Register*, 1848, pp. 320 f.

Fellow citizens:

We have conquered. We have compelled the enemy to fly, oppressed by his own shame as much as by our valour; but scattered in our fields—wandering like wild beasts—united in bands of plunderers, he prolongs for us all the horrors of war without affording any of its sublime emotions. This makes it easily to be understood that the arms we have taken up—that we still hold—can never be laid down as long as one of his band shall be hid under the cover of the Alps. We have sworn, we swear it again, with the generous Prince who flies with the common impulse to associate himself with our glory—all Italy swears it, and so it shall be!

To arms then, to arms, to secure the fruits of our glorious revolution —to fight the last battle of independence and the Italian Union.

A moveable army shall be at once organised. . . .

II.9 THE COMMUNIST MANIFESTO

At a congress of the Communist League held in London in November 1847, Marx and Engels were commissioned to prepare a party programme for publication. The manifesto was drawn up in German during January 1848, and sent to the printer in London shortly before the French February revolution.

II.9.A Extract from Karl Marx and Friedrich Engels, *The Communist Manifesto*, authorised English translation, edited and annotated by Friedrich Engels, Toronto: Progress Books (no date), pp. 8 ff.

... A spectre is haunting Europe—the spectre of Communism. All the powers of old Europe have entered into a holy alliance to exorcise this spectre: Pope and Czar, Metternich and Guizot, French Radicals and German police-spies.

Where is the party in opposition that has not been decried as communistic by its opponents in power? Where the Opposition that has not hurled back the branding reproach of Communism, against the more advanced opposition parties, as well as against its reactionary adversaries?

Two things result from this fact:

1. Communism is already acknowledged by all European powers to be itself a power.

2. It is high time that Communists should openly, in the face of the whole world, publish their views, their aims, their tendencies, and meet this nursery tale of the spectre of Communism with a manifesto of the party itself.

To this end, Communists of various nationalities have assembled in London, and sketched the following manifesto, to be published in the English, French, German, Italian, Flemish and Danish languages.

The history of all hitherto existing society is the history of class struggles.

Freeman and slave, patrician and plebeian, lord and serf, guildmaster and journeyman, in a word, oppressor and oppressed, stood in constant opposition to one another, carried on an uninterrupted, now hidden, now open fight, a fight that each time ended, either in a revolutionary reconstitution of society at large, or in the common ruin of the contending classes.

In the earlier epochs of history, we find almost everywhere a complicated arrangement of society into various orders, a manifold gradation of social rank. In ancient Rome we have patricians, knights, plebeians, slaves; in the Middle Ages, feudal lords, vassals, guildmasters, journeymen, apprentices, serfs; in almost all of these classes, again subordinate gradations.

The modern bourgeois society that has sprouted from the ruins of feudal society, has not done away with class antagonisms. It has but established new classes, new conditions of oppression, new forms of struggle in place of the old ones.

Our epoch, the epoch of the bourgeoisie, possesses, however, this distinctive feature. It has simplified the class antagonisms. Society as a whole is more and more splitting up into two great hostile camps, into two great classes directly facing each other—bourgeoisie and proletariat. ...

The Communists turn their attention chiefly to Germany, because that country is on the eve of a bourgeois revolution that is bound to be carried out under more advanced conditions of European civilisation and with a much more developed proletariat than what existed in England in the 17th and in France in the 18th century, and because the bourgeois revolution in Germany will be but the prelude to an immediately following proletarian revolution.

In short, the Communists everywhere support every revolutionary movement against the existing social and political order of things.

In all these movements they bring to the front, as the leading question in each case, the property question, no matter what its degree of development at the time.

Finally, they labour everywhere for the union and agreement of the democratic parties of all countries.

The Communists disdain to conceal their views and aims. They openly declare that their ends can be attained only by the forcible overthrow of all existing social conditions. Let the ruling classes tremble at a Communist revolution. The proletarians have nothing to lose but their chains. They have a world to win.

Workingmen of all countries, unite!

II.10   INDUSTRIALISATION AND POLITICAL RIGHTS

In Germany, as elsewhere in Europe, the economic, social and political consequences of industrialisation were causing grave concern.

II.10.A   In the following extract, translated from German, an anonymous writer in the encyclopaedia *Die Gegenwart*, I, Leipzig: Brockhaus, 1848, pp. 84 ff., examines the effect of changing economic conditions on political rights.

. . . Up to the end of the last century all production work—with few and unimportant exceptions—was done by human hand. Now this merely personal work has a decisive influence on the attitude of those working which, however, only became really apparent in the period of the rule of machines that followed. It is not the main characteristic of personal labour that it can only seldom or never employ so great a number of workers and does not assemble them easily for any length of time in a particular place; there are enough cases and conditions where this may nevertheless happen. It is rather that personal labour forms a workshop relationship; that is a relationship in which the employee stands to the employer partly as somebody to be instructed, as a journeyman or even as a lad, but partly also ranks as a member of the household and subordinates himself to it. It therefore gives little encouragement to the idea of personal independence; by far the greatest number of those working, the journeymen and lads, are in any case dependent owing to their position. This dependence is easily tolerated here, mainly for the two reasons peculiar to this personal workshop labour. For first of all the employer is always there as the teacher and master, and has the reputation of being the more experienced and the better; but then he has, next to the right of directing the work, at the same time the duty to care for the maintenance of his workers. The workshop is the family at work. This is quite different where the machines function. Here, the master and employer is, because the machine is mainly capital and demands capital, above all a capitalist. He does not work himself and very often does not even understand anything of the work. The tie between worker and master therefore does not exist at all; right from the beginning, the employer is a stranger to the worker. Furthermore, machine work is of necessity simple; the higher the development of human beings, the more work will be restricted to parts of a whole and will therefore more easily be done through monotonous repetition. The factory worker is therefore in a certain sense to the machines what the day labourer is to the field; nothing ties him except the need for work and wages. Above all the employer, initially for the purely material reason that he has too many workers, has no family relationship with his workers. He does not undertake, like the master of a workshop, any obligation for feeding his people, nor even to give them always work and wage. He takes them on and lets them go as he thinks fit. The consequence, therefore, is . . . that the machine workers largely become independent persons who are thrown from the beginning on their own individual resources. And as the machine-operated industry necessarily needs a great number of such workers, it therefore has as its immediate consequence the accumulation of a mass of independent workers at certain points. These were, indeed, the first results of the introduction of machines, not only in England, but equally in France and Germany. The population increased rapidly, particularly in towns with factories; but this growth consisted mainly in the increase of the estate of workers, which gradually began to form in many places the mass of the people.

At the beginning of this development this state of affairs had no special consequences. But already after a short time a result became apparent which increasingly formed the central point of the whole matter. As is known, the workers of handicrafts undertake their period of apprenticeship and as journeymen in the hope of being able to found, after a certain time, an independent family and an independent workshop. Most of them succeed in this; but for all artisans the principle is valid that personal efficiency, diligence and skilfulness of the individual form the main basis of their advancement. In handicrafts, therefore, the worker himself is in a way the originator of his own fate, and as all depends on him, he has no reason to complain of the course of things and of the laws relating to property if he does not make progress. . . . It is quite different in factory industry. The machine . . . can only be built and maintained by means of significant capital; while the artisan has in his personal work the possibility of himself acquiring his tools and his workshop by means of his work and thus to create capital, the factory worker can never achieve possession of a machine. The whole estate of factory workers is, therefore, from the beginning destined by the nature of its work to remain an estate cut off from the acquisition of capital. It has nothing but its labour and can never gain more than that. There is a further factor in the position of the workers' estate. As the labour of the factory worker cannot be applied without the machine, it is worth something for the worker only if the owner of a factory wants to use it. Work, therefore, becomes a pure commodity, and the price of this commodity is fixed by the same principles which govern it in the case of any other commodity, by the law of supply and demand. But competition for this commodity is greatest because, as already mentioned, it produces and accumulates an enormous estate of workers. Capital, therefore, has the possibility of depressing this price as low as possible, to the limit of pure personal necessity. Now the factory worker, as has just been shown, is almost always on his own; he is completely dependent on this worker's wage and usually even with a family. . . . Capital and through it capitalists have it in their hands to dominate the whole life of the factory workers through fixing the worker's wage. And in this manner the development of machine work leads to a difference between capital and labour which takes its most important significance from the fact that as a rule the worker can never, thanks to his work and to great diligence, pass into the group of capitalists. This fact makes two estates of workers and capitalists, which are separated by the law of the movement of property as sharply the one from the other, as the nobility and citizens were under the rule of the feudal system. Thus has been caused that which forms the basis of the social movements of our time—not yet the proletariat, but certainly the body of the proletariat. . . .

Here is now the place to explain the content of a much-used and known expression: we mean that of the social danger. . . . First of all one understands by the social danger frequently only the possibility of a purely violent activity of the proletariat against those with possessions, with robbery and plundering, destruction of machines, etc. It is indeed highly regrettable that the proletariat still believes to some extent that it is able to improve its position through such outbreaks of savage fury, or that it even enjoys the satisfaction of its wild desire. However, we cannot call this the real social danger; for if a community were so weak that it could not deal with such excesses, there would hardly be any deliverance for it. The danger is quite another. As in fact a certain measure of ownership of possessions has become a condition of the whole social position of all, there can only be hope for improvement in the position of the proletariat if it somehow manages to achieve in some way a higher level of possessions. But all property is only capable of achieving that through its value. The value of a possession is that which others give or do in return for it. Now the proletariat has no other possessions but its working capacity. However one formulates the demand, in the end one will, if one wants to improve the lot of the workers, arrive at the demand that a higher value should be attached to work—or briefly that one must pay them better than has so far happened. But one can only then pay labour, and particularly factory labour, on which all depends, better if the buyer pays more for the product of work, the commodity.

This can, indeed, happen in a very simple way. The raising of the worker's wage will at once result in a rise in the price of the commodity, and therefore that demand of the workers' estate may be satisfied easily, if the state commands that for a shorter time of work the same wage should be paid as for the longer. However, for this really to help it must be assumed that the buyers are prepared to buy or are capable of buying at the new price as much as at the old. To this end the whole fortune of the people would have to experience an increase; for nobody can, merely to help labour, buy more than he can pay. Furthermore, if the price of a commodity rises, at the same time the price for the needs of the worker goes up; he consumes on the one hand what he takes in on the other. An increase in the wage of labour therefore diminishes the labour [needed]; the immense mass of labour which is at present consumed, depends precisely on the low price of the commodity: and thus really that demand of the proletarians is a contradiction in itself. But in spite of that the demand will be made. However, it will not be possible to satisfy it. The entrepreneurs will declare themselves unable to do the impossible, and with that moment danger to society begins to operate. For then only two means are possible. Either the workers understand the position of things and in a calm and sensible way seek a way out (which, however, we do not yet observe), and then any danger is avoided in this common striving of worker and capitalist; or they want the impossible from the start, an immediate and lasting higher wage for labour, and then they will of necessity go on to attack existing personal property. This notion that the abolition of personal property or capital, and a new distribution of wealth or its common ownership will help the situation for the proletariat, is the only truly dangerous aspect, but is indeed so on a tremendous scale; for then something which cannot be predicted will ensue. Against that there will always remain a means—the full and honest enlightenment of the people about what is possible and what is impossible. And he serves his people as his Fatherland best who contributes his own solution to this question. . . .

Then came the mighty events at the end of the last century. The overthrow of the old order of things was by no means a mere change in the form of government. Its main significance lay in the fact that it raised the poor class, and in it above all the estate of workers characterised earlier, to a never previously suspected importance. The republic was proclaimed for the first time in France; its form changed, but its principle remained: namely that the person without property should in the state have the same right as the one with property. It is true that the immaturity of this idea overthrew the whole constitution; the Empire followed it; however, even it fell. In place of the old rights and privileges came in the constitutional monarchies. But in this constitutional monarchy lay a deep and not by any means overcome contradiction. They recognise the equality of the rights of the citizen of the state, but they only acknowledge it for those with property. Whoever has the franchise [Wahlcensus] is a citizen of the state, whoever does not have it is only a subject. The division in the state was no longer the consequence of birth; but a no less sharp division came about through property. The distribution of property ruled state and society; the principles and laws according to which wealth is acquired and lost became the principles governing the realisation of the highest ideals, those of freedom and equality. The sharpness of this contradiction was even further increased by the impossibility, arising from the structure of industry, of the workers' estate arriving at such a fortune; whoever was a worker was thereby excluded from participation in the highest goods. And in addition, impartial research showed that the real lot of these workers was worst wherever the highest development of industry had accumulated the highest mass of material goods for the exclusive enjoyment of a part of the people. Under the shadow of these mighty contradictions the old ideas of equality continued; where was now their home? Were they not because of the revolution itself farther away from their goal than before? It is clear that now they faced not only the law of the state. Their opponent was the law which dominated the distribution of property, and this law, manifested through industry, was apparently the rule of capital over labour. This, however, was not all. The actual distributed wealth, the real individual possession, was protected through a second law; this was the law of inviolable personal property. Property produced capital, capital ruled; the rule of capital again includes property as legally inviolable: both principles stood in reciprocal action to each other. If one wanted a new order, realising the idea of an equal society, one had to begin with the recognition that both these laws had to be abolished. On that rested the internal and constantly recurring relationship of both movements; however, they appeared at first quite independent of each other. The whole succession of those theories which aim as their main task at the rule of labour over capital and through this

rule at the realisation of the idea of equality by means of the equal distribution of goods, dependent on labour, form Socialism. But those
theories and ideas which aim to achieve this equality through the abolition of the principle of personal property and an absolute community
of wealth following from this, form Communism. . . .

III

THE UNFOLDING
(GENERALLY APRIL TO JUNE 1848)

DURING THESE THREE months the forces of change reached the high-water mark of their success, but in June there were signs of a reaction. In Germany, the first national assembly, the Frankfurt Parliament, began its session in the middle of May. In the Habsburg Monarchy, great concern was caused to the authority by recurrent disorder in Vienna and by the war in Italy. But, in June, the forces of order began to rally. The Austrian army had some successes in Italy. A radical rising was crushed in Berlin. And, not the least important, an attempt at a second revolution was crushed in Paris.

III.1   GERMAN PRE-PARLIAMENT, FRANKFURT
PARLIAMENT, AND VICAR OF THE EMPIRE

The Pre-Parliament, which was to prepare the election of the first German national assembly, began a meeting of a few days on the last day of March. The extremists, led by Hecker and Struve, failed. Their rising in April was crushed. The Frankfurt Parliament soon turned to the establishment of a provisional central power for Germany and the Austrian Archduke John was elected Vicar of the Empire on 29th June.

III.1.A   The extracts from the programme put forward by Gustav von Struve to the Pre-Parliament on 31st March 1848—but not accepted—are translated from the German text in Wilhelm Mommsen (ed.), *Deutsche Parteiprogramme*, Munich, 1960, pp. 125 ff.

We . . . put the motion to the German Parliament at Frankfurt-on-Main that it should approve at once the following compilation of rights of the German people and watch over their realisation. . . .

A long period of the deepest humiliation weighs on Germany. It can be characterised as the subjugation, reduction to a state of ignorance and exploitation of the people. Arbitrary rule, riches and honours for those in power and their instruments. Under the influence of the system of tyranny which still continues even if essentially broken in its strength, Germany has more than once been brought close to the brink of disaster. It has lost several of its best provinces, others are most severely threatened. The misery of the people has become intolerable. In Upper Silesia it has taken on the proportions of a famine.

Security of property and of the person, prosperity, education and freedom for all irrespective of birth, of estate and religious faith, is the goal for which the German people strives. The means for attaining it are:

1. The abolition of the standing army of soldiers and its fusion with the civic guard, for the purpose of forming a true people's militia comprising all men capable of bearing arms.

2. Abolition of the existing armies of officials and their replacement by an economically run government consisting of freely elected men of the people.

3. Abolition of the standing armies of dues which waste the substance of the people, particularly those tolls which hinder the internal communications of Germany, inland customs duties and levies on shipping which weigh on agriculture, tithes, ground rents and compulsory services, etc. which burden trade, trade dues, excises, etc., and their replacement by
   (a) a progressive income and wealth tax, in which the necessary subsistence remains free from all dues;
   (b) a customs duty levied at the frontiers of Germany for the protection of its trade, its industry and its agriculture.

4. Abolition of all special rights, whichever name they may bear, particularly of the nobility, of the privileges of wealth, of the census,[1] of preferred estates with special judicial privileges, and their replacement by a universal German citizenship.

5. Abolition of the tutelage of municipalities and its replacement by a local government law on the basis of self-administration.

6. Dissolution of all monasteries and monastic institutions.

7. Dissolution of the alliance which has existed so far between church and state, and church and school, and its replacement by:
   (a) the principles of equal rights for all confessions of faith, of the undiminished freedom of faith and conscience, of the right of free association, of the self-government of communities and especially of their right freely to elect their spiritual ministers, their teachers and their mayors;
   (b) improvement of the position of the teaching profession and uniform regulation of the pay of ministers of religion;
   (c) abolition of school fees and surplice fees.

8. Abolition of censorship, of concessions and of caution money, and replacement of these institutions of oppression by the principle of freedom of the press in its widest extent.

[1] Franchise based on wealth.

9. Abolition of the secret courts of inquisition, transacting their business in writing, and their replacement by public, orally conducted jury courts.

10. Abolition of the hundreds of limitations on the personal freedom of Germans of the various estates and their safeguarding by a special law (habeas corpus in the fullest sense of the word) which in particular regulates the right of the people to association and assembly.

11. Removal of the distress of the working classes and of the middle class, improvement of commerce, of the estate of artisans and of agriculture. The immense hitherto existing civil lists and apanages, the unearned and too high remunerations and pensions, the manifold foundations and possessions of many bodies now lying idle, as well as the domains of the country, offer rich resources for this.

12. Correction of the disproportion between labour and capital by means of a special ministry of labour which regulates usury, protects labour and particularly secures for it a share in the profit.

13. Abolition of the in thousands of ways mutually diverging laws relating to private law, to criminal litigation law, to church law and state law, to that pertaining to money, measure, weight, post, railways, etc., and their replacement by laws which, deriving from the spirit of our age, establish the inner unity of Germany uniformly in spiritual and material respects, as well as its freedom.

14. Abolition of the dismemberment of Germany and restoration of the division into Reich circles [Reichskreise] with adequate regard to the situation of the time.

15. Abolition of the hereditary monarchy (rule by one man) and its replacement by freely elected parliaments at whose head stand freely elected presidents, all united in the federal constitution according to the pattern of the North American Free States.

German people, these are the principles with whose help alone, in our opinion, Germany can become happy, respected and free.

German brothers in East and West, we ask you to support us in the endeavour to secure for you the . . . inalienable human rights.

We will remain united in Frankfurt-on-Main until a freely elected parliament can take charge of the destiny of Germany. In the meantime we will draft the necessary law proposals and will prepare the great work of the restoration of Germany through a freely elected executive committee.

III.1.B Bismarck had been one of the leaders of the Extreme Right in the first Prussian United Diet in 1847. In March 1848, he advised resistance to the revolution. The speech in the second Diet on 2nd April is particularly noteworthy for his reference to a united German Fatherland. Extract translated from the German in Otto von Bismarck, *Gedanken und Erinnerungen*, I, Stuttgart, 1915, pp. 35 f.

I am one of the few who are going to vote against the [loyal] address, and I have merely asked to speak in order to give my reasons and to explain to you that I fully accept the address in so far as it is a programme for the future, but only for the sole reason that I cannot do otherwise. I do it not voluntarily, but driven by the pressure of circumstances; for I have not changed my view since six months ago; I believe that this ministry is the only one which can lead us out of the present situation to an ordered and lawful state of affairs, and for this reason I will devote to it my small support wherever this is possible for me. What, however, induces me to vote against the address are the expressions of joy and thanks for that which happened during the last days. The past is buried, and I regret more painfully than many of you that no human power is capable of calling it back to life after the crown itself has thrown earth on its coffin. But if I accept this, forced by the power of circumstances, I still cannot cease my activity in the United Diet with the lie that I could give thanks and be joyful about that which I must regard as at least an erroneous way. If there is really to be success along the new path which has been taken in achieving a *united German Fatherland*, a happy or at least a lawfully ordered state of affairs, then the moment will have arrived when I can express my thanks to the originator of the new order of things, but at present this is not possible for me. . . .

III.1.c The resolutions of the Frankfurt Pre-Parliament of 4th April 1848, are of considerable importance because they formed the basis of the regulations issued by the Federal Assembly of the German Confederation for the holding of elections to the German Parliament. Extract translated from the German in Huber, *Dokumente*, pp. 271 ff.

TASK OF THE ASSEMBLY

. . . The assembly has seen as its task the laying down of the manner in which the constituent national assembly is to be formed.

It has expressed clearly that the decision about the future constitution of Germany is to be left exclusively and solely to the constituent assembly which is to be elected by the people.

. . . Schleswig, in state and national matters indivisibly joined to Holstein, is to be accepted at once into the German Confederation, and is to be represented in the constituent assembly like every other German federal state by freely elected deputies.

East and West Prussia is to be included in the German Confederation in the same manner.

The assembly declares the partition of Poland a shameful injustice. It recognises the sacred duty of the German people to collaborate in the restoration of Poland. In this connection it expresses the wish that the German Governments may grant to the Poles returning to their Fatherland without arms free transit and, as far as necessary, support.

Numbers of representatives of the people in the German constituent assembly
One representative in the German constituent assembly will be elected for every 50,000 inhabitants.
A state with less than 50,000 inhabitants chooses one representative. The Bundesmatrikel [the official population table drawn up by the German Confederation] is authoritative for the calculation of the number of inhabitants.

Mode of election of representatives in the German constituent assembly
In respect to the mode of elections, the following conditions apply to each of the German states:
The right to vote and eligibility may not be limited by an election census, by preference being given to a particular religion, by an election according to certain estates.
Every citizen [Staatsangehörige] who is of age and is [economically] independent, is to be entitled to vote and to be elected.
The person to be elected need not belong to the state which he is to represent in the assembly.
The political refugees who return to Germany and resume their state citizenship are entitled to vote and to be elected.
In all other respects it is left to each German state to decide the mode of election deemed appropriate: the assembly, however, regards direct election in principle as the most suitable.

Meeting place of the constituent national assembly
The constituent national assembly holds its sessions in Frankfurt-on-Main.

Date of meeting
Elections are to be arranged in the individual states in such a manner that the national assembly may hold its first session on 1st May of this year.

Permanent committee of the assembly
The present assembly elects a permanent committee of fifty members which remains in Frankfurt until the meeting of the constituent assembly.

The committee will be elected from members of the assembly in such a manner that each ballot designates fifty persons, concerning whom the assembly assumes that each voter will want to see all parts of the Fatherland represented on the committee.

This committee of fifty is commissioned to:

—invite the Federal Assembly [Diet] to consult with it until the meeting of the constituent assembly;

—advise the Federal Assembly independently in connection with the preservation of the interests of the nation and the administration of federal affairs until the meeting of the constituent assembly, and to put the necessary motions to the Federal Assembly; to recall the present assembly at once in case of any danger arising to the Fatherland.

The committee will use its influence with the governments to ensure that a general arming of the people will be effected in all German states as quickly as possible.

The committee has to ensure that it will be joined by six men from Austria.

The negotiations of the committee with the Federal Assembly are to be published by the press.

The assembly demands that the Federal Assembly, when it undertakes the task of founding a constituent assembly, should renounce the unconstitutional emergency decrees and expel the men from its midst who took part in their initiation and execution.

Basic rights and demands of the German people

The assembly recommends with its approval in principle to the constituent parliament for examination and appropriate consideration the following motions which demand certain basic rights as a minimum measure of German popular freedom, and which express the wishes and demands alive in the German people:

Equality of political rights for all without distinction of religious confessions, and independence of the Church from the state.

Full freedom of the press.

The right of free association.

The right of petition.

A free state constitution with representation of the people and a decisive voice of the deputies of the people in legislation and taxation, and with responsibility of ministers.

Just assessment of taxable duty according to taxable capacity.

Equality of the duty and the right to bear arms.

Equal eligibility of all citizens for communal and state offices.

Unconditional right to emigrate.

General German state citizenship.

Freedom of teaching and learning.

Protection of personal freedom.

Protection from the refusal of justice.

Independence of justice.

Public and oral administration of justice and trial by jury in criminal matters. . . .

A complete credit system with agricultural and workers' schemes.

Protection of labour through institutions and measures which preserve those incapable of working from want, which secure gainful occupation to the unemployed, which adapt the organisation of crafts and factories to the needs of the time.

School education for all classes, trades and professions from state resources.

Finally, recognition of emigration as an affair of the nation and its regulation for the protection of the emigrant.

Frankfurt-on-Main
4th April 1848

> In the name of the Committee
> of Fifty
> Soiron as Chairman
> H. Simon as Secretary

III.1.D　The Czech historian F. Palacky was invited by the Committee of Fifty left behind as caretaker by the Pre-Parliament to join its deliberations. His reasons for refusal are an interesting tribute to the Habsburg Empire from a leading non-German. The letter, written from Prague on 11th April 1848, is translated from the original German text, reproduced in F. Palacky (ed.), *Gedenkblätter*, Prague, 1874, pp. 149 ff.

. . . To the Committee of Fifty, for the attention of President Soiron at Frankfurt-on-Main.

P.P.

The letter of 6th April in which you, greatly esteemed gentlemen, did me the honour of inviting me to Frankfurt in order to take part in the business concerned 'mainly with the speediest summoning of a German Parliament' has just been duly delivered to me by the post.

With joyful surprise I read in it the most valued testimony of the confidence which Germany's most distinguished men have not ceased to place in my views: for by summoning me to the assembly of 'friends of the German Fatherland', you yourselves acquit me of the charge which is as unjust as it has often been repeated, of ever having shown hostility towards the German people. With true gratitude I recognise in this the high humanity and love of justice of this excellent assembly, and I thus find myself all the more obliged to reply to it with open confidence, freely and without reservation.

Gentlemen, I cannot accede to your call, either myself or by despatching another 'reliable patriot'. Allow me to expound the reasons for this to you as briefly as possible.

The explicit purpose of your assembly is to put a German people's association [Volksbund] in the place of the existing federation of princes, to bring the German nation to real unity, to strengthen German national feeling, and thus to raise Germany's power both internal and external. However much I respect this endeavour and the feeling on which it is based, and particularly because I respect it, I cannot participate in it. I am not a German—at any rate I do not consider myself as such—and surely you have not wished to invite me as a mere yes-man without opinion or will. Consequently, I would have in Frankfurt either to deny my feelings and to play the hypocrite or to contradict loudly at the first opportunity which offers itself. For the former I am too frank and outspoken, for the latter not sufficiently bold and ruthless; for I cannot find it in my heart by ugly sounds to disturb the harmony which I find desirable and gratifying not only in my own house but also in my neighbour's.

I am a Bohemian of Slav descent [Stamm] and with the little which I possess and can do have devoted myself totally and for ever to the service of my people. This people is, indeed, a small one, but has always been a distinct one and one existing for itself.

Its rulers have for centuries participated in the German union of princes [Fürstenbund]; it has never, however, counted itself as part of this people, and it has not been considered as belonging to it by others, during the course of centuries. The whole association of Bohemia, first of all with the Holy Roman Empire, then with the German Confederation, has always been a pure matter of the royal prerogative [Regale], of which the Bohemian people, the Bohemian estates, have never been accustomed to take any notice. This fact is known equally well to all German historians as to me; and if it should be doubted by anybody, I am prepared to secure the evidence in due course. Even granting the full assumption that the Bohemian crown has ever been in a feudal relationship with Germany (which, incidentally, has always been denied by Bohemian writers), nobody versed in history can possibly doubt the former internal sovereignty and autonomy of Bohemia. The whole world knows that the German emperors as such have never had anything to do with the Bohemian people; that they possessed in and over Bohemia neither the legislative nor the judicial or executive power; that they were never entitled to draw either troops or anything else based on their royal prerogative [Regalien] out of the country, that Bohemia with its crown lands was not part of any of the former German circles

[Kreise], that the competence of the Supreme Imperial Court [Reichs-kammergericht] never extended over it, etc.; that thus the whole con-nection of Bohemia with Germany so far must be considered as a relationship not of people with people, but of ruler with ruler. If it is now demanded that, going beyond the hitherto existing union of princes, the people of Bohemia should join together with the German people, then this is a new demand lacking any basis in historical right, to which I for my part do not regard myself as justified in acceding, so long as I do not receive for it an explicit and complete mandate.

The second reason which prevents me from taking part in your de-liberations is the circumstance that, judging by everything that has so far been published about your purposes and views, you will of necessity intend to weaken Austria as an independent empire, even to make it impossible—a state whose maintenance, integrity and strengthening is and must be a high and important affair not only of my people, but of the whole of Europe, nay, of humanity and civilisation itself . . .

. . . You know which power possesses the whole great East of our continent; you know that this power, which has already grown to a colossal size, strengthens itself inwardly in greater measure with each decade than is or can be the case in Western countries; that—in its interior almost unassailable and inaccessible—it has long adopted a threatening position externally, and, though aggressive even in the North, driven by its natural instinct it seeks and will seek preferably to expand towards the South; that every further step which it could take along this way threatens with increased speed to produce and to lead to a new *universal monarchy* that is an incalculable and unutterable evil, a calamity without measure and end, which I, a Slav body and soul, would therefore in the interest of humanity mourn no less, even though it would be primarily a Slav one. With the same injustice with which I am viewed as an enemy of the Germans in Germany, I am designated by many in Russia as an enemy of the Russians. No, I say it loud and openly, I am no enemy of the Russians. Quite the contrary, I have always followed with attention and joyful participation each step which this great people takes forward within its natural frontiers on the path of civilisation. As, however, notwithstanding all fervent love for my people, I have always put the interests of humanity and science above those of nationality: the mere possibility of a Russian universal mon-archy finds no more decided opponent and person fighting against it than me; not because it is Russian, but because it would be a universal monarchy.

You know that the south-east of Europe along the frontiers of the Russian Empire is inhabited by several peoples significantly different in origin, language, history and culture—Slavs, Wallachians, Magyars, and Germans, not to mention the Greeks, Turks and Schkipetars—of whom none is strong enough by itself to put up a successful resistance in the future against the overpowering neighbour in the East; they can do that only when a single and firm bond unites them all with one another. The true life blood of this necessary union of peoples is the Danube: its central power, therefore, must not be too far distant from this stream if it wants to be and to remain at all effective. Truly, if the Austrian Empire had not already existed for a long time, then one would have to hurry in the interest of Europe and the interest of humanity to create it.

But why did we see this state, which by nature and history is called to be Europe's shield and refuge against Asiatic elements of all kinds— why did we see it in the critical moment surrendered to every impetuous onslaught, unsteady and almost helpless? Because it has in unhappy delusion for so long itself misjudged and denied the actual legal and moral basis of its existence: the principle of the complete equality of rights and the equality in respect of all nationalities and confessions united under its sceptre. The law of nations is a true natural law: no nation on earth is entitled to demand for its benefit from its neighbour its self-sacrifice; none is obliged to deny itself or to sacrifice itself for the good of its neighbour. Nature knows no ruling, as well as no servile peoples; for the bond which unites several peoples to a political whole to be firm and lasting, none must have a reason for fearing that it would lose by unification any of its dearest blessings: quite the contrary, each must harbour the secure hope that it will find from the central power protection against any encroachments of its neighbours; then it will hasten, too, to endow this central authority with so much power that it could give such protection effectively. I am convinced that it is not yet too late for Austria to proclaim aloud and without reserve this principle of justice, the sacred anchor [sacra ancora] when shipwreck threatens, and to give it practical emphasis everywhere: but the moments are precious, not an hour is to be lost! Metternich did not fall only because he was the worst enemy of freedom, but also because he has been the most irreconcilable enemy of all Slav nationality in Austria.

When I cast my glance beyond the frontiers of Bohemia I am impelled by natural as well as historical causes to direct them not towards Frankfurt but towards Vienna, and there to seek the centre which is natural and is called to secure and to protect for my people peace, freedom and justice. Your tendency, gentlemen, however, now seems openly designed to weaken incurably this centre from whose strength I expect salvation not only for Bohemia, and even to destroy it. Or do you believe that the Austrian monarchy will still continue if you forbid it to possess in its hereditary lands its own army independent of the federal head [Bundeshaupt] in Frankfurt? Do you believe that the Austrian Emperor will even then be able to maintain himself as sovereign if you oblige him to accept all the more important laws of your assembly, and thus to make illusory the institution of the Austrian Reich estates as well as the provincial constitutions of the associated kingdoms, which are offered by nature itself? And if then Hungary, for instance, following its urge, secedes from the monarchy, or, which is almost the same, becomes its centre of gravity—will this Hungary, which does not want to know anything of equal rights of nations within its own frontiers, in the long run remain free and strong? Only the just is truly free and strong. But there can be no question of the Danube Slavs and the Wallachians, nay the Poles, voluntarily joining the state which proclaims the principle that one has first to be a Magyar and only then a human being; and even less can there be any question of a compulsory union. For the salvation of Europe, Vienna must not sink down to the level of a provincial city! But if there are even in Vienna people who desire your Frankfurt as the capital, they must be told, Lord forgive them, that they do not know what they want!

Finally I must hesitate for a third reason to collaborate in your deliberations: for I believe that all the existing plans for the reorganisation of Germany on the basis of the will of the people cannot be carried out and are in the long run untenable, unless you decide on a true Caesarean operation [Kaiserschnitt]—I mean the proclamation of a German republic, if only as a transitional form. All attempts to draft rules for a division of power between sovereign princes and the sovereign people remind me of the theories of phalanstery which equally make the assumption that all those participating will behave like figures in an arithmetical problem and will claim no other rights than those which theory designates for them. Possibly my view is unfounded, I may be wrong in my conviction—sincerely I desire myself that such may be the case—but the conviction is there, and I may not abandon its compass for a single moment, unless I want to get lost in the tempests of the day. So far as the introduction of a republic in Germany is concerned—this question lies completely outside the sphere of my competence, so that I do not want even to express an opinion on it.

I must, however, reject expressly and emphatically in advance the idea of a republic within the frontiers of the Austrian Empire. Think of an Austria divided into a lot of republics and small republics [Republikchen]—what a welcome basis for the Russian universal monarchy...

The demand that Austria (and with her Bohemia) should nationally unite with Germany, that is merge in Germany, is to expect it to commit suicide, and therefore lacks all moral and political sense; conversely the demand that Germany should join Austria, that is to say enter the Austrian monarchy under the conditions sketched above, makes much more sense. But if this expectation is inadmissible to the German national sentiment, then there only remains for the two powers—Germany and Austria—to constitute themselves next to each other on the basis of equality of rights, to convert their existing federation into an eternal defensive and offensive alliance [Schutz und Trutzbündnis] and in case of need, if it suits their mutual material interests, to conclude a customs union between them.

I shall always be glad to co-operate in all measures which do not endanger Austria's independence, integrity and the development of her power, particularly towards the East. . . .

III.1.E One of the most notable developments in Germany during 1848 was the beginning of a Roman Catholic political organisation. The following document contains the programme for the foundation of a Catholic newspaper, the 'Rheinische Volkshalle' in Cologne, dated 13th May 1848. Extract translated from the German in Mommsen, *Parteiprogramme*, pp. 200 ff.

. . . The new freedom achieved for the press has strengthened the power which it already possessed, but has also created great new obligations for those who are capable of handling this power. The appeal to external obstacles as an excuse for their inactivity or the imperfection of their performance will no longer be possible. The new freedom which has been gained demands of them that they should enter with all their strength into the struggles of the present, and collaborate, by their participation in the mighty influence of the daily press, in the salutary development of the great advances from which we benefit, and in the glorification of our Fatherland.

In the realisation of this obligation the undersigned have met together for the foundation of a new political newspaper which is to appear in Cologne under the name *Rheinische Volkshalle*. In publishing the views which form the basis for the enterprise, they are hopeful that they will enjoy the applause and support of many of their fellow citizens.

To the forces affecting the present day belongs above all the *idea of freedom*. To realise it in every respect and to make it at home in a mankind which is to be rejuvenated through its spiritual inspiration is the high aim, the attainment of which forms the main task of the daily press.

In the struggles of the present, *social questions* have above all pressed themselves into the foreground. The means by which a dam can be raised against a pauperism, which in our day has increasingly spread and hampered free intellectual development, must form a main topic of the discussion on this subject. By giving its most heartfelt participation to those most urgent interests of humanity, but also by exposing clearly and thoroughly all the difficulties of the tasks to be solved, the daily press should arouse the forces of common interest for what is attainable, as well as inform about what is unattainable, should destroy dangerous illusions and thus contribute to a calming of our excited condition.

The political system is capable and in need of a speedier reconstruction than the social. In trying to collaborate in the timely adaptation and further development of these movements according to its strength, our newspaper will above all bear in mind the principle: *freedom in all and for all*. It should fight for a constitution which, resting on truly popular foundations, secures for all citizens of state the equal civic and political rights, confines itself to the minimum limitation of the free and independent development of the individual and offers the greatest guarantee against any undue tutelage by the state authority.

Religion, that secret power which fills the human being it enters with love and the most unselfish sacrifice for everything that is noble, truly sublime and in furtherance of the common weal, thus forms in this time, when political arts and forms have impotently disintegrated into nothingness, that power on which the regeneration of the social order will turn. Thus the political daily press must also devote its attention to the religious element, and it appears as one of its most important duties to understand correctly and assess every development in religion and church in its relation to our social and political conditions. The *Catholic* Church especially has a great deal to do in this connection, to correct prejudices and to make good injustices. The strength which lies in religion, however, demands above all liberation from those delicate and in many ways intertwined ties of tutelage and dependence, arising from a narrow-minded, distrustful government system, a misplaced delight in governing, and inter-denominational aversion, particularly on the part of the Catholic Church. The feeling of *church freedom* has during the last twenty years, in spite of the efforts of short-sighted statecraft to ignore it or to appease it with deception, through the struggles in England, Belgium, France and on the Rhine, matured to a power which now makes itself felt in the generally voiced demand for the *independence of the church from the state*, in the full consciousness of its strength and justification. It can now only be a question of grasping and carrying out this principle in all its consequences without reservation and without predilection for or aversion to any religious confession. The only hope for the final re-unification of the separate confessions lies on the basis of freedom—a goal, however distant it may seem, for which the intellectual developments and even the differences of the time appear to pave the way, and towards which all those who are looking around for a thorough healing of our political want of union are already drawn for this reason.

Another force which has, beside the constantly increased striving for freedom, been involved in the struggle of the present and gained the greatest significance, is the sentiment of *nationality* and of the inalienable rights lent to it by nature itself. All the more, however, the friend of truth must concede that in this point, through earlier events and the mutual faults of the princes no less than of peoples, the natural relationship has in many ways been unsettled: all the more is it necessary that, in discussion of the facts and in endeavours relating to it, the correct measure should be observed, and that the balance, which inclines every noble heart so strongly towards the nationalities involved in the struggle of rebirth, should be accompanied by prudence of judgement.

We wish ourselves good fortune in the struggle into which we see nearly all European nations drawn, the struggle for freedom and national independence. We hope that from this fight the German people will go forth free and united. We hope for an international brotherhood between all free nations, in which we see the most secure guarantee for the freedom and national independence of all. . . .

III.1.F   Pending the completion of the work of unification, the Frankfurt Parliament established a Provisional Central Power on 28th June. The document is translated from the German text in Huber, *Dokumente*, pp. 276 f.

1. Until the definite foundation of a government authority for Germany, a provisional central power for all common affairs of the German nation is to be established.

2. This is:
   (a) to exercise the executive power in all affairs which concern the general security and welfare of the German federal state;
   (b) to take supreme command of the complete armed force, and particularly to appoint its Commander-in-Chief;
   (c) to exercise the international and commercial representation of Germany and for this purpose to appoint ministers and consuls.

3. The establishment of the constitution remains excluded from the sphere of the Central Power.

4. Concerning war and peace, and treaties with foreign powers the Central Power decides in agreement with the National Assembly.

5. The Provisional Central Power is to be entrusted to a Vicar of the Empire, who will be elected by the National Assembly.

6. The Vicar of the Empire exercises his authority through ministers appointed by him and responsible to the National Assembly. All his dispositions require for their validity the countersignature of at least one responsible minister.

7. The Vicar of the Empire is not responsible.

8. The National Assembly is to make a special law about the responsibility of the ministers.

9. The ministers have the right to attend the deliberations of the National Assembly and to be heard by it.

10. The ministers are obliged to appear in the National Assembly at its request and to give information.

11. The ministers have the right to vote in the National Assembly only if they have been elected as its members.

12. The position of Vicar of the Empire is incompatible with that of a member of the National Assembly.

13. The existence of the Federal Assembly ceases with the beginning of the functioning of the Provisional Central Power.

14. In connection with executive measures, the Central Power has to come to an understanding, in so far as is possible, with the plenipotentiaries of state governments.

15. The activity of the Provisional Central Power ceases as soon as the constitution for Germany has been completed and put into operation. . . .

III.1.G   The Archduke John of Austria was elected Vicar of the Empire on 29th June. The scene in the Parliament which met in St. Paul's Church is described in a letter of 1st July 1848, by Clotilde Koch-Gontard, a Frankfurt hostess, at whose salon the President of the Assembly, Heinrich von Gagern, was a frequent visitor. Extract from W. Klötzer (ed.), *Clotilde Koch-Gontard an ihre Freunde, Briefe und Erinnerungen aus der Zeit der deutschen Einheitsbewegung 1843–1869*, Frankfurt 1969, p. 66.

The election of the Vicar of the Empire was a magnificent moment. . . .

Gagern gave the act a high consecration through the most beautiful introductory words, spoken with deep emotion. When the vote began and when during a great silence in the Church the dull sound 'Archduke of Austria' rang from almost every corner of the Church, I was moved to the depths of my soul. When Gagern proclaimed the Archduke, when the bells sounded, the guns thundered, all were compelled to feel the high significance of this hour. Gagern said yesterday that the best he could do now was to die, for this day had been the greatest of his life. The wonderful consecration Gagern gave the whole has almost reconciled all hearts to him. There is only one of his sterling worth. . . .

III.2   THE MAY TROUBLES IN VIENNA

Vienna developed during 1848 into one of the great centres of European radicalism. After a renewal of disturbances in May, the Emperor Ferdinand I left the capital for Innsbruck, where he could count on more loyal support.

III.2.A   The sudden departure of the Emperor left the Government, which included some moderate liberals, in an awkward situation. The ministerial declaration issued in Vienna on 17th May 1848, is taken from *The Times*, 24th May 1848, p. 5, col. 2.

. . . This day, about nine o'clock in the evening, have the Ministers been verbally and most unexpectedly informed that His Majesty the Emperor, from motives of health, with the Empress and the Archduke Francis Charles and his Royal Consort, and three Princes, have left the capital and proceeded in the direction of Innsbruck.

The undersigned Ministry, being ignorant of the reasons and details of this journey, feel it their duty to bring the same to the cognisance of the inhabitants of this capital.

The Ministry have likewise thought it their duty to send the Commander of the National Guard, Count Hoyos, as a trustworthy man, to His Majesty with the urgent request to dispel the apprehensions of the people, either by the Emperor's return, or a statement of the reasons which make it impossible. The same urgent request will be laid before the Archduke by Count Wilczek.

The Council of Ministers are, moreover, fully sensible of the duty they have to fulfil at this important moment—namely to devote their undivided care and attention to the interests of the country, and to act on their own responsibility as circumstances shall demand. Whatever information the ministers may receive respecting this event, they will at once faithfully and completely publish. If direct commands or communications from the Monarch should reach them, they will likewise publish them.

Vienna, May 17, 1848.

Pillersdorf	Latour
Sommaruga	Doblhoff
Kauss	Baumgartner

III.2.B The Emperor issued a declaration from Innsbruck, extracts of which are taken from *Annual Register*, 1848, p. 408.

. . . The events which took place at Vienna forced the painful conviction upon me that factious rioters, assisted by the Academical Legion and part of the National Guard, misled by foreigners, and unmindful of their wonted allegiance, conspired against my liberty with a view of enthralling my provinces. The inhabitants of these provinces, and, indeed, all well-meaning citizens of my capital, must of necessity resent so daring an outrage with unlimited exasperation. No alternative was left to me, beyond recurring to measures of violence, except to withdraw for the moment to one of my provinces. These, God be thanked, have all remained true to their Monarch. . . .

I will not grant anything to the forcible exactions of unauthorised and armed individuals. My departure from Vienna was intended to impress this upon my painfully excited people and likewise to remind them of the paternal love with which I am ever ready to receive my sons, even though they be prodigal ones. . . .

III.3   THE SLAV CONGRESS IN PRAGUE

An attempt to formulate a common policy of the Slavs was made, with
limited success, at a congress in Prague. It proved difficult to reconcile
the interests of the various nationalities and the divergent ideological
views.

III.3.A   The following extracts are translated from the German text of the
declaration issued at the end of the congress on 12th June 1848,
reproduced in H. Reschauer and M. Smets, *Das Jahr 1848:
Geschichte der Wiener Revolution*, II, Vienna, 1872, pp. 340 ff.

. . . For the first time since history records us, we, dispersed members
of a great family of peoples, have joined together in great numbers from
distant regions in order to acknowledge ourselves once more as brethren
and to deliberate peacefully about our common affairs; and we have
come to an understanding, not only by means of the wonderful language
spoken by eighty million members of our people, but also through the
harmony of our heart-beats, through the harmony of our intellectual
interests.

The Latin and Germanic peoples, at one time famous in Europe as
mighty conquerors, have for thousands of years not only secured with
the strength of their swords their political independence, but they also
knew how to obtain manifold satisfaction of their lust for power. . . . In
the case of the Slavs, however, . . . one people after another sank into
dependence in the course of the centuries; . . . but . . . their spirit has
finally won the day, the spell is removed. . . . Now the long oppressed
Slav again raises his head, . . . he does not *want any rule, any conquest*,
he wants freedom for himself as for everybody; he demands it in
recognition of the holiest right of man. Therefore we Slavs condemn
and despise any rule of force which wants to assert itself outside the law,
we condemn all privileges . . . as well as all political distinctions of
estates, and we demand absolute equality before the law; we demand the
same degree of rights and duties for everybody; . . . we have proposed
to the Emperor of Austria, under whose constitutional regime the
majority of us live, to convert the Empire into a Federation [Bund] of
nations all with the same rights, which should take equal account of the
divergent needs of the latter as of the unity of the Monarchy. . . .

The enemies of our nationality have succeeded in alarming Europe
with the spectre of political panslavism which allegedly threatens to
destroy all achievements of freedom, culture and humanity. . . . We
raise our voice loudly for our unhappy brethren, the Poles, who have
been deprived of their independence by the most despicable tricks of
violence; we urge the cabinets finally to expiate this old sin, this curse,

which hereditarily burdens their policy, and in this we count on the sympathies of the whole of Europe. We protest against the arbitrary dismemberment of countries, which is sought these days in the Grand-Duchy of Posen, and we expect of the Prussian and Saxon Government that it should desist henceforth from the denationalisation of the Slavs living in Silesia, Lusatia, Posen, East and West Prussia, which has so far been carried out according to plan; we call upon the Hungarian ministry to cease at once the shocking measures of force which it has taken against the Slav peoples in Hungary, particularly against the Serbs, Croats, Slovaks, and Ruthenes, and to strive to grant them as soon as possible the national rights due to them; we hope that a heartless policy will not for long prevent our Slav brethren in Turkey from developing their nationhood politically. . . .

We, who appear again on Europe's political stage as the youngest, but not by any means the weaker actors, propose at once the sending of delegates to a general European Peace Congress for the settlement of all international questions; for we are convinced that free peoples understand each other better than paid diplomats. May attention be paid in good time to this proposal, before the reactionary policy of individual courts again succeeds in bringing about that the nations, goaded by envy and hate, tear each other to pieces.

In the name of the freedom, equality and fraternity of all peoples.

III.4   THE JUNE RISING IN PARIS

Many of the promises of the French Provisional Government, particularly that of the right to work, proved difficult to fulfil. Disappointed, though probably quite unrealistic, hopes combined with the determination of a radical group in Paris to force a second revolution, led to the June rising, the suppression of which was a major landmark in the defeat of European radicalism.

III.4.A   The following document translates from the French a letter from the Minister of Public Works to M. Emile Thomas, the director of the National Workshops, of the 24th May. The order was not, however, made public until 20th June 1848. The extract is taken from Marriott, *The French Revolution*, II, pp. 271 ff.

Sir, I have the honour to announce to you that the Commission for the Executive Power has adopted the following measures with regard to the National Workshops:

1. Unmarried workers aged from eighteen to twenty-five years will be invited to enrol under the flag for the Republic in order to fill the different regiments of the Army; those who refuse to take on a voluntary engagement will at once be struck from the lists of brigadement of the National Workshops.

2. A new census of the workers of Paris will be carried out without delay. This census will be undertaken concurrently by the mayoralties and by the employees of the Central Office of the National Workshops which are delegated to this task. The workers who cannot show that they have had a regular residence of six months before 24th May will be dismissed and will cease to receive wages and relief.

3. Lists of workers, arranged by arrondissement and by profession, will be deposited in an office to be especially established as soon as possible in the centre of Paris, where information will be provided to the employers by the employees of the administration. Employers will be able to ask for such a number of workers as they declare necessary for the resumption and continuation of their work. Those who refuse to obey will at once be struck from the general list of the National Workshops.

4. The workers who do not find themselves included in the cases of exclusion provided by the above articles and who for a transitional period continue to form part of the National Workshops, will be put to work on the basis of tasks and not of days.

5. There will be organised in the shortest possible time brigades of workers who will be directed in the Departments to be employed under the direction of engineers of bridges and roads in the execution of great public works.

I ask you, Sir, to occupy yourself with the greatest possible speed with the application of the measures decreed by the Commission for the Executive Power. You must prepare the necessary lists in order to single out the workers who by reason of their age will have to enrol in the armies of the Republic; all those who will have to be sent back to their respective Departments owing to the lack of six months' regular residence; those who may be asked for again or taken back by their employers; and, finally, those whom it will be convenient to enlist for great works in the province and the suburbs of Paris. I will let you know tomorrow the place where lists of workers of various professions not excluded from the National Workshops by virtue of the first two stipulations will be deposed and communicated to employers.

You will have to designate two or three employees of our administration who will have to constantly have this place manned in order to put at the disposal of the employers the workers asked for by them.

I leave it to you to inform the public by means of placards and of announcements in the newspapers, of the day on which one will have to present oneself at the information office. You will see that this measure is one of extreme urgency and that not an instant must be lost to execute it.

I attach great importance to the stipulation which re-establishes the task as the basis of wage. You must put it into practice at once.

I will, in due course, address to you instructions about the organisation of workers' brigades who will have to be directed in the Departments. . . .

> For the Minister of Public Works,
> By Order,
> The Secretary General,
> Boulage.

III.4.B The removal of the Director, Emile Thomas, and the dissolution of the National Workshops, was followed by the Paris rising from 23rd to 26th June, crushed by General Cavaignac, the Minister of War. The famous writer and politician Alexis de Tocqueville was a member of the French National Assembly during the rising. Extracts from *The Recollections of Alexis de Tocqueville*, translated by A. T. de Mattos, edited by J. P. Mayer, New York, 1949, pp. 172 ff., by kind permission of the Harvill Press Ltd.

. . . I found the Assembly agitated by a thousand sinister reports. The insurrection was gaining ground in every direction. Its headquarters, or, so to speak, its trunk, was behind the Hotel de Ville, whence it stretched its long arms farther to right and left into the suburbs, and threatened soon to hug even us. The cannon was drawing appreciably nearer. And to this correct news were added a thousand lying rumours. Some said that our troops were running short of ammunition; others, that a number of them had laid down their arms or gone over to the insurgents.

M. Thiers[2] asked Barrot,[3] Dufaure,[4] Rémusat,[5] . . . and myself to follow him to a private room. There he said: 'I know something of insurrections, and I tell you this is the worst I have ever seen. The insurgents may be here within an hour, and we shall be butchered one and all. Do you not think that it would be well for us to agree to propose to the Assembly, as soon as we think necessary and before it becomes too late, that it should call back the troops around it, in order that, placed in their midst, we may all leave Paris together and remove the seat of the Republic to a place where we could summon the army and all the National Guards in France to our assistance?'

He said this in very eager tones and with a greater display of excitement than is, perhaps, advisable in the presence of great danger. I saw that he was pursued by the ghost of February. Dufaure, who had a less

---

[2] A former minister and opposition leader under Louis Philippe, an anti-republican conservative in 1848, President, 1871–73.

[3] On the Right in 1848, Prime Minister in December.

[4] Also on the Right in 1848, Minister of the Interior shortly afterwards.

[5] An anti-republican.

vivid imagination, and who, moreover, never readily made up his mind to associate himself with people he did not care about, even to save himself, phlegmatically and somewhat sarcastically explained that the time had not yet come to discuss a plan of this kind; that we could always talk of it later on; that our chances did not seem to him so desperate as to oblige us to entertain so extreme a remedy; that to entertain it was to weaken ourselves. He was undoubtedly right, and his words broke up the consultation. I at once wrote a few lines to my wife, telling her that the danger was hourly increasing, that Paris would perhaps end by falling entirely into the power of the revolt, and that, in that case, we should be obliged to leave it in order to carry on the civil war elsewhere. I charged her to go at once to Saint-Germain by the railroad, which was still free, and there to await my news; told my nephews to take the letter; and returned to the Assembly.

I found it discussing a decree to proclaim Paris in a state of siege, to abolish the powers of the Executive Commission, and to replace it by a military dictatorship under General Cavaignac.

The Assembly knew precisely that this was what it wanted. The thing was easily done: it was urgent, and yet it was not done. Each moment some little incident, some trivial motion interrupted and turned aside the current of the general wish; for assemblies are very liable to that sort of nightmare in which an unknown and invisible force seems always at the last moment to interpose between the will and the deed and to prevent the one from influencing the other. Who would have thought that it was Bastide[6] who should eventually induce the Assembly to make up its mind? Yet he it was.

I had heard him say—and it was very true—speaking of himself, that he was never able to remember more than the first fifteen words of a speech. But I have sometimes observed that men who do not know how to speak produce a greater impression, under certain circumstances, than the finest orators. They bring forward but a single idea, that of the moment, clothed in a single phrase, and somehow they lay it down on the rostrum like an inscription written in big letters, which everybody perceives, and in which each instantly recognises his own particular thought. Bastide, then, displayed his long, honest, melanchoy face in the tribune, and said, with a mournful air:

'Citizens, in the name of the country I beseech you to vote as quickly as possible. We are told that perhaps within an hour the Hôtel de Ville will be taken.'

These few words put an end to debate, and the decree was voted in the twinkling of an eye.[7]

I protested against the clause proclaiming Paris in a state of siege; I

[6] Briefly Foreign Minister under the Second Republic.
[7] On 24th June.

did so by instinct rather than reflection. I have such a contempt and so great a natural horror for military despotism that these feelings came rising tumultuously in my heart when I heard a state of siege suggested and even dominated those prompted by our peril. In this I made a mistake in which I fortunately found few to imitate me.

The friends of the Executive Commission have asserted in very bitter terms that their adversaries and the partisans of General Cavaignac spread ominous rumours on purpose to precipitate the vote. If the latter did really resort to this trick, I gladly pardon them, for the measures they caused to be taken were indispensable to the safety of the country.

Before adopting the decree of which I have spoken, the Assembly unanimously voted another, which declared that the families of those who should fall in the struggle should receive a pension from the Treasury and their children be adopted by the Republic. . . .

III.5 ITALY IN APRIL 1848

The next two documents illustrate some of the many developments taking place in Italy at this time.

III.5.A The following resolution was carried by the Sicilian Parliament on 13th April. Extract from *Annual Register*, 1848, p. 336.

. . . The Parliament declares:

1. Ferdinand and his dynasty are for ever fallen from the throne of Sicily.

2. Sicily shall govern herself constitutionally, and call to the throne an Italian Prince, as soon as she shall have reformed her *statuto*. . . .

III.5.B For a time Pope Pius IX had hoped to reconcile a role in Italian unification with his position as Supreme Pontiff. It was, however, an anomaly that Papal troops were ranged against the army of the Emperor of Austria, the leading Roman Catholic sovereign in Europe. The allocution of Pope Pius IX delivered in the Secret Consistory of 29th April 1848, marked the turning away of the Pope from the ideal of Italian unity and one of the first steps in his disenchantment with liberalism. Extract taken from L. C. Farini, *The Roman State from 1815 to 1850*, translated from the Italian by W. E. Gladstone, I, London, 1851, pp. 106 ff.

. . . Venerable Brothers!

More than once have We, in this our Assembly, denounced the audacity of some persons who, Venerable Brothers, had not scrupled to inflict wrong upon Us, and through Us upon this Holy See, by concluding falsely that We had departed, and not in one point alone, from the ever sacred maxims of our Predecessors; nay, horrible to say, from the very doctrine of the Church. Nor, in truth, at this day are there wanting men who thus speak of Us, as though We had been the especial authors of the public commotions which have recently occurred, not only in other parts of Europe, but likewise in Italy. And, particularly, we have learned, from the Austrian dominions in Germany, that it is there bruited and disseminated among the people, that the Roman Pontiff has dispatched emissaries, and has by the employment of other arts excited the populations of Italy to introduce strange alterations into the course of public affairs. We have learned, furthermore, that some enemies of the Catholic religion have hence taken occasion to inflame the minds of the Germans, and to separate themselves in the heat of resentment from the unity of this Holy See. We, indeed, have not the smallest doubt that the people of Catholic Germany, and the highly distinguished Bishops who govern it, vehemently abhor the wickedness of such men. . . .

It is not unknown to you, Venerable Brethren, that ever since the later years of our Predecessor, Pius VII, the chief Sovereigns of Europe have sought to induce the Apostolic See to adopt, in the administration of civil affairs, such and such modes of proceeding, as more conciliatory, and more comfortable to the wishes of the laity, than those in use. . . .

Accordingly, . . . We at the outset, not stimulated by encouragements or advice, but prompted by our own singular affection towards the people placed under the temporal dominion of the Church, granted more large indulgence to those who had departed from their duty of allegiance to the Pontifical Government; and We subsequently made speed to adopt certain measures, which We had judged conducive in themselves to the prosperity of that people. And the whole of the acts which We have thus performed at the very commencement of our Pontificate, are in thorough correspondence with those most anxious desires of the European Sovereigns.

But after that, by the help of God, our plans had been brought to effect, not only our own people but those of neighbouring States manifested an exulting joy, and applauded Us with public congratulations and testimonials of respect, in such a mode as made it our duty to take care, even in this exalted City, to keep within due bounds popular outbursts, acclamations, and assemblages, that broke forth with an excess of vehemence.

. . . the above-mentioned people of Germany could not be incensed with Us, if it has been absolutely impossible for Us to restrain the ardour of those persons, within our temporal sway, who have thought fit to applaud the acts done against them in Upper Italy, and who, caught by the same ardour as others for the cause of their own Nation, have, together with the subjects of other Italian States, exerted themselves on behalf of that cause.

For several other European Potentates, greatly excelling Us in the number of their troops, have been unable at this particular epoch to resist the impetus of their people.

Moreover, in this condition of affairs, We have declined to allow the imposition of any other obligation on our soldiers, dispatched to the confines of the Pontifical State, except that of maintaining its integrity and security.

But, seeing that some at present desire that We too, along with the other Princes of Italy and their subjects, should engage in war against the Austrians, We have thought it convenient to proclaim clearly and openly in this our solemn Assembly, that such a measure is altogether alien from our counsels, inasmuch as We, albeit unworthy, are upon earth the viceregent of Him that is the Author of Peace and Lover of Charity, and, conformably to the function of our supreme Apostolate; We reach to and embrace all kindreds, peoples, and nations, with equal solicitude of paternal affection. But if, notwithstanding, there are not wanting among our subjects those who allow themselves to be carried away by the example of the rest of the Italians, in what manner could We possibly curb their ardour?

And in this place We cannot refrain from repudiating, before the face of all nations, the treacherous advice, published moreover in journals, and in various works, of those who would have the Roman Pontiff to be the head and to preside over the formation of some sort of novel Republic of the whole Italian people. Rather, on this occasion, moved hereto by the love We bear them, We do urgently warn and exhort the said Italian people to abstain with all diligence from the like counsels, deceitful and ruinous to Italy herself, and to abide in close attachment to their respective Sovereigns, of whose good-will they have already had experience, so as never to let themselves be torn away from the obedience they owe them. For if they should do otherwise, they not only would fail in their own duty, but would also run a risk of rending Italy herself, every day more and more, with fresh discords and intestine factions. As to what concerns Us, We declare again and again, that the Roman Pontiff bestows all his thoughts, cares, and anxiety, towards quickening the daily increase of the Kingdom of Christ, which is the Church: not towards the enlargement of the boundaries of the temporal Sovereignty, which it has pleased Divine Providence to confer on this Holy See, for its own dignity and in order to secure the free exercise of the Supreme Apostolate. In grievous error, then, are those involved, who imagine that our mind can be seduced, by the alluring grandeur of a more extended temporal sway, to plunge into the midst of war and its tumults. This on the contrary would be most delightful to our paternal heart, if it were granted to Us to contribute ever so little by our exertions, our cares, and our zeal, towards quenching the incentives to discord, reconciling the minds that are in mutual conflict, and restoring harmony among them. . . .

III.6 GREAT BRITAIN AND EUROPE

III.6.A The views of the British Foreign Secretary, Lord Palmerston, concerning the situation on the European continent are summed up in his letter of 15th June 1848, to King Leopold I of the Belgians. Extract from E. Ashley, *The Life of Henry John Temple, Viscount Palmerston*, I, London, 1876, pp. 96 ff.

. . . Sire,

I was much obliged to Your Majesty for the letter which I had the honour of receiving from Your Majesty some little time ago; and I am happy to have the opportunity which is thus afforded me of congratulating Your Majesty upon the continued tranquillity and stability of your kingdom. It would seem as if the storms which have shaken everything else all over the continent of Europe had only served to consolidate more firmly the foundations of Your Majesty's throne. As to France, no man nowadays can venture to prophesy from week to week the turn affairs may take in that unfortunate country. For many years past the persons in authority in France have worked at the superstructure of monarchy without taking care of the foundation. Education and religion have been neglected, and power has now passed into the hands of a mob ignorant of the principles of government, of morality, and of justice; and it is a most remarkable fact in the history of society that in a nation of thirty-five millions of men, who have now for more than half a century been in a state of political agitation, which, in general, forms and brings out able men, and who have during that time been governed by three dynasties, there is no public man to whom the country looks up with confidence and respect, on account of his statesmanlike qualities and personal character combined; and there is no prince whom any large portion of the nation would make any considerable effort to place as sovereign on the throne. The principle of equality seems to have been fully carried out in one respect, and that is that all public men are equally without respect, and all candidates for royalty equally without following.

As to poor Austria, every person who attaches value to the maintenance of a balance of power in Europe must lament her present helpless condition; and every man gifted with ever so little foresight must have seen, for a long time past, that feebleness and decay were the inevitable consequences of Prince Metternich's system of government: though certainly no one could have expected that the rottenness within would soon and so completely have shown itself without. Lord Bacon says that a man who aims at being the only figure among ciphers is the ruin of an age: and so it has been with Metternich. He has been jealous of anything like talent or attainment in individuals, and of anything like life in communities and nations. He succeeded for a time in damming up and arresting the stream of human progress. The wonder is not that the accumulated pressure should at last have broke the barrier and have deluged the country, but that his artificial impediments should have produced stagnation so long.

I cannot regret the expulsion of the Austrians from Italy. I do not believe, Sire, that it will diminish the real strength nor impair the real security of Austria as a European Power. Her rule was hateful to the Italians, and has long been maintained only by an expenditure of money and an exertion of military effort which left Austria less able to maintain her interests elsewhere. Italy was to her the heel of Achilles, and not the shield of Ajax. The Alps are her natural barrier and her best defence. I should wish to see the whole of Northern Italy united into one kingdom, comprehending Piedmont, Genoa, Lombardy, Venice, Parma, and Modena; and Bologna would, in that case, sooner or later unite itself either to that state or to Tuscany. Such an arrangement of Northern Italy would be most conducive to the peace of Europe, by interposing between France and Austria a neutral state strong enough to make itself respected, and sympathising in its habits and character neither with France nor with Austria; while, with reference to the progress of civilisation such a state would have great advantages, political, commercial, and intellectual. Such an arrangement is now, in my opinion, Sire, inevitable; and the sooner the Austrian Government makes up its mind to the necessity, the better conditions it will be able to obtain. If Austria waits till she be forcibly expelled—which she will soon be—she will get no conditions at all.

I have the honour to be, Sire,
Your Majesty's most obedient and humble Servant,
PALMERSTON

IV

THE DEFEAT OF THE REVOLUTION
(JULY TO DECEMBER 1848)

IN JULY, THE Austrians were beginning to get the upper hand in Northern Italy. In August, Prussia concluded an armistice with Denmark at Malmö, an event which led to the September massacres in Frankfurt and aggravated the situation in Germany. In October, Vienna had its biggest rising of the year. With its crushing the way was clear for a reassertion of the authority of the Habsburg Monarchy under the new Prime Minister Felix, Prince Schwarzenberg, not least in Germany. Hungary, however, was to continue her struggle for independence well into 1849. In November the Prussian Government began a series of measures against the radical Prussian National Assembly. The recovery of the dynasties was made possible by the extremism of the Left which forced the moderate liberals into the arms of the traditional guardians of law and order, the princes and the armies.

IV.1   MALMO ARMISTICE AND FRANKFURT RIOTS
Prussia's armistice with Denmark in August was regarded as a betrayal of the German national cause by many. The provisional Reich Government in Frankfurt, charged with responsibility but without possessing power, was placed in an awkward position. The Frankfurt Parliament eventually found itself obliged to give up its opposition to the armistice, but was now challenged by the more extreme forces on the Left. The Frankfurt disorders and their suppression left behind a deep split between moderates and radicals. In October, the President of the Frankfurt Parliament, Heinrich von Gagern, tried to give a new impetus to German unification by a plan concerning the relationship with the Habsburg Empire.

IV.1.A   Stephan Born, a collaborator of Karl Marx, founded a central committee for workers in Berlin during April 1848. On 10th July, Born published the petitions his committee had addressed to the national assemblies in Frankfurt and Berlin. Extract translated from the German text in Mommsen, *Parteiprogramme*, pp. 292 ff.

I. *For manufacturers or masters*
1. The state ministry is to make it its task to find ways and means for an increased export of our manufactures into the markets which have so far been closed to our country.
2. Export drawbacks.
3. Free importation of all raw products belonging to industry.
4. No encouragement of new industry which has to be artificially imported, but strong promotion of existing industry in keeping with conditions in the country.
5. Increased award of patents for inventions in the sphere of industry, protection against industrial imitation of goods.
6. Regulation of credit arrangements through expanded state banks.

II. *For the small masters or artisans*
1. Formation of corporations to which each independent worker has access, through which all common trade affairs are directed and arranged.
2. The work awarded by the governmental authorities to them should mainly be given to the smaller masters, wherever this is not impossible. The number of journeymen may here serve as a criterion.
3. Appointment of commissions through the corporation which look after the distribution of work, but serve in the offices only for one-quarter of a year.
4. Interest-free loans in return for work to be done or ready work.
5. Gratis trade courts, as well as gratis justice for all without means.
6. The state should support the acquisition of machines wherever these are required for preparatory work and serve for the common use of the corporation.

III. *For the workers*
1. The fixing of the minimum working wage and of the hours of work through commissions of workers and masters or employers.
2. Union of workers for the maintenance of the fixed wage.
3. Abolition of indirect taxes, introduction of progressive income tax, with exemption of taxation for those who only have the necessities of life.
4. The state undertakes the gratis instruction and, where necessary, the education of youth free of charge, taking into account its ability.

5. Gratis public libraries.

6. Regulation of the number of apprentices which may be kept by a master, by commissions of masters and workers.

7. The lifting of all special laws concerning the movement of workers, particularly those indicated in the travelling journeymen's book [Wanderbuch].

8. Eligibility for [election to] the Prussian chamber to be lowered to the 24th year.

9. Occupation of the unemployed in state establishments, in which the state ensures a living appropriate to their human needs.

10. Establishment of model workshops by the state and extension of the already existing public art printing-works for the training of efficient workers.

11. The state cares for all helpless people and therefore also for disabled workmen.

12. General right of settlement and of choosing one's domicile.

13. Limitation of the arbitrariness of officials in relation to workmen. The latter may only be dismissed from their work by the clear judgement of the commission. . . .

IV.1.B The principal provisions of the Treaty of Malmö concluded by Prussia with Denmark on 26th August 1848, are taken from *Annual Register*, 1848, pp. 351 f.

. . . The blockade established by the naval forces of His Danish Majesty shall cease, and orders to this effect shall at once be sent to the commander of the Danish men-of-war.

All prisoners of war, and all political prisoners, shall at once be liberated without delay or restriction.

All vessels, that have been captured since the commencement of the war, and on which an embargo has been laid, shall be returned with their cargoes within ten days after the signing of the armistice. This space of time has been thought necessary, on the one hand to prepare these vessels for sea, and on the other to effect the evacuation of the Duchies. Prussia admits the indemnity claimed by Denmark for the requisitions levied on Jutland, and Denmark engages to refund the value of the cargoes that have been disposed of and which cannot be restored *in natura*.

The two Duchies, as well as the islands belonging to them, shall at once be altogether evacuated by the Danish and by the German federal troops. But the King of Denmark shall be allowed to guard with 400 men the hospitals, and storehouses, and military establishments on the Island of Alsen. On the other hand, an equal number of federal troops shall be allowed, for a similar purpose, to remain in the city of Altona, and in other places where there are military hospitals and establishments.

The two contracting parties, being desirous as speedily as possible to restore order and tranquillity in the Duchies, are agreed that the mode of administration which was in force previous to the events of March shall be re-established while the armistice lasts. The collective Administration of the two Duchies shall be composed of five Members, to be taken from the gentry of the Duchies, and who enjoy general respect and consideration. They shall administer the affairs of the Duchies after the existing laws and ordinances, in the name of the King of Denmark, in his quality as Duke of Schleswig and Holstein, and with the same authority, always excepting the Legislative Power.

Two of these Members shall be chosen by the King of Denmark for the Duchy of Schleswig, and two by the King of Prussia, acting in the name of the Germanic Confederation, for the Duchy of Holstein. These four Members shall choose a fifth, to be the President of the collective Administration of the Duchies; and, if they cannot agree on this choice, then shall Great Britain, in her quality as mediating Power, be invited to nominate this fifth Member from among the inhabitants of one of the Duchies. It is understood that neither the Members of the Administration of and before the 17th of March, nor of those of whom the Provisional Government was since composed, can form part of this new Administration. The same shall with all possible speed enter upon its functions—that is to say, at the latest a fortnight after the signature of this present Convention.

The contracting parties claim the guarantee of Great Britain for the strict execution of the articles of this present Convention of an armistice.

It is expressly understood that the articles of this Convention shall nowise prejudice the conditions of a definitive peace, and that neither Denmark nor the Confederation give up any of the pretensions or rights which they have respectively asserted. . . .

IV.1.c The decision of the Reich Ministry under the presidency of Charles, Prince Leiningen, taken on 3rd September 1848, is translated from the German text in Huber, *Dokumente*, p. 461.

It is clear that Prussia has exceeded its authority by the conclusion of the treaty under discussion, and that no obligations can arise from the treaty either for the Central Power which issued the authority, or for third powers, or towards Prussia, before the Reich Government has given its approval. This approval can be given by the Central Power only in consequence of a decision of the National Assembly, to which the concluded treaty has to be submitted as going beyond the limits of an armistice in the narrower sense, and as bearing a political character already prejudicing the peace negotiations.

IV.1.D The extracts from the debates of the Frankfurt Parliament on 18th and 19th September are translated from the short-hand reports F. Wigard (ed.), *Stenographischer Bericht über die Verhandlungen der deutschen constituirenden Nationalversammlung zu Frankfurt-am-Main*, Frankfurt, 1848, III, 2163, and 2185.

(i) 18th September

Berger (Extreme Left) from Vienna: '. . . This morning I saw two battalions of infantry, Austrians and Prussians, and it has been reported to me, artillery is stationed in Bockenheim. I do not see the reason for the urgency of such a stationing of troops. . . .'

Reich Minister v. Schmerling (Right Centre): '. . . The incidents which took place in the city of Frankfurt on the evening of the day before yesterday, as well as those at a numerous meeting of the people which was held yesterday quite close to Frankfurt, should be known to most of the High Assembly. The Senate of the Free City of Frankfurt, as a result of these incidents sent a communication to the Minister of the Interior at midnight . . .: ". . . In view of current conditions where a threatening agitation exists against the National Assembly, where this is increased by popular meetings . . . augmented by numerous accessions from outside, . . . where finally from many sides . . . appeals are made for physical intervention, nay, even for the outlawing and violation of a part of the National Assembly; the Senate wishes to express its view that the Reich Ministry would have to take care of the protection of the Assembly. . . . The Senate has, in order to counter the danger actually threatening the National Assembly, made precautionary use of the military help put at its disposal by the Reich War Ministry. . . .

Frankfurt-on-Main,

17thSeptember 1848.

Mayor and Council of the Free City of Frankfurt Signed, von Heyden."

Gentlemen, the troops which this morning at three o'clock moved into Frankfurt, were called, as can be seen from the contents of this communication which came to me at midnight from the Senate of the City of Frankfurt . . ., for the protection of the National Assembly. Amongst other matters the Senate has expressed its view that the protection of the High Assembly is a matter for the Reich and the duty of the Reich Ministry, and has therefore asked the Ministry to respond to this duty. The Ministry which was then meeting had no misgivings, it actually regarded itself as unanimously obliged to respond to the request. The Ministry recognises it as the most sacred duty of the Central Power to protect the High Assembly. It will exercise this most sacred duty as widely as is necessary for the lasting peace of the High Assembly. The Reich Ministry declares plainly to you that all preparations which are necessary to protect the Assembly against any attack from outside . . . to maintain law and order in Frankfurt, the seat of the National Assembly, that all these measures have been taken over by the Reich Ministry with full responsibility and that they will be executed. (Cheers on the Right.) Gentlemen! I recognise only too vividly that amidst this High Assembly there will be nobody who does not know how to appreciate in a high degree the duty of this Ministry, I therefore do not have to appeal to anybody in this High Assembly in this respect, but I may expect also that those outside the Assembly who possibly, led astray as always, intend to make that violent attack on the Assembly, will on closer scrutiny of those proceedings recoil from the idea, [realising] that every attack on the German National Assembly is high treason.' (Cheers on the Right.)

(ii) 19th September
Fuchs (Right Centre) from Breslau: 'I miss the mention of two matters in the record. First that attempts were made to enter this house by force, secondly that we have been called traitors to the people in the declaration made to the National Assembly by a popular meeting held outside. I asked that these two facts be entered in the protocol.' (Approval on the Right and in the Centre.)
President (Heinrich von Gagern): 'The first fact will not encounter contradiction. So far as the second is concerned, I have regarded the petition, or whatever I should call it, which has been handed in, as part of the record and as such it must be printed with the protocol. . . . Gentlemen, it is under the impression of the saddest events that I open today's sitting. The movement in our Fatherland, its new formation, has demanded new victims. I said: demanded. That is an incorrect expression, they have been wantonly and barbarously slaughtered. Among the victims we have to mourn are two highly honoured excellent members of this Assembly and I am deeply shaken to have to announce to you the death of Herr v. Auerswald and of Prince Lichnowsky. These chivalrous men were not destined to find death for the Fatherland in defence of its honour against external foes, for which they would gladly have been ready. They have not fallen in the struggle for the maintenance of lawful internal order, for the suppression of the rising; they were murdered treacherously in the vilest manner, they were slaughtered. (Manifold expressions of indignation.) Gentlemen, I do not want to excite you, but I cannot suppress a feeling of shame for the disgrace which such a deed brings over the nation. . . .'

IV.1.E A member of the moderate Left, Theodor Paur, witnessed the scene in Parliament on 18th September. The extract is translated from the German of his letter of 19th September 1848, published in *Mitteilungen aus dem Literaturarchive in Berlin*, Neue Folge, 16, Berlin, 1919, p. 57.

. . . I was supposed to give a speech on this day [18th September]; . . . suddenly the gate on the right, which has a three-vault door, is broken through, fists or axes already struck the innermost [door]. As in a storm, the Assembly jumped up; members of the Right particularly wanted to rush out. The President calmed them and thundered the words to those who broke in: 'I declare every transgressor against this holy place a traitor to the Fatherland!' Curiously enough, they withdrew at once.

IV.1.F   The following extract from the letter of 23rd September from Clotilde Koch-Gontard of Frankfurt (see III.1.G), is translated from the German text in W. Klötzer (ed.), *Clotilde Koch-Gontard*, pp. 70 f.

. . . The end of Auerswald and Lichnowsky has taught us how base, how demoralised our nation is. There are persons who are capable of anything. If anything happened to Gagern, we should all be lost, and with him the future of Germany. I have been so very much disillusioned with our German people. Here, where the sense of justice maintained itself so strongly for so long, the ground has become decayed by political agitation, so that the civic guard no longer wants to do its duty. The armistice was only a pretext. Even without it, civil war would have broken out, and we have it, so much must be clear to us. This Left cannot justify its sins against Germany, and the Right and the Centre should at least give up German stubbornness and pettiness. Thus, today again the Left scored a victory, so that no address to the German people will be issued, because the others could not agree on details. . . .

IV.1.G   The speech by Heinrich von Gagern, President of the Frankfurt Parliament, on 26th October 1848, is notable not only for his plan on the future relationship of Germany with the Habsburg Empire, but also for his general assessment of the situation in Europe. Extract translated from the German of F. Wigard (ed.), *Stenographischer Bericht*, IV, pp. 2896 ff.

. . . Heinrich von Gagern, from Darmstadt: '. . . which were the obstacles because of which our people could not rise to the power which is its due? Among these causes there is above all the relationship of mixed states, that relationship according to which German and non-German states were united in one state unit under one government. . . . In the case of the mixed states as created by the Federal Act there is a substantial difference according to whether the German territory is a subsidiary one which is joined together with the non-German mainland; or

whether the German land is the mainland to which non-German territories belong as subsidiary ones. . . . It may appear dubious what is the
main national component in the composition of the Austrian state complex; but this is not in doubt, that, even if the German element is in the
minority by number of population, it is yet the most influential in this
monarchy and must be even more so. Therefore . . . I cannot share the
view which demands that Austria should be forced to separate herself
constitutionally from the states with which she has so far been joined
together in one state unit, thus to dissolve the whole Monarchy. In the
case of the realisation of paragraphs 2 and 3, it would be a matter of
this separation of German from non-German Austria, of the dissolution
of the whole Austrian Monarchy . . . As even men who are experienced
in political matters . . . assert that a personal union of the crowns could
secure a continuing connection, and as they asked why it would amount
to a dissolution: so I must answer that they do not seem to have considered the mutual relationship of paragraphs 2 and 3 . . . For paragraph 2 prohibits a common state life, it commands that whatever was
so far united in a state—German and non-German—should separate,
that the non-German should be left to itself, to an independent state
or even national life. With states of such independent existence, it is
evident that the continuing union in a mutually agreeing political direction of one constitutional state with another by means of the personal
union of crowns is only accidental; that through the possibly different
political directions of the majorities of states merely associated in a
personal union, the executive power could be forced into different directions and even into [mutual] hostility. . . . It is not enough to say: we
want to declare paragraphs 2 and 3 as law and then wait and leave it to
events whether they are carried out. I believe if we declare that something should or should not be, that we regard it as appropriate in the
interests of the Fatherland, that it should be so and not otherwise, then
we must in advance be agreed about the means of making good this
assertion, not to let the decision hang in the air. It is true that we have the
calling to give the nation, the entire German people, a constitution; but
with this calling we have also assumed the obligation to take that account
of conditions, facts, which must be considered if we are to create a
viable constitution. What would be the consequence of the realisation of
paragraphs 2 and 3 for Austria?—We draw the German–Austrian
provinces into the German federal state; we separate them from the
non-German provinces and territories of Austria. These other parts of
Austria, however, do not remain a united state, but according to the
nature of things they will disintegrate as soon as they have lost their
common centre of gravity which lies within the German hereditary
lands. There would thus be an independent organisation of Galicia, of
Hungary, . . . possibly, too, of the subsidiary territories of Hungary, of

Italy. I now ask . . . whether passing the paragraphs which lead to such results is appropriate to the conditions to be considered? . . . The obligation we have seems to me to be that in the moment when a civil war has come about in a federal state, when the fire flares up, we should not throw further firebrands on to those already burning. (Great movement on the Left.) We will act in a spirit of alliance if we contribute to putting out the fire, provided that we do not start from the premise that the existence of the whole Monarchy is put in question, and that we act on the conviction that the entire Austrian Monarchy, whose continued existence as a state lies equally in the interest of the whole Fatherland, will continue to exist, strengthened by freedom, a mighty empire, closely allied with Germany for the great national task. In this sense we must act, or we do not fulfil the duty of a good neighbour, much less that of an ally of kindred nationalities. Should we, however, accept paragraphs 2 and 3 without reservation as they stand, and should we be able to force Austria into this, then we would break up a great empire, leave its non-German parts without any connection with each other, uncertain what would become of them, uncertain which role these parts would find in the context of the European family of peoples, which influences would get hold of them. Other nations would regard it as their first duty not to put in question through a constitution even the possession of a village, and are we frivolously to abandon the whole seed of the future, to alienate from the existing connection a rich expectancy of future national development, to abandon it to chance? That . . . cannot be our intention and task. But it would be the consequence if we apply paragraphs 2 and 3 to Austria and want to force the dynasty into a relationship of purely personal union with the individual parts. That would only be a dynastic connection, the very objection erroneously made to the Pragmatic Sanction, which is actually something quite different. If states can have nothing else in common but personal union, then it is better they have nothing more in common and each goes his own way. (Voices: "Quite right!") And this, too has been the feeling of those who advocate this personal union and who actually intend complete separation. . . . Under personal union in Austria, we would in future see four Austrian [diplomatic] ministers, four Austrian armies, everything now common would be multiplied fourfold; such chaotic conditions we would project into a Europe already subverted many times, and we would sin against the obligation which a great nation has towards the European family of peoples if it attempts a transformation so incalculable in its effects. . . . This first obligation is that we do not deceive the hope and entitlement of people to peace, along with secured freedom, by sowing the new revolutions which would arise from such chaotic conditions. This would apply to the non-German provinces of Austria which have not yet demanded independent statehood, such as

Dalmatia and the Küstenland, Croatia and even Galicia. It is true the assertion has been made that all these provinces are only kept down by Austrian bayonets, but we have so far been owed the proof for this allegation. . . . With such inevitable consequences from articles 2 and 3, if they should become effective in the Austrian states, we thus violate the first obligation in relation to Europe, we offer no guarantee for the existence of peaceful conditions, rather we destroy the hope for them, and we would thus presently undertake an act which shows no consideration for the law of nations, which violates the international relationship. I ask further: can we be acting thus in the national interest, to leave the non-German provinces of Austria in future to themselves and to chance? I have regarded the calling of the German people as a great one, commanding the world. One may ridicule it, one may cynically deny such a calling for our people. I believe in it and I would lose the pride of belonging to my people if I had to surrender my faith in such a higher destiny. It is not the limit of our task to create a constitution which is confined to the narrow bounds of our present political circumstances; to accept a principle of unity into the constitution which cuts us off from that which unitary power demands; that, while other nations grow in power and influence, condemns us, as long as our neighbours leave us the peace and freedom for it, in quiet retirement to warm ourselves by the stove. (Bravo!) For what unity should we strive? That we can live for the destiny which has been set for us towards the Orient; that we fit those peoples who along the Danube have neither calling nor right to independence like satellites into our planet system. There is talk about the rights of nationalities. These rights I concede in the fullest extent where they exist, for instance in Italy. Therefore, according to my conviction, in the general interest of the nation the troubles in Italy will find a solution only if Austria withdraws from Lombardy. To maintain the secure connection with the Adriatic is the task which has been set for our national development. We must strive with the whole strength of our national unity to stipulate the requisite frontier for ourselves, and by doing so, by limiting ourselves to that, we do not oppose the right to nationality. The Italians may then order their own affairs, united like ourselves, and we shall then, mutually associated, want to rejoice with each other when this Italian federation, or federal state [Bund], as the case may be, has been established and offers, with the guarantee of independence, that of future peaceful relations.

A veil has been cast over conditions in Poland, over what could become of Galicia. We will not claim a desire to draw Galicia into our national development. But the moment has not arrived now to leave it to itself; now we must wish to keep it with Austria and in connection with Austria. Through any independent mode of organisation, even if it were possible in view of the hostile position which the peasant estate has taken up towards the nobility, a focus of revolution would be created in Galicia which would give cause for a war with Russia. A war which appears as a political necessity we would want to wage with the whole energy of the reborn strength of our people. But we do not want to conjure it up arbitrarily. This would, however, be the case if an independent organisation of Galicia took place today. There would then prevail similar conditions, only with increased cause, to those which resulted in the annihilation of the Free State of Cracow. Hungary enjoys constitutional independence from Austria, and whatever was put in question through the latest troubles by one side or the other, will be ordered again in the old spirit of brotherhood, if the Magyars do not themselves interfere with the rights of nationalities. In the other non-German provinces of Austria there exists no right to, or pre-condition of, or claim to, independent national development. Any violent separation, particularly of the southern provinces, would only play into the hands of foreign influences, of foreign powers, to our own immeasurable disadvantage. . . . Every constitutional state has the duty of self-preservation. By any dissolution of the unity of the state *vis-à-vis* provinces which have not yet come to a conclusion as to how their future could shape as a result of the separation from the general monarchy, the Austrian Government would fail in its most important obligations. I believe, therefore, . . . that we must seek a relationship which would not force Austria to detach its German from its non-German provinces, but would keep it in the most intimate association with Germany. The question is therefore: is it more in the interest of Germany that the whole of Germany should only so organise itself, only engage in so lax a unity, that Austria, without being forced to break up the union of its German and non-German provinces in one state, could belong to the Reich on the same terms as the other German states? Or is it not in the general interest of the nation of Austria as well as of the rest of Germany, that at least the rest of Germany should form a closer connection; even if Austria because of its non-German provinces cannot enter into this narrowest union on the same terms; but that nevertheless a close federal relationship be maintained between Austria and the rest of Germany? The terms, federal state for the one, confederation [Staatenbund] for the other, are vague; *one can also imagine federal relationships which lie midway between both and which form transitions.* What has been the reason hitherto for the fact that in the union which the Federal Act created in Germany the formation of a closer relationship did not take place for a long time? Because there were no common interests, because these interests were deliberately kept apart and because particularism was taken to extremes. Since when did the need and the consciousness of unity begin to develop in Germany in increased measure? From the moment when common national *interests* united a great part of Germany, and excluded the possibility of a separate policy among these more closely associated states, from the beginning and the development of the Zollverein. Let us have an eye to material interests, to the possibility of their fusion between the rest of Germany and Austria. In this way we will be able to join Austria to us, without having to use force (even if we could do so) to separate its German provinces from the non-German ones. . . . In this way there are connections possible which lie half-way between confederation and a federal state. But, once more, are we in a position to force Austria to separate its German provinces from the non-German ones? And if we cannot do that should we think of Austria as completely detached from the rest of Germany? We cannot and do not want the former, we may not do the latter. Whatever has been said by others about the attitude of the Austrians to this question, I believe the majority of Austrians desire the continuation of the Empire, as the Tirolese have just said in their proclamation. . . . The Austrians want to be with Germany, but they also want to have Austria maintained, to make possible these two unions. But we must not delay the task which has been set for the remainder of Germany, which is so necessary, to found unity in the federal state, while Austria maintains its world position with and next to us. It has been said that if German-Austria unites with Germany in a federal state, if non-German-Austria is abandoned to a dubious fate, then the united German people will be able to fulfil its destiny in the East with all the greater vigour. This argument has not convinced me. By dissolving the state connection which exists between the German and the non-German, new ties with . . . Germany will not be formed at once. The intimate relations which have existed for centuries between the Austrian provinces and between the dynasty and the non-German provinces will, once destroyed, not so soon be replaced by new ones. A government of the whole of Germany, the more distant Reich power, would not command the means of operating in the same beneficent way, of exercising influence, as the Austrian Government. . . . Decades would pass before the Reich authorities would be able to appropriate to themselves this heritage under such changed conditions, and we would not be able for so long a time to do without the influence in the East at present put at our disposal by Austria's world position. The Eastern question, on whose solution that world position of Austria and, through Austria, of Germany, can and must have so great an influence, is at present in the background. It will soon once more come into the forefront, as the domestic political conditions of the European powers are again put in order. Germany will then not be stronger if on the one hand it associates the German provinces of Austria more closely with itself, but separates itself from the non-German ones and from their manifold connections with the lands of the Southern Danube. We would, however, be able to take a powerful part in the solution of this question if Austria, separated from Italy, had only one policy with Germany, if their political interests were united. It has been said, and actually on this (the Right) side that Germany should follow a national policy, that it should withdraw from that of Austria, from Austria itself, if the latter is not prepared to separate its German from its non-German provinces. I ask, however, what national policy can Germany have if it does not enter into the mission of Austria, the spreading of German culture, language and civilisation along the Danube up to the Black Sea, into lands inhabited thinly by so many different peoples and yet so full of hope, whose whole civilisation is already accustomed to lean upon the German, who long for German-Austrian protection and increased German-Austrian influence, and for whom German efficiency would open up a rich market? And what a prospect there is for this if behind the total Austrian power, which is in the first place called to give a mighty impulse, stands the remaining united Germany and like a wedge presses with its interests, with its strength! The emigrants who at present go to the West will turn there. There, too, will be and is already freedom. Why should not the person desirous of emigrating, set up his home—rather than in distant America—on the banks of the nearby Danube, make labour and capital profitable among friendly peoples for centuries already familiar with German culture and language, where the ways have already been paved [for him], where the acquisition of free property is facilitated, and where German protection, progress and influence is secured? How much more quickly will German civilisation then spread, so that we will be able to take up and maintain that rank which is our due in the company of European nations! If we resign from the mission of bearing German civilisation along the Danube—and we do that if we undermine the constitutional relations of German Austria with the countries of the Eastern Danube, or if we actually fear that in Austria the Slav element might get the better of the German in the case of the continuation of the unity of the Monarchy—if we do not accept this mission for Germany in union with Austria, then others will accept it; if we do not strengthen our influence along the Danube, that of the Russians has already been organised; and they will be ahead of us until we have made up our minds whether we want to leave Austria freedom to maintain its existing constitutional and neighbourly relations with the lands of the Danube and to cultivate them. Starting from such views I am not for delaying the arrangement of the relationship between Austria and the rest of Germany. I believe that we must at once bring this question to a decision and recognise that Austria, for the time being, cannot enter the narrow federal state which the rest of Germany desires, on the one hand because the majority of Austrians do not accept the conditions of entry into the narrower federal state, [namely] the constitutional separation of the German provinces from the non-German ones; on the other hand because this separation, the dissolution of the Austrian Monarchy and the abandonment of its world historical calling, only to be fulfilled in the closest union with Germany, lies just as little in the German national interest. I have, therefore, in accordance with this view, formulated a motion which I am honoured to announce to the High Assembly:

> "In view of its constitutional connection with non-German territories and provinces, Austria remains in permanent and indissoluble union with the rest of Germany. The organic stipulations for this federal relationship made necessary by the changed circumstances will be contained in a special federal act."

I allow myself a few words to justify this motion. As the motion has been formulated, it would have to find its place after paragraph 1, that is to say it would have to be inserted between paragraphs 1 and 2. For I am of the opinion that the ensuing clauses of paragraph 2 are in part not applicable to Austria, while nevertheless I wish to see these stipulations maintained in order that the federal state be established for the remainder of Germany. It has been said that it is against our mandate to establish or to allow a dual federal relationship. We are called on to carry out unification in so far as it is useful in existing circumstances; our task can go no further. But if we pass paragraphs which, we can foresee, will not satisfy Austria, and that Austria would be forced by them to secede from Germany, no longer to belong to the German Reich (some voices: "Oh!") then—Gentlemen, we have not created unity, but torn it up, and it is this destruction of unity which I oppose. The question of the future position of Austria in and in relation to Germany has been linked with that of the future supreme head, the possessor of the future Reich authority. I publicly stated some months ago how I think about this question, but I would regard it as anticipating and as inappropriate if I were to read aloud what I voiced about it at the beginning of our revolution. Through my amendment I have in no way sought to prejudice the decision on this question. I am certainly of the opinion that a uniform supreme head has to be put at the summit of the federal state, which already excludes the concept of the hegemony of Prussia. But for the general direction of Germany, including Austria, a further institution will have to be created, and it is true that this would be a very important and difficult task which awaits its solution in the future. We would have to create an organism responsible, with the collaboration of its united representatives, for the central direction of the common interest of the whole of Germany. I have also not specified in my motion whether the organic stipulations for the further federal relationship which are to be arranged anew, are to be included in the constitution. I desire that they should form part of the constitution. But as a relationship of this kind so far has lain outside the sphere of the committee, I do not want to anticipate the view of the committee in this respect by my motion even in case it found support. The more closely Austria can be associated with the rest of Germany, without removing the constitutional unity of its provinces, the more room is allowed also for the non-German provinces of Austria to enter a closer confederate relationship with Germany, the more completely our task will be solved. The federal state remains our aim; for that transitions are necessary. We cannot circumvent them without tearing up, without doing the opposite of what we ought to do: to create the unity of interests of which the unity formula in the constitution may only be the appropriate expression, the means to an end, not an end in itself. As we are called to create that kind of unity, we ought to guard against choosing too narrow formulae which press national interests into a strait-jacket against their nature; let us rather open the gate wide so that entry into the German family and into its great hospitable house is not made difficult.' (Persistent applause, call for end and adjournment.)

IV.2 THE SARDINIAN RETREAT

Charles Albert of Sardinia had been unwilling or unable to hold together the heterogeneous alliance striving for Italian unity. Furthermore, the Sardian army was no match for the Austrians. Milan fell to the Austrians on 6th August 1848, and soon after an armistice was concluded between Sardinia and Austria.

IV.2.A The extracts from the proclamation of Charles Albert to the 'People of the Kingdom', on 10th August, are taken from *Annual Register*, 1848, p. 326.

. . . The enemy increased; my army was almost alone in the struggle. The want of provisions forced us to abandon the positions we had conquered. . . . With my army I had retired to the defence of Milan; but, harassed by long fatigues, it could not resist a new field-battle, for even the strength of the brave soldier has its limits. The interior defence of the town could not be sustained. Money, provisions, and ammunition were wanting. The courage of the citizens might perhaps have resisted for some days, but only to bury us under the ruins, not to conquer the enemy. A convention was begun by me; the Milanese followed it up and signed it. . . . The throbs of my heart were ever for Italian independence; but Italy has not yet shown to the world that she can conquer alone. People of the kingdom! show yourselves strong in a *first* misfortune. Employ the free institutions that have arisen among you. . . .

Repose confidence in your King. The cause of Italian independence is not yet lost. . . .

IV.3 THE CROAT INVASION OF HUNGARY

On 11th September, the Ban of Croatia, Jelačič, crossed the river Drave and marched rapidly across Southern Hungary. The Austrian court could not at first openly come out against the attempt by the Hungarian Government to secure a maximum of independence from the Habsburg Empire. The measures of the radicals in Budapest benefited the Magyars, but were badly received by the other nationalities in the Kingdom of Hungary, including the Croats. Jelačič, who had been ostensibly dismissed as Ban of Croatia by the Austrian court in the summer, was still secretly encouraged. Kossuth, who was acquiring a leading influence in the Hungarian Government, recommended the Hungarian Parliament to send a deputation to the Austrian court.

IV.3.A The extracts from the address of the Hungarian delegation to the Emperor at his palace in Schönbrunn, outside Vienna, are from *Annual Register*, 1848, pp. 414 f.

. . . It is in the name of that fidelity we have shown for centuries to your ancestors that we now come to demand of you the maintenance of the rights of the kingdom. Hungary has not been united to your crown as a conquered province, but as a free nation, whose privileges and independence have been insured by your Majesty's coronation oath. . . . The wishes of the people have been satisfied by the laws enacted by the last Diet; why are the rights of the nation menaced by an insurrection, the leaders of which declare openly that they are in arms on your Majesty's behalf? Whilst the blood of Hungary is flowing in Italy in defence of the Austrian monarchy, one portion of her children is perfidiously excited against the other, and casts off the obedience due to the legal Government of the country. Insurrection threatens our frontiers, and, under the pretence of upholding your authority, it is actually assailing the integrity of the kingdom, and our ancient and new liberties. . . . It is in the name of the people we call on your Majesty to order the Hungarian regiments to obey the Hungarian Ministry, without reserve and notwithstanding all other orders. We desire that Croatia be freed from military despotism, in order that it may unite fraternally with Hungary. Finally, we demand that your Majesty, discarding the reactionary counsels of those about you, give your immediate sanction to all the measures voted by the Diet, and come and reside in Pesth among your people, where your royal presence is necessary to save the country. Let your Majesty hasten. The least delay may occasion indescribable calamities. . . .

E

IV.3.B Jelačič crossed the River Drave into Hungary proper on 11th September. The extracts from the proclamation he addressed to the Hungarian people are from *Annual Register*, 1848, p. 415.

. . . It is in vain to call by the name of revolt or treason a proceeding which is inspired only by pure love of country and fidelity to our King. And let it not be feared that I wish to retract any of the concessions or privileges lately accorded by the royal word to the Hungarian nation. All that has been done legally shall be upheld: it is not an enemy who invades the plains of Hungary; it is a friend who comes to the aid of the loyal subjects of the constitutional King. They will hold out to me the hand of brotherhood, and, with God's aid, we will deliver the country from the yoke of an incapable, odious, and rebel Government. . . .

IV.3.c After the invasion by Jelačič, Kossuth called for resistance to the invader. Extracts from his article published on 18th September 1848, in the journal Kossuth Hirlapja, taken from P. C. Headley, *The Life of Kossuth*, Auburn, 1852, pp. 113 ff.

. . . Hear! patriots hear!

The eternal God doth not manifest himself in passing wonders, but in everlasting laws.

It is an eternal law of God's that whosoever abandoneth himself will be of God forsaken.

It is an eternal law that whosoever assisteth himself him will the Lord assist.

It is a Divine law that swearing falsely is by its results self-chastised.

It is a law of God's that he who resorteth to perjury and injustice, prepareth his own shame and the triumph of the righteous cause.

In the name of that Fatherland, betrayed so basely, I charge you to believe my prophecy, and it will be fulfilled.

In what consists Jellachich's power?

In a material force, seemingly mighty, of seventy thousand followers, but of which thirty thousand are furnished by the regulations of the military frontier.

But what is in the rear of this host? By what is it supported? There is nothing to support it!

Where is the population which cheers it with unfeigned enthusiasm? There is none.

Such a host may ravage our territories, but never can subdue us.

Batu-Chan deluged our country with his hundreds of thousands. He devastated, but he could not conquer.

Jellachich's host at worst will prove a locust-swarm, incessantly lessening in its progress till destroyed.

So far as he advances, so far will be diminished the number of his followers, never destined to behold the Drave again.

Let us—Hungarians—be resolved, and stones will suffice to destroy our enemy. This done, it will be time to speak of what further shall befall.

But every Hungarian would be unworthy the sun's light if his first morning thought, and his last thought at eve, did not recall the perjury and treason with which his very banishment from the realms of the living had been plotted.

Thus the Hungarian people has two duties to fulfil.

The first, to rise in masses, and crush the foe invading her paternal soil.

The second, to remember!

If the Hungarian should neglect these duties, he will prove himself dastardly and base. His name will be synonymous with shame and wickedness.

So base and dastardly as to have himself disgraced the holy memory of his forefathers—so base, that even his Maker shall repent having created him to dwell upon this earth—so accursed that air shall refuse him its vivifying strength—that the cornfield, rich in blessings, shall grow into a desert beneath his hand—that the refreshing well-head shall dry up at his approach!—Then shall he wander homeless about the world, imploring in vain from compassion the dry bread of charity. The race of strangers for all alms will smite him on the face. Thus will do that stranger-race, which seeks in his own land to degrade him into the outcast, whom every ruffian with impunity may slay like the stray-dog—which seeks to sink him into the likeness of that Indian Pariah, whom men pitilessly hound their dogs upon in sport to worry.

For the consolations of religion he shall sigh in vain.

The craven spirit by which Creation has been polluted will find no forgiveness in this world, no pardon in the next.

The maid to whom his eyes are raised shall spurn him from her door like a thing unclean; his wife shall spit contemptuously in his face; his own child shall lisp its first word out in curses on its father.

Terrible! terrible! but such will be the malediction, if the Hungarian race proves so cowardly as not to disperse the Croatian and Serbian invaders, 'as the wild wind disperses the unbound sheaves by the way-side'.

But no, this will never be; and, therefore, I say the freedom of Hungary will be achieved by this invasion of Jellachich. Our duty is to triumph first, then to remember.

To arms! Every man to arms; and let the women dig a deep grave between Veszprem and Fehervar, in which to bury either the name, fame, and nationality of Hungary, or our enemy.

And either on this grave will rise a banner, on which shall be inscribed, in record of our shame, 'Thus God chastiseth cowardice'; or we will plant thereon the tree of freedom everlastingly green, and from out whose foliage shall be heard the voice of the Most High, saying, as from the fiery bush to Moses, 'The spot on which thou standest is holy ground'.

All hail! to Hungary, to her freedom, happiness, and fame.

He who has influence in a county, he who has credit in a village, let him raise his banner. Let there be heard upon our boundless plains no music but the solemn strains of the Rakoczy march. Let him collect ten, fifty, a hundred, a thousand followers—as many as he can gather, and marshal them to Veszprem.

Veszprem, where, on its march to meet the enemy, the whole Hungarian people shall assemble, as mankind will be assembled on the Judgement Day....

IV.3.D Any hope of a settlement passed with the murder of the imperial emissary, Count Lamberg, in Budapest on 27th September. On 3rd October, the Emperor issued a firm rescript. Extract from Headley, *Life of Kossuth*, pp. 123 ff.

... We, Ferdinand I, Constitutional Emperor of Austria, &c., King of Hungary, Croatia, Sclavonia, Dalmatia the Vth of this name, to the Barons, to the High-Dignitaries of the Church and State, to the Magnates and Representatives of Hungary, its dependencies, and the Grand Duchy of Transylvania, who are assembled at the Diet, convoked by ourselves in our free and royal town of Pesth, our greeting:

To our deep concern and indignation the House of Representatives has been seduced by Kossuth and his adherents to great illegalities; it has even carried out several illegal resolutions against our royal will, and has lately, on the 27th of September, issued a resolution against the commission of the Royal Commissary, our Lieutenant Field-Marshal, Count Francis Lamberg, appointed by ourselves to re-establish peace. In consequence of which, this our Royal Commissary, before he could even produce his commission, was in the public street violently attacked by the furious mob which murdered him in the most atrocious manner. Under these circumstances, we see ourselves compelled, according to our royal duty, for the maintenance of the security and the law, to take the following measures, and to command their enforcement:

First. We dissolve the Diet by this our decree; so that after the publication of our present Sovereign Rescript, the Diet has immediately to close its sessions.

Secondly. We declare as illegal, void, and invalid, all the resolutions, and the measures of the Diet which we have not sanctioned.

Thirdly. All troops, and armed bodies of every kind, whether national guards, or volunteers, which are stationed in Hungary, and its dependencies, as well as in Transylvania, are placed by this our decree under the chief command of our Ban of Croatia, Sclavonia and Dalmatia, Lieutenant Field-Marshal Baron Joseph Jellachich.

Fourthly. Until the disturbed peace and order in the country shall be restored, the Kingdom of Hungary shall be subjected to martial law; in consequence of which, the respective authorities are meanwhile to abstain from the celebration of congregations, whether of the counties, of the municipalities, or of the districts.

Fifthly. Our Ban of Croatia, Sclavonia and Dalmatia, Baron Joseph Jellachich, is hereby invested and empowered as Commissary of our Royal Majesty; and we give him full power and force, that he may, in the sphere of Executive Ministry, exercise the authority, with which as Lieutenant of our Royal Majesty, we have invested him in the present extraordinary circumstances.

In consequence of this our Sovereign plenipotence, we declare that whatsoever the Ban of Croatia shall order, regulate, determine and command, is to be considered as ordered, regulated, determined and commanded by our royal authority. In consequence of which, we likewise by this graciously give command to all our ecclesiastical, civil and military authorities, officers, and High Dignitaries of our Kingdom of Hungary, its dependencies, and Transylvania, as also all their inhabitants, that all the orders signed by Baron Jellachich as our empowered Royal Commissary, shall be by them obeyed, and enforced, in the same way as they are bound to obey our Royal Majesty. . . .

IV.4 THE VIENNA OCTOBER RISING AND ITS SUPPRESSION

The conflict with Hungary in turn contributed to setting off a revolution in Vienna. The Austrian minister of war, Count Latour, was in secret contact with Jelačić and stripped Vienna of troops in order to muster them against Hungary. On 6th October, revolutionaries interfered with the departure of a military unit for Hungary and a series of incidents led to an outbreak of fighting. The minister of war, Latour, was murdered by the mob and members of the Government as well as members of the court fled from the capital.

IV.4.A Like his countrymen and many other non-Magyars, Jelačić was deeply resentful of the tyranny of the Magyars over the other nationalities in the Kingdom of Hungary. In the middle of October, Jelačić gave his views in a proclamation to his Slav brethren in Bohemia. Extract from *Annual Register*, 1848, pp. 419 f.

... It was my duty, as a faithful and sincere Slav, to oppose in Pesth the anti-Austrian party which hostilely rose against Slavism. But as I approached Pesth, that nest of the Magyar aristocracy, our common enemies arose; and had they conquered in Vienna, my victory in Pesth would have been incomplete, and the mainstay of our enemies would have been Vienna.

Therefore I turned, with the whole of my army, to Vienna, in order to chastise the enemies of Slavism in Austria's capital. I was led solely by the conviction that I was approaching Vienna against the enemy of Slavism. . . .

IV.4.B On 23rd October, the Commander-in-Chief, Prince Windisch-grätz, who was besieging the city, announced to the Viennese the terms on which he would accept their submission. Extract from *Annual Register*, 1848, p. 422.

. . . 1. Within forty-eight hours after receipt of this present, the city of Vienna, with its faubourgs and neighbourhood, are to surrender; and by detachments the inhabitants are to give up their arms at some place appointed for that purpose, with the exception of private firearms.

2. The dissolution of all armed corporations, and of the Academical Legion; the University to be closed; the President of the Academical Legion and twelve students to be made hostages.

3. Certain individuals, hereafter to be named, are to be given up to me. . . .

IV.4.C Robert Blum, the leader of the Left in the Frankfurt Parliament, was executed by the Austrian military authorities on 9th November. The story of Blum's mission to Vienna is described more fully in document IV.4.D. Extract from *Annual Register*, 1848, pp. 423 f.

. . . According to sentence by court-martial of the 8th inst., Robert Blum, bookseller, from Leipsic, convicted by his own avowal, on the ground of seditious speeches and armed resistance against the Imperial troops, has been, in pursuance of the proclamation issued by Prince Windischgrätz on the 20th and 23rd of October, sentenced to death, which sentence was executed by powder and lead in the Brigittenau, on the morning of the 9th instant, at half-past eight o'clock. . . .

IV.4.D Unlike Robert Blum, his fellow parliamentarian and emissary to Vienna, Julius Fröbel, was reprieved. Their story is told in Fröbel's statement to the Frankfurt Parliament on 18th November 1848. Extract from F. Wigard (ed.), *Stenographischer Bericht über die Verhandlungen der deutschen constituirenden National-versammlung zu Frankfurt am Main*, V, pp. 3419 ff.

. . . Fröbel from Reuss (strongly cheered by the Left and by the Left Centre): '. . . There is only one question which belongs before this High Assembly, which is whether and to what extent the Reich law of 30th September has been violated by the complications I, in common with Robert Blum, experienced in Vienna.

. . . After the defeat of the motion by the deputy Berger, that the National Assembly should resolve that the City of Vienna had by its last rising deserved well of the Fatherland, the Left of the Assembly decided to send a deputation of its own to Vienna in order to express its sympathy with the Vienna revolution. The two groups of the Left which met in the "Donnersberg" and in the "Deutscher Hof" united for this purpose. Robert Blum was elected by the one [Deutscher Hof], I by the other [Donnersberg] to take a short address to Vienna in the sense of what I have said. Two others members, Herr [Moritz] Hartmann [Donnersberg] and Herr [Albert] Trampusch [Deutscher Hof] accompanied us and joined our deputation. We departed from here on the 13th [of October] and arrived in Vienna on the 17th. There we conveyed these addresses to the permanent committee of the Reichstag, to the Commander-in-Chief, to the municipal council and to the student committee. The permanent committee of the Reichstag already on the same day, one hour later, in its daily report, informed the Reichstag itself of our address, which was received with general acclamation. After we had employed the 17th, 18th and 19th October in executing our commission, we were ready on the 20th to leave Vienna again.

. . . I myself went with Blum to the Saxon Minister, where Blum had a passport given to him at his request, which I intended to have done, too, since a card proving my identity as a member of the National Assembly did not seem to secure me sufficiently, even Viennese deputies have been maltreated on the journey by the military because of this attribute. The passport was refused to me because I was not a Saxon. I thereupon went to the Commander-in-Chief and requested passes for myself and my three companions, which were valid for three days and which I carried with me because we were constantly thinking of leaving Vienna. We did not, however, do this, because we constantly heard that it was impossible to get through [the besieging Austrian Army] without maltreatment. In this manner the days from the 20th to the 26th passed in uncertainty as to whether it would be possible to depart. I will be completely frank in my report, even in the relations which put me in an unfavourable light with the Right side of the Assembly. I therefore remark frankly, that after we had convinced ourselves that it was not possible to depart, I resolved to take part in the fighting.

. . . It was on the 26th that Blum and I were asked by a retired captain of the name of Hauk, who had been ordered to form an élite corps, to join his corps. We were appointed captains by this commandant of the corps, which consisted of four companies. Blum had the first, I the third company. According to its organisation patent, it was the task of this corps to secure calm and order in the city. This was a truly important and no less dangerous task than to be stationed opposite the troops. Already on the day before, shots had been fired on passers-by from several houses; these houses were taken by storm, the persons found in them seized, and it was intended to hang them without any further ado. On this day, all men who were discovered in the streets without arms were rounded up and forced to join some corps of the mobile guard. There was thus a chance that disorders would break out in the city itself. . . . We believed that as strangers who were staying in the hard-pressed city as guests, we had the duty and owed it to our honour to participate in the general burdens, particularly as we had been told that . . . importance was attached to our names. The corps, however, was at once employed differently, which greatly surprised us. Blum and I were separated from each other. We were sent to the farthest opposite points of the city, where barricades had been built, to the most dangerous places which existed. . . . We had the conviction which was later proved to be correct, that the city would not be able to hold out because it had been betrayed. I use this expression without reference to any particular party, simply to describe an ambiguity in the management of things which cannot be denied. I will only mention a few facts, and you will agree that there is no other word to designate this procedure than the word betrayal. Robert Blum stood opposite the Croats. He had five guns but the strictest order in his pocket not to employ them. On the barricade where I was stationed blank cartridges had been distributed to my men. I myself delivered gun cartridges filled with sawdust. After such occurrences you can imagine that we wanted to cease fighting. Our activity had begun on the 26th; on the evening of the 28th we decided to hand in our resignation. At six o'clock on the morning on the 29th this was done in writing by us, and the resignation was accepted by the commandant of the corps. After this had been done we took no further part in what happened afterwards. I must draw your attention to this because I have heard that newspaper reports said Blum had still been under arms after the capitulation and during the capture of the town, and had fought; that is an untruth. We spent the whole time from the 29th October to the 4th November in our inn, with a few excursions into the city. On the first day, actually, we had still dared several times to go into the street. But as atrocities were committed in the town and there was a risk of being massacred if somebody had a physiognomy which did not please the soldiers, we decided not to go out any more, and kept quietly to the house. During this time—I no longer have the date, probably it was the 2nd [of November]—we wrote to the General Tshoritsch who we heard had become commandant of the town. In this letter we declared that we had been kept back in Vienna against our wish, and wanted to travel back to Frankfurt as quickly as possible, and we asked him for the necessary permit in order to be able to make the journey safely. We received in reply a communication which referred us to General Cordon. We therefore directed our request to the latter on the afternoon of the 3rd, and on the morning of the 4th at six o'clock an official of the town commandant accompanied by a captain and six to eight soldiers appeared in front of our door. When we opened, we were shown the warrant of arrest which had been written on the reverse of our letter to General Cordon. We asserted our rights as members of the German National Assembly by a short oral declaration, but received the reply that the order for our arrest permitted no consideration of any protests, whereupon we allowed ourselves calmly to be removed to the prison in the Stabsstockhaus. There we spent the time from the 4th to the evening of the 8th under quite a considerate treatment. We had all the comfort which one can expect in a situation like that. We occupied the best room of the house, which was not actually a prison. On the afternoon of the 8th at four o'clock we handed a protest to the Central Investigating Commission in which we drew attention once more, in writing, to our capacity as deputies, and reserved the rights of this Assembly solemnly against our arrest and further judicial procedure against us. Here I must report an earlier event. On the 5th we addressed a communication to the presidency of this Assembly. It was handed in to the Commission. I do not believe that it arrived here. In this letter we announced our arrest, stated the probable reasons for it, and asked the Assembly to assert its rights regarding us. The protest, however, which we handed in on the 8th, forms a decisive turning point in the matter. This protest was certainly taken into consideration. You see in the death of Blum in what way this was done. Blum's death is the instant reply to this protest. The protest was written at four o'clock, at six o'clock Blum was called to the interrogation, at eight o'clock the interrogation was over, the following morning at six o'clock the sentence was announced to him, and at seven o'clock he was shot. I did not see Blum again, from the moment he was led away to the interrogation, with the exception of half a minute during which he entered into the room. But he was at once removed again. I must remark on something else with reference to the protest. You may judge yourselves what value to attach to it. Until early on the 8th we were alone in the prison, then another prisoner was put in with us, who explained to us that he had been the Adjutant-General von Messenhauser, that he, too, was under investigation, and that we had him put in with us as there was no more room in the house. This man behaved in a very obtrusive manner; he asked the provosts, who supervised us, for all sorts of things and his demands were satisfied in an extraordinary manner. This man constantly led the conversation to the time that we had been under arms, and in spite of the hints I made to Blum, the latter was frank and told him much. Amongst other things he asked Blum if we had worn waist belts as captains and where he had left his. In short, it appeared to me that he was looking for evidence against us. This man urged on Blum that we had made a mistake in not protesting with sufficient energy and in not sufficiently emphasising our position as deputies. "You do not know the Austrian authorities," he said. "If you proceed energetically, you will see—you will be free tomorrow." I had a different opinion than Blum about this, and I did not like the protest which Blum drew up. When it was copied, one passage at the end which contained a threat was left out at my request. I copied the protest and retained a copy which I kept in my wallet although all [personal] effects were taken from me, until the moment that my sentence had been promulgated and I was acquitted. When I was led away to be sentenced, I had put my papers and odds and ends which had been left to me into my hat, and I asked the provost who had left the door of the prison open whether I should leave the things, to which he assented. I went away with him, and when I re-entered the prison after my freedom had been given to me, in order to collect my effects, everything was there with the exception of the copy of the protest. This is the reason that I cannot inform you of the wording of the protest.

. . . on the 8th at four o'clock we had handed in the protest. The time of two hours is roughly that which was necessary in order to bring the protest to Prince Windischgrätz at Hetzendorf and to receive an order in reply. Two hours afterwards Blum was interrogated, and the following day the sentence and execution took place. So far as I was concerned I, too, had to feel the consequences of the protest, for you will see in the way in which I was treated a certain refinement, which I interpreted to mean that they thought they had enough with one victim but that they wanted to punish me at least as severely as possible. Otherwise I do not see why Robert Blum was treated mildly up to the last moment, whereas I was put into the most rigorous detention and was deliberately left for four days in the belief that I had to expect death by the rope! (Movement.) At midnight I was suddenly taken out of the prison in which I had been together with Blum, the staff provost in full uniform, accompanied by four soldiers, conducted me down to a carriage which had stopped in front of the door, two soldiers sat down inside opposite me, the provost next to me, and one man went on to the box and another behind on the carriage. We drove through the city without knowing whither. We came to a house where I had to descend, I was led to an official to whom a sealed order was handed. Concerning the contents of the papers, I could not guess. But I could detect such consternation in the official, that I believed that I had to fear the worst. The man looked at me for a long time with obvious alarm, I could look sideways at the paper in which I read the words "at 5 o'clock". In combination with the other circumstances, I believed this was to be the time of my execution on the following day. After this official had done his reading, he wrote a second order. With this I was transported in the carriage to another building and put into a cell with one sentry inside and one sentry in front of the door. Here I had to undress, my clothes were examined most carefully, all my effects, down to the smallest papers, were taken from me, and I would not have had the opportunity to retain one tooth pick. In this prison I remained up to the afternoon of the 10th. Then the staff provost from the Stabsstockhaus came to me, this time in mufti, and asked me to follow him, with the remark that we would go through the city freely and without escort. In this way I was actually led by him through the town and we came back to the former house, where I was put into a very small cell. In this I remained for a couple of hours until I was called to the interrogation. The interrogation was on the 10th at six o'clock in the evening. . . . The aspect to which the questions were directed was whether I had borne arms after the 23rd [October], that is to say, after Prince Windischgrätz had, on arriving before the city, declared it in a state of siege, and when I admitted this instantly, it was remarked that this was the essential question, the rest did not matter. I objected to this that the declaration of the state of siege had not been published in the city, that the municipal council had declared that the few copies which could be seen on street corners had been stolen from it, and that the Reichstag had declared this measure illegal. The reply made to me was whether I did not know what a state of siege signified, and that with it all civil authorities, including the authority of the Reichstag, ceased. When matters stood like this, I remarked to the judges that if extenuating circumstances could not be considered before the court, I had nothing else to say. However, I received as a reply the humane invitation to continue speaking and to mention everything which could be in my favour. I now defended myself as well as I could, without on the one hand giving up any of my principles or on the other committing the imprudence of provoking my judges. In my defence I referred to my having been in Vienna some months previously, mentioned that I had given many speeches and had had something printed, and that the conservative press had acknowledged me as a man of moderate views. I drew attention to a pamphlet, "Vienna, Germany and Europe" [Wien, Deutschland und Europa], in which I developed the opinion that the Austrian-German question had to be solved not through the partitioning of Austria, but through a connection of the whole Austrian territorial complex with Germany. When I made this remark, the lieutenant-colonel who was the

president of the court said that this was a very important point in my
defence, and that I should depose it in evidence. (Sympathetic movement in the Assembly. So I dictated into the record everything which
I had said orally and referred particularly to the pamphlet I have
named. As it was a court martial before which I stood, there was no
time to produce the pamphlet, and it appeared as if the appeal to it
would pass without benefit. At that point a member of the court pulled
out the pamphlet from among the papers. I had given it to Blum to
read, and when I was led away it had been left on the table, had been
removed and had come to the files. I have had to engage in these details
because I have heard that I owed the remission of the death penalty to
this pamphlet. Prince Windischgrätz, I was told, along with several
generals, read it attentively, which took several hours, and had then
signed the pardon. I was led back after the interrogation and remained
undisturbed in prison until the next morning. At that time, however, I
was once more summoned before the commission. Martial law allows
twelve hours, and this time had expired since the interrogation on the
previous day, so that I had already been hoping that the worst had
passed. With the new summons the matter changed again in that the
files were read to me once more and, although I had already signed on
the previous day, I was asked afresh whether I recognised them, so that
I could only assume that this was the final interrogation from which the
period had to be reckoned within which I must expect execution. Soon
after somebody unknown to me knocked gently on my door, asked me
for my name and informed me of Blum's fate. . . . Up to that time I had
not been able to find out what had become of him. In the evening I was
finally summoned and the judgement was promulgated to me with the
usual military ceremonies. Perhaps you saw the official announcement
in the *Wiener Zeitung*. It says, "N.N., convicted by his own confession
of having borne arms against the Imperial troops, has been sentenced
unanimously by the court martial to death by hanging". The conclusion
was immediately followed by a sentence which during the reading aloud
immediately followed it but whose exact wording I cannot repeat. I do
not know whether the word "pardon" occurred in it or not. The essence
lay more or less in the words, "Prince Windischgrätz commands in consideration of extenuating circumstances that the death penalty be re-
mitted completely to the condemned prisoner, and that he be set at
liberty immediately". I have allowed no expression of sentiment to flow
into my account, because it would not have belonged here; but I permit
myself to say just this, that the members of the Court expressed to me
their warm sympathy and joy for my delivery and that this sympathy
touched me deeply. After my freedom had been announced to me, I was
asked to go, in the company of a judge advocate and a lieutenant, to the
Town Commandant's office, where I was bidden by the Town Com-

mandant to leave Vienna at once. A police official in civilian clothes was attached to me who in my presence was instructed to treat me with all consideration and to take me to the Saxon border without regarding me as a prisoner. With this official I departed immediately and made my journey here as quickly as possible. The route via Breslau was refused to me. When I inquired about the reason for the refusal it was remarked to me that this would probably become clear to me. Gentlemen! To this report I have simply nothing to add, because it would be quite unfitting if I allowed myself to make a motion in this matter.' (Strong cheering on all sides of the house.)

IV.4.E On 27th November 1848, the new and forceful Austrian Prime Minister, Prince Schwarzenberg, submitted his programme to the Austrian Reichstag at Kremsier in Moravia. Schwarzenberg made it clear that Austria would have to be consulted on any reorganisation in Germany. Extract from Huber, *Dokumente*, p. 291.

. . . The great work we have to do in concert with the peoples is the creation of a new bond which will unite all the territories and tribes of the Monarchy into one great state body.

This point of view at the same time shows the course which the Ministry will pursue in the German question. The greatness of Germany does not lie in the destruction of the [Habsburg] Monarchy, the strengthening of Germany does not lie in its weakening. The continuance of Austria as a state unit is a German, as it is a European need. Penetrated by this conviction, we look forward to the natural development of the not yet completed process of transformation. Only when the rejuvenated Austria and the rejuvenated Germany have found new and firm forms, will it be possible to regulate their mutual state relations. Until then Austria will continue to fulfil faithfully its federal duties. . . .

IV.5.A On 26th September 1848, Louis Napoleon, nephew of the Emperor Napoleon I, and later himself President and Emperor, took his seat in the French Chamber to which he had been elected. Extracts from his maiden speech are from *Annual Register*, 1848, p. 296.

Citizen Representatives,
    It is impossible that I can keep silence after the calumnies of which I have been the object. I must express frankly, and at the earliest moment of my taking my seat amongst you, the real sentiments which animate, and which have ever animated me. After thirty-three years of proscription and exile, I am at last entitled to resume my rights as a citizen. The Republic has bestowed on me happiness; to the Republic I tender my oath of gratitude, my oath of devotion; and my generous countrymen, who have returned me to this place, may be assured that I will endeavour

to justify their choice by exerting myself with you to maintain tranquillity, the first necessity of the country, and the development of democratic institutions, which the people have the right to demand. For a long time I have been unable to consecrate to France anything but the meditations of exile and captivity. At last the career which you pursue is open to me. Receive me, then, my dear colleagues, into your ranks, with the same sense of affectionate confidence which I bring here. My conduct—always inspired by duty, always animated by respect for the law —my conduct will prove the falsehood of those who have attempted to blacken me for the purpose of still keeping me proscribed, and will demonstrate that no one is more firmly resolved than myself to establish and defend the Republic. . . .

V

1849

THE YEAR 1849 saw the gradual defeat of radicalism and constitutionalism in Italy, Germany and Hungary.

V.1. ITALY

In Italy, war continued. In March, Charles Albert resumed fighting, only to have to ask for an armistice with Austria after his defeat at Novara the same month. He abdicated in favour of his son, Victor Emmanuel II, later to be the first king of the united Italian kingdom. After the Pope's flight from Rome, a Roman republic was proclaimed in February.

V.1.A   On 1st January 1849, Pope Pius IX addressed a message to his subjects in Rome from his exile in Gaeta in the Kingdom of Naples. Extracts from *Annual Register*, 1849, pp. 292 f.

. . . We have waited in the hope that the protests and decrees which we have issued would recall to their duties as subjects, and as part of the faithful, those who in the very capital of our States have despised these duties and trampled them under foot. But, instead of returning, a new and still more monstrous act of hypocritical felony and genuine rebellion, audaciously committed by them, has filled the measure of our grief, and excited our just indignation, as it will afflict the universal Church. We speak of that act, so detestable in all its bearings, by which it has been pretended to order the convocation of a *soi-disant* general Assembly of the Roman States by a decree of the 29th of December last, for the purpose of establishing new political forms in the Pontifical States. Thus heaping iniquity upon iniquity, the promoters of demagogical anarchy are endeavouring to destroy the temporal authority of the Roman Pontiff over the domains of the Holy Church, believing, and seeking at the same time to make it believed, that his sovereign power is subject to controversy, and depends upon the caprice of factions, although its rights are so irrefragably founded upon the most ancient and solid bases, and although they are acknowledged, defended, and venerated by all nations. We will spare our dignity the humiliation of dwelling upon all the monstrosity of this abominable act, arising from the absurdity of its origin, the illegality of its forms, and the impiety of its object. But it certainly belongs to the Apostolic authority with which unworthily we are invested, and to the responsibility with which we are bound by the most sacred oaths, taken in the presence of the Almighty, not only to protest, as we now do, in the most energetic and efficient manner, against this act, but, moreover, to denounce it in the face of the universe, as a monstrous and sacrilegious attempt against our independence and sovereignty—an attempt which merits the chastisements inflicted by divine and human laws. We are convinced that, on receiving this audacious appeal, you have cast it far from you with indignation as an insult and a crime. Nevertheless, that none of you may hereafter have the pretext of having been deceived by fallacious seductions and by artful preachers of subversive doctrines, or of having been ignorant of the machinations of the enemies of all order, of all law, of all right, of all true liberty, of even your own felicity, we have this day again raised and exalted our voice, so that you may be rendered perfectly assured of that absolute command, by which we forbid you, whatever may be your ranks or conditions, from taking any part in the elections of persons to be sent to the Assembly which we have condemned. In the mean time we remind you that this absolute interdiction is sanctioned by our predecessors and by councils, especially by the Holy Council of Trent . . . in which the Church has repeatedly fulminated its censures, and particularly that of the greater excommunication, as incurred without the necessity of any previous declaration, by whomsoever shall render himself guilty of any atempt whatever against the temporal authority of the Sovereign Pontiffs of Rome, as we declare all those have unhappily incurred it who contributed to the abovementioned act, and those which preceded it, to the detriment of the same sovereignty, or who, in any other manner, and under false pretences, have disturbed, violated, and usurped our authority. But, if we feel ourselves compelled by our conscientious duties to preserve and defend the sacred deposit of the patrimony of the spouse of Jesus Christ, confided to our care, and to employ the sword of just severity which God Himself, our Judge, has given into our hands to be thus used, we cannot, however, at any time forget, that we hold on earth the place of Him who in the exercise of His justice never failed to use mercy. . . .

V.1.B   The Roman constituent assembly, which the Pope as sovereign regarded as illegal, did not allow itself to be deterred from its course. It passed the following decree on the 8th of February. Extract from *Annual Register*, 1849, pp. 293 f.

Article 1. Papacy has fallen, *de facto,* and *de jure,* from the temporal throne of the Roman State.

Article 2. The Roman Pontiff shall enjoy all the guarantees necessary for the exercise of his spiritual power.

Article 3. The Government of the Roman State is to be a pure democracy, and to assume the glorious name of the Roman Republic.

Article 4. The Roman Republic shall maintain with the rest of Italy relations required by a common nationality.

V.1.c   In reply the Pope issued the following declaration. Extract from *Annual Register,* 1849, pp. 294 f.

. . . The long and uninterrupted series of attempts committed against the temporal dominion of the States of the Church, acquiesced in by many from ignorance, and following up by the malign and evil spirit of those who for a long time past have imposed on the too easy kindness of the first, have touched the last stage of crime by a decree of the sitting Roman Constituent Assembly under date of the 9th of February, which declared the Popedom deprived in right and fact of the temporal Government of the Roman States—thus converting that Government into a pure Democracy under the name of the Roman Republic. We are compelled by it again to raise our voice against an act which presents itself before the civilised world with all the characters of ingratitude, injustice, ignorance and impiety; and against which—thus surrounded by the Holy College, and by the worthy representatives of the Powers and Governments friendly to the Holy See—we do protest, and in the most solemn manner declare its nullity, as we have done all preceding acts. You, gentlemen, have been witnesses of the equally deplorable acts of the 15th and 16th of November of last year, and in concert with us have deplored and condemned them. You comforted our hearts in those unhappy days. You have followed us to this land, where we have been guided by the hand of God, who exalts the humble, but never abandons those who have confidence in Him. To you who still surround us—to you we address these words, in the hope that you will convey our sentiments to your Courts and to your Governments. Fallen as many of our pontifical subjects are, in consequence of the artifices of that faction, enemy of all human society, into the abyss of profound misery, we, as temporal Prince, and still more as Head of the Pontificate of the Holy Catholic religion, expose the lamentations, and at the same time the prayers of our Pontifical subjects, who anxiously desire to see broken the chains which oppress them. We ask at the same time the maintenance of the sacred rights of the temporal dominion of the Holy See, which it has enjoyed for so many ages, and which by all have universally been recognised—rights which by order of Divine Providence, are rendered needful for the free exercise of the Catholic religion of the Holy See. The lively interest manifested through the world in favour of our cause is a luminous proof that it is one of justice, and we cannot doubt but that this our protest will be received with all fitting interest and sympathy by the nations you represent. . . .

V.1.D　The writer Mazzini, a life-long revolutionary, who had spent many years in exile, was the leading spirit in the new Roman Government, which attempted to carry out many overdue reforms. Attention was paid to the necessities of the social question, as the following decree of 4th April 1849, shows. Extract from *Life and Writings of Joseph Mazzini*, V, London, 1869, pp. 371 f.

Whereas it is the office and duty of a well-organised Republic to provide for the gradual amelioration of the condition of the most necessitous classes;

Whereas the improvement most urgent at the present moment is that of withdrawing as many families as possible from the evils resulting from crowded and unhealthy habitations;

Whereas, while the Republic is occupied in endeavouring to destinate proper localities, both in the provinces and in Rome itself, for the use of the indigent classes, it is a work of republican morality to cancel even the vestiges of past iniquity by consecrating to benevolence that which past tyranny employed for torture, the Constituent Assembly, at the suggestion of the Triumvirs [the executive committee], decrees:

1. The edifice hitherto used as the *Holy Office*, is henceforth dedicated to the use of necessitous families or individuals, who shall be allowed to have lodgings therein on payment of a small monthly rent.

2. A commission is instituted, composed of three representatives of the people, and two civil engineers, to provide with all due speed for the execution of the present decree:

(a) By receiving applications from Roman families or individuals asking for lodging in the above-mentioned locality, and selecting those who are proved to be the most necessitous.

(b) By causing such alterations to be made in the above-mentioned locality as are necessary in order to adapt it to its new destination.

(c) By appropriating the necessary amount of space to those whose applications shall have been granted, fixing the rent they will be required to pay, and putting them in possession of their lodging.

(d) By drawing up rules for the maintenance of order and discipline within the building, and for the general administration and preservation of the locality.

3. No sub-letting of the aforesaid lodgings will be permitted.

4. The Commission will commence its sittings within the building

itself on the 9th inst., for the immediate execution of the duties with
which it is entrusted. . . .

V.1.E Another decree issued in April concerned land reform. Extract
from *Life and Writings of Mazzini*, V, pp. 373 f.

. . . Whereas there is no more appropriate and speedy method of
rendering the labours of the agriculturist lucrative, and of benefiting a
most numerous and useful class; of strengthening their affection for
their country, and interesting them in the organisation of the great
reform; of improving the soil and its cultivators at one and the same
time, by the emancipation of both, than that of parcelling out a large
portion of the vast rural possessions now actually administered, or to be
administered by the State, into small leasehold allotments at a moderate
annual rent, redeemable at any given time, to one or several families of
the poorest peasants; under such regulations and conditions as shall be
deemed most fitting to ensure the speediest, most just, and most stable
execution of so salutary a purpose, it is decreed:
Article 1. A large portion of the rural domains belonging to religious
corporations . . . in whatsoever portion of the Roman territory, which
either are or are to be placed under the administration of the State,
shall be immediately divided into a given number of portions, sufficient
for the maintenance of one or more necessitous families having no other
means of subsistence; who shall hold them in free and permanent leasehold in consideration of a moderate *canon* payable to the State, redeemable at any given time from the leasehold.
Article 2. A special regulation will distinctly determine the method of
proceeding by which this wholesome provision shall be effectuated.
Article 4. The measures already announced with regard to the fitting
payment of the expenses of public worship, the pastoral administration
of parishes, and other establishments of public interest, either through
payment in kind, the produce of leaseholds or other public monies
belonging to the provincial or municipal authorities, will remain in
force.
Article 5. The Ministers of Finance and of the Interior, are respectively charged with the execution of the present law. . . .

V.1.F The idealism of the new regime was not sufficient to deal with the
practical problems which arose, as the proclamation of the republican authorities on 4th May shows. Extract from *Life and
Writings of Mazzini*, V, pp. 379 ff.

Romans!—Infrequent, but grave disorders have arisen. Some acts of
devastation and injury to property have been committed, which
endanger the majestic tranquillity with which Rome has sanctified her

victory. For the honour of Rome and the triumph of the sacred principle we defend, it is necessary that such disorders should cease.

Everything must be great in Rome: alike the energy in battle, and the conduct of the people after victory.

The weapons of those who dwell amid the eternal monuments of their fathers' greatness, may not be turned against the unarmed, nor used to enforce arbitrary acts. The repose of Rome should be as the repose of the lion, a repose as majestic as his rage is terrible.

Romans! Your triumvirs have solemnly pledged themselves to prove to Europe that you are superior to your assailants,—that the accusations cast upon you are calumnious,—that the Republican principle has destroyed the germs of anarchy sown by the former Government, and to which the renewal of the past alone could give life,—that you are not only brave but virtuous, that law and courage are in your eyes the breath and soul of the Republic.

On these conditions your triumvirs are proud to remain at your head; on these conditions, they will, if need be, join you on the barricades. Be these conditions inviolable as the love that unites the people with its Government, as the resolution of both people and Government to maintain the banner of the Republic unsullied and pure from every stain.

Persons are inviolable. The Government alone has the right to punish.

Property is inviolable. Every stone of Rome is sacred. The Government alone has the right to modify the inviolability of property when public utility renders it necessary.

No one is allowed to make arrests, or domiciliary perquisitions, without the direction or assistance of the head of a military post.

Foreigners are under the special protection of the Republic. All the citizens are responsible for the reality of this protection.

The military commission recently organised will deliver speedy judgement, according to the necessities of the exceptional state of affairs and the public safety, upon all acts of sedition, reaction, anarchy, or violation of the laws.

The National Guard, which has shown itself ready to fight for the Republic, will also be ready to keep our honour pure from all reproach in the face of Europe. The National Guard is specially charged with the preservation of order, and with the execution of the above-mentioned regulations. . . .

V.1.G   The Pope appealed to the Catholic powers to reduce Rome to
         obedience. The French Republic, in which Louis Napoleon had
         been elected President by popular vote in December 1848,
         responded first and its troops appeared before Rome in May. The

---

Roman Republic appealed to the French soldiers on 10th May. Extract from *Life and Writings of Mazzini*, V, pp. 381 f.

Soldiers of the French Republic.

You are for the second time led as enemies beneath the walls of Rome, of the republican city that was at once the cradle of liberty and of military valour.

Your leaders are urging you to fratricide.

And that fratricide, were it possible to effect it, would be a mortal blow to the liberties of France. The peoples are securities for one another. The destruction of our Republic would leave an ineffaceable stain upon your banner, would deprive France of an ally in Europe, would be a new step taken upon the path of monarchical restoration, towards which your great and beautiful country is being led by a Government either deceiving or deceived.

Rome, therefore, will fight as she has fought. She knows how to fight for your liberty and for her own.

Soldiers of the French Republic, while you are advancing against our tri-coloured flag, the Russians, the men of 1815, are advancing against Hungary and looking towards France.

A few miles distant from you, a body of Neapolitan troops, defeated by us a few days since, yet bears aloft the flag of despotism and intolerance. A few leagues to our left, Leghorn, another republican city is, at the time of writing, engaged in resisting an Austrian invasion. Your post is there.

Tell your leaders to fulfil what they said to you. Remind them that they promised in Marseilles and Toulon to lead you against the Croats. Remind them that French soldiers bear the honour and liberties of France upon the point of their bayonets.

French soldiers! Soldiers of liberty! Do not attack men who are your brothers. May the two tri-colour banners entertwined advance to the emancipation of the peoples and the destruction of tyranny! God, France, and Italy will bless your arms.

Long live the French Republic! Long live the Roman Republic! ...

V.1.H   In the meantime, the Venetian republic continued on its uneasy course under the leadership of the lawyer and politician Manin. The desperate situation of the republic is described in a despatch from the British Consul-General to Lord Palmerston of 6th May 1849. Extract from G. M. Trevelyan, *Manin and the Venetian Revolution of 1848*, London, 1923, pp. 252 ff.

... On the morning of yesterday, the 5th, a summons was sent in to the Venetians by Marshal Radetsky, who had arrived the day before in the neighbourhood of Mestre, giving them until eight o'clock on the following morning, the 6th, to surrender.

This summons contained an offer, I am assured, of a full and complete pardon to all non-commissioned officers and soldiers, and liberty to all those persons who chose, without exception, to leave the place, but neither these terms nor any others that it may have contained have been made public by the Government.

In the afternoon of the same day, the 5th, M. Vasseur, the French Consul here, called upon me to inform me that a French steamer just arrived from Ancona had brought him a despatch from Paris, dated the 17th April, a portion of which he read to me, desiring him to make clearly known to the Provisional Government of Venice, that notwithstanding the sympathy it felt for them, the French Government could not take any measures for their support; and that the mediation of the two Governments of England and France being now at an end, all that those Governments could do would be to urge the Austrian Government to show as much moderation as possible to the Venetians. . . .

M. Vasseur, who fairly admits that his sympathies are with the Venetians, then left me to execute the instructions he had received, it being arranged between us that I should see Signor Manin afterwards. M. Vasseur returned to give me an account of his interview, from which it appeared that Signor Manin, although fully admitting the difficulties of his position, was nevertheless unprepared to take any steps whatever for a surrender.

I then went myself to Signor Manin, and pointed out to him the perfect inutility of further resistance, the utter hopelessness of relief being afforded to him by any Foreign Government, the additional sacrifices which each day's opposition would infallably entail upon Venice, and lastly the immense responsibility which he personally would incur by causing the loss of so many lives.

I found Signor Manin much cast down and disposed to receive my representations in a very friendly spirit, but although admitting the truth of them, I regret to say they entirely failed in producing the desired effect.

Signor Manin said that on learning the total discomfiture of the Piedmontese Army, the Venetian Government addressed themselves again early in April to the French and English Governments, entreating them to interfere in behalf of Venetian Independence; that the reply of the French Government had been received, in which, although stating that the time for such a project was gone by, allusion was made to the possibility (M. Manin did not say whether present or past possibility) of a Lombardo-Venetian Kingdom under the protection of Austria, and that the Venetian agent at Paris had been forthwith instructed to enter into communication with the French Government upon this point. To

the despatch sent to England, Signor Manin said he knew Your Lord-
ship had replied in writing, but that the reply had not yet reached him.

Although evidently not placing much reliance in the result of these
appeals to the English and French Governments, Signor Manin still
seemed unwilling to abandon all hope that something might result from
them, favourable to Venice. He then returned to the language already
used by him to me, viz.: that it was impossible to put any faith in
Austria; that the utter ruin of Venice if it fell again into her hands was
certain; that it would be better to die than to survive and witness such a
state of things; that although under present circumstances resistance
did appear hopeless, yet that, powerful as was the Austrian besieging
force, the position of Venice gave it still the means, if well defended, of
resisting for sometime longer; that the ill success of the French Expedi-
tion to Rome would probably produce a change of Ministry in France;
that the successes of the Hungarians might require the entire withdrawal
of the Austrian force from Italy, etc. etc.

Admitting the possibility of these events coming to pass I besought
Signor Manin to consider that Austria having now seriously undertaken
the reduction of Venice would be only all the more determined to effect
her object without loss of time, and again urged him to take some step
in a conciliatory sense; I also begged him to consider his own position. I
told him, what I have reason to know is perfectly true, that he was now
accused by many of sacrificing them to his own ambition, that a very
large portion of the inhabitants of Venice were most anxious to come
to terms, and I entreated him to make use of the influence he possessed
over the people while that influence yet remained in his hands, begging
him to beware lest it should fall from him altogether.

To all my representations, though received in a friendly and grateful
manner, Signor Manin's constant reply was: 'It is impossible—I cannot surrender—I cannot surrender—I cannot trust the Austrians—I am
here to resist.'

Then said I: 'What is the reply you will send to Marshal Radetsky's
summons?' 'We shall send no reply whatever,' answered he, 'and the
operations of the siege of Malghera must therefore be continued.'

Notwithstanding the determination expressed by Signor Manin to
persevere in his resistance, a determination I believe him to have been
perfectly sincere in expressing, I am inclined to suspect that if anything
like a popular demonstration in favour of a surrender were to be made,
Signor Manin would not oppose himself to it. His position is becoming
daily more difficult. . . .

V.1.J   Garibaldi, the greatest citizen-general of 1848, inspired the de-
        fenders of Rome with great enthusiasm. When finally, on 2nd
        July 1849, capture of the city by the French became inevitable,

Garibaldi led five thousand soldiers out of Rome into the hills. Before leaving Rome, Garibaldi addressed the crowd. Extract from G. M. Trevelyan, *Garibaldi's Defence of the Roman Republic, 1848–9*, London, 1920, p. 223.

Fortune, who betrays us today, will smile on us tomorrow. I am going out from Rome. Let those who wish to continue the war against the stranger come with me. I offer neither pay, nor quarters, nor provisions; I offer hunger, thirst, forced marches, battles and death. Let him who loves his country in his heart and not with his lips only, follow me.

V.1.K The definitive peace treaty between Austria and Sardinia was signed at Milan on 6th August 1849. Extract from Hertslet, *The Map of Europe by Treaty*, II, pp. 1110 ff.

Article 1. There shall be from henceforth and for ever, Peace, Friendship, and good understanding between His Majesty the King of Sardinia and His Majesty the Emperor of Austria, their Heirs and Successors, their respective States and Subjects.
Article 2. All Treaties and Conventions concluded between His Majesty the King of Sardinia and His Majesty the Emperor of Austria which were in force on the 1st March 1848, are fully renewed and confirmed, in so far as they are not altered by the present Treaty.
Article 3. The limits of the States of His Majesty the King of Sardinia on the side of the Po, and on the side of the Tessin, shall be . . . such as they existed previous to the beginning of the War in 1848.
Article 4. His Majesty the King of Sardinia, as well for himself as for his Heirs and Successors, renounces all Rights and Pretensions whatever over the Countries situated beyond the Limits mentioned . . . above. . . .

V.2 REICH CONSTITUTION, IMPERIAL CROWN AND END OF FRANKFURT PARLIAMENT

Heinrich von Gagern took over the presidency of the provisional Reich Government in December 1848. There was opposition in many quarters to a 'Little Germany' without Austria, even if closely linked to the Habsburg Empire in accordance with the Gagern plan (see IV.1.G). The Frankfurt Parliament finally passed the Reich constitution and the electoral law on 27th March 1849. The following day the assembly elected Frederick William IV hereditary German Emperor, but the King of Prussia declined early in April. The Frankfurt Parliament broke up at the end of May. A radical rump continued for a little longer in Stuttgart during June. The summer saw a series of further revolutions in Germany which were crushed.

V.2.A   The Right Centre deputy and historian Arneth from Vienna, in his speech to the Frankfurt Parliament on 11th January, which followed one by Heinrich von Gagern, put the 'Great German' point of view. Extract translated from F. Wigard (ed.), *Steno-graphischer Bericht*, VI, pp. 4566 ff.

. . . Arneth from Vienna: '. . . At the beginning of your constitution you have put stipulations by which you force a third of our common Fatherland, . . . the German-Austrian territories, out of Germany. Whether you thus acted justly, whether you thus acted wisely, I will not decide; I will not determine whether you would not have done the Fatherland a greater service, if you had tightened the bonds of its future constitution a little less firmly, if you had not steered beyond the federal state to the unitary state, but had constructed your constitution in such a way that under its protecting roof room had remained, too, for your brothers in Austria. I believe, gentlemen, the constitution you are building must be adapted to the peoples to whom it will apply,—if you carry out the contrary, if you want to adapt the peoples to the constitution, then you will not attain your goal for a long time; . . . I believe the Fatherland will not be grateful to you for those regulations at the moment when it is striving not only for internal unity, but also for external might and greatness; I believe the Fatherland will not be grateful to you for those stipulations which rob it of a third of its might and greatness, and history will take severely to task this assembly through whose resolutions no village, no house, no inch of territory has been won for Germany, but many millions of its best citizens, many thousands of square miles of its most beautiful land carelessly pushed away; yes, gentlemen, *pushed* away, it is a hard but it is a true word: you yourselves drive away Austria from Germany by the acceptance of those stipulations; you yourselves have largely alienated the sympathies of the Austrian people by their acceptance. You yourselves have been the worst enemy of Germany in Austria. The Austrian people, so often ridiculed because of its small political education, has understood well the importance of those regulations; it has protested against them in its overwhelming majority, and it was this temper of the people which empowered the Austrian Government to take up its present position towards Germany. In view of this situation, gentlemen, if you really want to preserve Austria for Germany, then you must above all decide to drop those regulations. (Voices in the Centre: Hear! Hear!) But you do not want that; quite the contrary, as in one of the most recent sittings one of the leading members of the assembly affirmed from the rostrum: quite the contrary, you are firmly resolved at this moment to accept those paragraphs for a second time and thus to renew the blow which you have dealt Austria. I, too, am an enemy of all mistrust, an enemy of any casting of suspicion, and therefore I do not approve, but I understand it if the Austrian people, indignant about those regulations and your rigid adherence to them, believes that you do not want to maintain Austria with Germany at all, and that from the beginning you have only been concerned about Austria's withdrawing, not with its remaining with Germany. If you, gentlemen, really believe that you must firmly persist in those stipulations, then I only see two ways of securing their acceptance by Austria; the first is the path of negotiation; the second way—is force of arms—is war. Neither of the two methods, I am firmly convinced, will lead you to the desired goal. Austria can never agree to negotiations on *this* basis, to any negotiations to enter the federal state on the basis of paragraphs 2 and 3, and if it does not do that it is, in my conviction, completely in the right; for it cannot, it may not offer its hand for its own destruction. (Voices in the Centre: 'Hear! Hear!'—On the most extreme Right: 'Bravo!') There thus remains only the second way, force of arms; there remains [the possibility of] war, in order to force Austria to accept these regulations through the might of the stronger, if it does not submit to them voluntarily. This method, that of calling up Reich troops against Austria, has been indicated several times to you by this side of the house (the Left) as the most suitable method of restoring Germany's unity. Gentlemen! Your provocative call for fighting and war will . . . have no other effect than to rob you of the rest of the sympathy which the Austrian people still feels for you. There is no idea which is rejected in Austria with deeper indignation and aversion that than of a war with Germany. Austria has waged war with individual German states. It resorted to arms when Bavaria, supported by France, greedily reached out its hand for the rock fortress Tirol. It resorted to arms when Prussia's bellicose King Frederick, against all right, snatched the Silesian provinces for himself (Voices: Oh!)—yes, against all right. But in a war with the whole of Germany, Austria never yet saw itself. . . . But should there be a party in this house which, under the pretext of founding German unity, tried again to conjure up a civil war in my unhappy Fatherland, should there be a party which intends to call forth a more successful edition of the October revolution, then the efforts of such a party would like the first fail a second time owing to the healthy sense of the inhabitants of the German–Austrian lands; and the Austrian army, accustomed to victory, which has defeated in so many battles the treacherous Welschen [in this case the Italians] (unrest), which is at present about to put down the Magyar rebellion, will reject with determination any endeavour directed against the integrity of Austria from wherever it may come. . . . This, gentlemen, is the not very pleasant, but true state of affairs. Austria cannot accept those regulations with which you lead off your constitution, and you, gentlemen, have no means in your hands to force it to accept them. At present you not only have not got the power, but you also lack the right. For what are those paragraphs, the world-famous paragraphs, as one most honourable member of the Assembly—not without pride to be able to consider himself their creator—has called them, the infamous paragraphs, as the Austrian people call them, full of the most just anger? They are nothing but a provisional decision which you will overthrow, which you must overthrow, if you really do not want those words to remain nothing else but empty sound which has been written on to the walls of St Paul's Church, if you have really come here in order to found a new greatness of the Fatherland, the happiness of the Fatherland.

Those paragraphs are nothing else but an inquiry from Austria, as the Minister-President has himself expressed it. Now, gentlemen, I believe this question has been sufficiently answered and it is now up to you, during the second reading of the constitution, to make proper use of the reply that you have received. Whichever way your decision goes, whether for or against the paragraphs, whether you pass the constitution in the second reading in the same form as in the first, or whether you change it, in any case you cannot demand from Austria a declaration as to whether it is in a position to submit to the stipulations of this constitution, until these clauses are absolutely definite. For one has to know the laws to which one will have to submit; or do you want to consider Austria as having withdrawn from the German federal state, because of the hints which the Austrian Ministry expressed in its programme, because of the interpretation which you have given to these hints in decided contradiction to the since then expressly announced will of that Ministry, or perhaps because of the protests against the paragraphs 2 and 3? Or do you want to consider it as having withdrawn because it has ignored the resolutions of this Assembly? Gentlemen, it hurts me to have to say this, but if you want to consider as having withdrawn from the German federal state all those states whose Governments have ignored your decisions, then you would only have very little room for applying the new constitution, which you are about to complete . . . even then, gentlemen, when you have sacrificed those paragraphs during the second reading of the constitution because of Austria's peculiar circumstances, if you take due account of these special conditions in a few other clauses of the constitution, without however interfering with the nature of the federal state, if then the entry of Austria into the German federal state should not be feasible, then, gentlemen, nothing remains, however painful it may be, but to accustom yourselves to the idea of the withdrawal of Austria. Then, but only then, will the time have come to negotiate with Austria about the conclusion of the projected act of union, then, but only then will the time have come when the Austrian deputies will no longer regard it as compatible with their honour to occupy their seats in this parliament. It need hardly be mentioned that we would then no longer have the right to deliberate in common on that act of union. It would have to be concluded by plenipotentiaries and would then have to be submitted to both Reich assemblies, the one in Frankfurt and the one in Vienna, for acceptance and incorporation in both constitutions. However grievous this result would be, it would not help to shut one's eyes to it and to say: we do not want it, therefore it does not exist. And as we are acting accordingly, I reject in my own name and that of the other deputies from Austria the accusation which has been made to us repeatedly, but always with the same injustice, that, although inwardly convinced of the recognition that Austria's entry into the German federal state was impossible, yet we want to participate in order to make the federal state an impossibility for Germany. I have always regarded it as my duty, and still do so, to counter those sad results of our mission to Frankfurt with all our strength. Equally I would regard it as my duty to look the situation manfully in the eye and to help and to save, where one can still help and save. Should it, however, not be possible to bring Austria into the most intimate relationship with Germany, then gentlemen, it would be our most sacred duty to make every effort—you in Germany but also we in Austria—that the bonds which indissolubly connect the two countries should be as close as possible, which for the sake of the welfare of both countries must connect them indissolubly, then, gentlemen, it will be our most sacred duty to strive so that the division which at present threatens to separate both countries should disappear, that this division should never widen into an irreparable breach. Then let us above all develop the strong bond of material interests between both peoples, then let us see to it that Austria and Germany should never face each other as foreign powers, but always as intimately connected countries, that they should always go hand in hand pursuing common purposes, that they should represent—if not internally yet externally—one whole, that they show the threatening countenance, the one to the enemy in the East, the other to the enemy in the West; then . . . one would not speak of a partition of Germany; then one would always be able to say truthfully: Austria and Germany joined together so closely are strong enough to enter the lists against the whole of Europe.'

V.2.B   The Reich constitution theoretically left open the possibility of the participation of Austria (see § 87). Though never implemented, this document formed the basis of all further constitutional thinking in Germany, including that of Bismarck's North German Confederation and Reich. Extracts translated from the German of the text in Huber, *Dokumente*, pp. 304 ff.

SECTION I: THE REICH
Article I

§ 1. The German Reich consists of the area of the heretofore existing German Confederation. The stipulation of the position of the Duchy of Schleswig remains reserved [for future arrangement].

§ 2. If a German territory has the same head of state as a non-German one, then the German territory must have its own constitution, government and administration separate from the non-German one. Only German citizens may be appointed to the government and administration of a German territory.

The Reich constitution and Reich legislation have the same binding force in such a German territory as in the other German lands.

§ 3. If a German territory has the same head of state as a non-German one, then the head of state must either reside in his German lands, or a regency must be installed in a constitutional manner to which only Germans may be appointed.

§ 4. Apart from already existing associations of German and non-German lands, no head of state of a non-German territory may at the same time take over the government of a German territory, nor may a prince governing in Germany, without resigning his German government, accept a foreign crown.

§ 5. The individual German states retain their independence in so far as it is not limited by the Reich constitution; they have all the state sovereignty and rights in so far as these are not expressly assigned to the Reich Authority.

SECTION II: THE REICH AUTHORITY
Article I

§ 6. The Reich Authority exercises the exclusive international representation of Germany and of the individual German states towards foreign countries. . . .

§ 7. The individual German governments do not have the right to receive or to maintain resident ministers. They may also not maintain any special consuls. . . .

Article II

§ 10. The Reich Authority has the exclusive right of war and peace.

Article III

§ 11. The Reich Authority has at its disposal the whole armed force of Germany.

§ 12. The Reich army consists of the entire land forces of the individual German states designated for the purpose of war. . . . Those German states which have less than 500,000 inhabitants are to be united by the Reich Authority to a greater military whole which will then be under the direct command of the Reich Authority or will be attached to an adjoining greater state. . . .

§ 14. The military oath is to contain in the first place the obligation of loyalty to the Head of the Reich and to the Reich constitution.

§ 17. The appointment of commanders and officers of their troops, in so far as their strength demands it, is left to the Governments of the individual states. For the greater military units to which the troops of several states are united, the Reich authority appoints the common commanders. For war the Reich authority appoints the commanding generals of the independent corps as well as the personnel of headquarters. . . .

§ 19. The Navy is exclusively a matter for the Reich. No individual state is allowed to maintain warships or to issue letters of marque. . . .

ARTICLE VI

§ 28. Over railways and their operation, in so far as the protection of the Reich or the interest of general traffic demands it, the Reich Authority has superintendence and the right of legislation. . . .

ARTICLE VII

§ 33. The German Reich shall form one customs and trading area, surrounded by a common customs frontier, with the abolition of all internal border dues. The exclusion of individual places and areas from the customs area remains reserved to the Reich Authority. It remains further reserved to the Reich Authority to attach even territories . . . not belonging to the Reich to the German customs area by means of special treaties.

§ 34. The Reich Authority has exclusive legislation over customs as well as over common production and consumption duties. . . .

§ 35. The levying and administration of customs duties, as well as of the common production and consumption duties, takes place on the orders and under the supervision of the Reich Authority. From the proceeds a certain part will, according to the ordinary budget, be allotted for the expenditure of the Reich, the rest will be distributed to the individual states. . . .

§ 36. On what objects the individual states may put production or consumption duties for the benefit of the state or of individual municipalities . . . will be determined by Reich legislation.

§ 37. The individual German states are not entitled to levy customs duties on commodities which pass into or out of the Reich frontiers.

§ 38. The Reich Authority has the right of legislation about trade and shipping and supervises the execution of the Reich laws issued about these.

ARTICLE IX

§ 45. The Reich Authority has the exclusive legislation and supervision of the monetary system. It is incumbent upon it to introduce the same monetary system for the whole of Germany. . . .

§ 46. The Reich Authority is obliged to establish in the whole of Germany the same system of weights and measures. . . .

§ 47. The Reich Authority has the right to regulate banking and the issue of paper money by legislation. . . .

ARTICLE X

§ 49. To cover its expenditure, the Reich Authority is in the first instance dependent on its share of the revenue from customs and from the common production and consumption duties.

§ 50. The Reich Authority has the right, in so far as the other revenues are not sufficient, to levy contributions from the individual states [*Matrikularbeiträge*].

§ 51. The Reich Authority is empowered to levy Reich taxes in extraordinary cases . . . as well as to contract loans or other debts.

ARTICLE XII

§ 53. It is incumbent upon the Reich Authority to maintain a supervisory watch over the rights guaranteed to all Germans by the Reich constitution.

§ 54. The Reich Authority is charged with the maintenance of the Reich peace. It has to take the measures required for the maintenance of internal security and order:

(1) if a German state is disturbed in its peace or endangered by another German state;

(2) if in a German state security and order is disturbed or endangered by natives or strangers. But in this case the Reich Authority should only intervene if the Government concerned invites it to do so, unless the State Government concerned is notoriously incapable of doing so, or unless the general Reich peace appears to be threatened;

(3) if the constitution of a German state is forcibly or unilaterally abolished or changed, and if immediate help cannot be secured by appealing to the Supreme Reich Court [*Reichsgericht*].

§ 55. The measures which may be taken by the Reich Authority for the preservation of the Reich peace are:

(1) Decrees

(2) The dispatch of commissioners

(3) The use of armed force. . . .

§ 56. The Reich Authority is charged with determining by a Reich law the cases and forms in which armed force should be used against disturbances of the public order.

§ 57. The Reich Authority has the task of fixing the legal norms for the acquisition and forfeiture of Reich and state citizenship.

§ 58. The Reich Authority is competent to issue Reich laws about the law of domicile and to watch over their execution.

ARTICLE XIII

§ 62. The Reich Authority has the power of legislation necessary for the execution of the tasks entrusted to it by the constitution and for the protection of the institutions made over to it.

§ 63. The Reich Authority is empowered, if it finds common institutions and measures necessary in the general interest of Germany, to issue the laws necessary for their establishment in the forms prescribed for the change of the constitution.

§ 64. The Reich Authority is charged with establishing unity of law in the German people by the issue of general law codes.

§ 66. Reich laws have precedence over the laws of the individual states, in so far as they are not expressly given only a subsidiary validity.

SECTION III: THE HEAD OF THE REICH

ARTICLE I

§ 68. The dignity of Head of the Reich will be assigned to one of the reigning German princes.

§ 69. This dignity is hereditary in the house of the prince to whom it is assigned. It devolves in the male line according to the right of primogeniture.

§ 70. The head of the Reich has the title: Emperor of the Germans.

§ 71. The residence of the Emperor is at the seat of the Reich Government. . . .

ARTICLE II

§ 73. The person of the Emperor is inviolable. The Emperor exercises the authority assigned to him through responsible ministers appointed by him.

§ 74. All government actions of the Emperor require for their validity the countersignature of at least one of the Reich Ministers, who thus assumes responsibility.

ARTICLE III

§ 75. The Emperor exercises the international representation of the German Reich and of the individual German states. He appoints the Reich ministers [resident] and the consuls and conducts diplomatic relations.

§ 76. The Emperor declares war and concludes peace.

§ 77. The Emperor concludes alliances and treaties with foreign powers, with the collaboration of the Reichstag in so far as this is reserved to it in the constitution.

§ 79. The Emperor summons and closes the Reichstag; he has the right of dissolving the popular chamber [*Volkshaus*].

§ 80. The Emperor has the right of proposing bills. He exercises the legislative power in common with the Reichstag under the constitutional limitations. He proclaims Reich laws and issues the decrees necessary for their execution.

§ 82. The Emperor is charged with the preservation of the peace of the Reich.

§ 83. The Emperor has the right of disposal over the armed forces.

SECTION IV: THE REICHSTAG

ARTICLE I

§ 85. The Reichstag consists of two houses, the House of States [*Staatenhaus*] and the House of the People [*Volkshaus*].

ARTICLE II

§ 86. The House of States will be formed from the representatives of the German states.

§ 87. The number of members is as follows:

Prussia	40
Austria	38
Bavaria	18
Saxony, Hanover, Wurtemberg, 10 each	30
Baden	9
Electoral Hesse, Grand-Duchy of Hesse, Holstein, 6 each	18
Mecklenburg-Schwerin	4
Luxemburg-Limburg, Nassau, 3 each	6
Brunswick, Oldenburg, Saxe-Weimar, 2 each	6
The 23 others, 1 each	23
	192 members.[1]

---

[1] There were to be certain modifications so long as Austria did not join.

F

§ 88. Members of the House of States are appointed one-half by the governments and one-half by the popular representation of the particular states.

§ 92. The members of the House of States are elected for six years. One-half of the seats are filled every three years. . . .

ARTICLE III

§ 93. The House of the People consists of the deputies of the German people.

§ 94. The members of the House of the People are elected initially for four years, thereafter for three years. The election is to be in accordance with the regulations contained in the Reich electoral law.[2]

ARTICLE IV

§ 95. The members of the Reichstag draw from the Reich exchequer uniform daily allowances and compensation for their travelling expenses.

§ 96. The members of both houses may not be committed by instructions.

§ 97. Nobody may at the same time be a member of both houses.

ARTICLE V

§ 98. For a resolution of each house of the Reichstag the participation of at least one-half of the legal number of its members and a simple majority are required. . . .

§ 99. Each house has the right of initiation, of legislation, of complaint, of address and of the investigation of facts, as well as of the impeachment of ministers.

§ 100. A resolution of the Reichstag can only validly be made by agreement of both houses.

§ 101. A resolution of the Reichstag which has not obtained the consent of the Reich Government may not be repeated in the same session. If the Reichstag in three immediately consecutive ordinary sessions makes the same resolution without change, it becomes law with the end of the third Reichstag, even if the Reich Government does not give its consent. . . .

§ 102. A resolution of the Reichstag is necessary in the following cases:

    (1) if it is a matter of the issue, abolition, alteration or interpretation of Reich laws.

    (2) when the Reich budget is fixed, when loans are contracted, when

[2] See document V. 2. C.

the Reich takes over expenditure for which provision has not been made in the budget, or levies contributions from the states [*Matrikularbeiträge*] or taxes.

(6) if territories not belonging to the Reich are included in the German custom area or particular places or areas are excluded from it.

(7) if German territories are ceded, or non-German territories incorporated in the Reich or to be associated with it in some other manner.

§ 103. . . . (3) the length of the financial period and of the grant of the budget is one year. . . .

ARTICLE VI

§ 104. The Reichstag assembles each year at the seat of the Reich Government. . . .

§ 106. The House of the People may be dissolved by the Head of the Reich. In case of dissolution, the Reichstag is to be re-assembled within three months.

ARTICLE VII

§ 111. The sessions of both houses are public. . .

ARTICLE VIII

§ 117. A member of the Reichstag may be neither arrested nor investigated because of criminal accusations during the session without approval of the house to which he belongs, with the sole exception of his being caught red-handed. . . .

§ 120. No member of the Reichstag may at any time be prosecuted or disciplined or otherwise called to account outside the assembly because of his vote or because of utterances made in the exercise of his profession.

ARTICLE IX

§ 121. The Reich Ministers are entitled to be present at the proceedings of both Houses of the Reichstag and to be heard by it at any time.

§ 122. The Reich Ministers are obliged at the request of either house of the Reichstag to appear in it and to give information, or to indicate the reason why it cannot be given.

§ 123. The Reich Ministers may not be members of the House of States.

§ 124. If a member of the House of the People accepts an office or a promotion in the service of the Reich, he must submit to a new election; he keeps his seat until the new election has taken place.

SECTION V
THE SUPREME REICH COURT [REICHSGERICHT]
ARTICLE I

§ 125. The jurisdiction belonging to the Reich is exercised by the *Reichsgericht*.

SECTION VI: THE BASIC RIGHTS OF THE GERMAN PEOPLE

§ 130. The following basic rights are to be guaranteed to the German people. They are to serve as the norm for the constitutions of the individual German states, and no constitution or legislation of an individual German state may ever abolish or limit them.

ARTICLE I

§ 131. The German people consists of the members of the states which form the German Reich.

§ 132. Every German has German Reich citizenship. He can exercise the rights arising from it in every German state. . . .

§ 133. Every German has the right to stay and reside at any place in the area of the Reich, to acquire immovables of any kind and to dispose of them, to engage in any form of livelihood, to gain municipal citizenship. . . .

§ 134. No German state may make a difference in civil and criminal law or in any litigation between its citizens and other Germans which discriminates against the latter as foreigners.

§ 136. The state does not limit the freedom of emigration; duties on removal may not be levied. . . .

ARTICLE II

§ 137. The law does not recognise any difference between estates. The nobility as an estate is abolished. All privileges of estates are abolished. All Germans are equal before the law. All titles, in so far as they are not connected with an office, are abolished and may not be re-introduced. . . . Public offices are equally accessible to all who are qualified. Military service is the same for all; performance of service by a deputy is not permitted.

ARTICLE III

§ 138. The freedom of the person is inviolable. The arrest of a person, except when caught red-handed, may only take place by virtue of an order from a judge stating the reasons. This order must be handed to the arrested person at the time of the arrest or within the following twenty-four hours. The police must either release or hand over to the judicial authority in the course of the following day every person whom it has taken into custody. . . .

§ 139. The death penalty—except where prescribed by martial law or allowed by maritime law in case of mutinies—as well as the penalties of the pillory, of branding and of corporal punishment, are abolished.

§ 140. The home is inviolable. . . .

ARTICLE IV

§ 143. Every German has the right of free expression by word, writing, printing and picture. Freedom of the press may not in any circumstances and in any way . . . be limited, suspended or abolished. . . .

ARTICLE V

§ 144. Every German has full freedom of faith and conscience. . . .

§ 146. The enjoyment of civil . . . rights does not depend on a religious confession and is not limited by it. The duties of the citizen may not be hindered by it.

§ 147. Every religious society . . . administers its affairs independently but remains subject to the general state laws. No religious society is given preference by the state over others; there is no state church. . . .

§ 150. The civil validity of marriage is dependent only on the execution of the civil act; church marriage may only take place after the civil act. Difference in religion is no obstacle to civil marriage.

ARTICLE VI

§ 152. Learning and its instruction is free.

§ 153. Education is under the superintendence of the state and is, apart from religious instruction, removed from the supervision of the clergy as such.

§ 157. No fees are payable for instruction in elementary schools and in the lower trade schools. Those without means will be instructed free of charge in all public educational institutions.

ARTICLE VIII

§ 161. The Germans have the right to assemble peacefully and without weapons; special permission for this is not necessary. Assemblies of the people out-of-doors may be prohibited in case of urgent danger to public order and security.

ARTICLE IX

§ 164. Property is inviolable. . . .

§ 166. All serfdom . . . is abolished forever.

§ 167. Abolished without compensation are:

(1) patrimonial jurisdiction and the seignorial police, including all powers, exemptions and dues flowing from these rights. . . .

§ 168. All dues and labour tariffs attached to the soil are commutable. . . .

ARTICLE X

§ 174. All jurisdiction is derived from the State. There are to be no patrimonial courts.

§ 175. The judicial authority is exercised independently by the courts . . . ministerial justice is not permissible. Nobody may be withdrawn from his legal judge. Emergency courts may never be held.

§ 176. There must be no privileged judicial estate or persons or property. . . .

§ 177. No judge may, except by judgement and law, be removed from his office or be prejudiced in rank and salary. . . .

§ 178. Court procedure is to be public and oral. . . .

§ 179. Criminal cases are dealt with through prosecution. In more serious criminal cases at any rate and in all political offences there is to be a trial by jury.

§ 181. Justice and administration are to be separate and independent from each other. . . .

ARTICLE XII

§ 186. Every German state is to have a constitution with popular representation. The ministers are responsible to the popular representatives of the people.

§ 187. The representation of the people has a decisive voice in legislation, in taxation, in the ordering of the budget; also it has—where two Chambers exist, each Chamber separately—the right of making proposals for laws, of complaint, of address, as well as that of impeachment of ministers. As a rule the sittings of the state parliaments are public.

ARTICLE XIII

§ 188. The non-German speaking peoples of Germany are guaranteed their national development, especially equality of the rights of their languages, as far as their areas extend, in church matters, in [school] instruction, in internal administration and jurisdiction.

SECTION VII: THE GUARANTEE OF THE CONSITITUTION

ARTICLE I

§ 190. At the beginning of a new reign, the Reichstag meets without being summoned—unless it is already assembled—in the manner in which it was composed the last time. The Emperor, before he takes over the Government, swears in a united session of both houses of the Reichstag an oath to the constitution. The oath reads: 'I swear to protect the Reich and the rights of the German people, to maintain the Reich constitution and to execute it conscientiously. So help me God'. Only after having sworn the oath is the Emperor entitled to carry out acts of government.

ARTICLE III

§ 196. Changes in the Reich constitution may only be made by a resolution of both houses and with the consent of the Head of the Reich. Such a resolution requires in each of the houses:
(1) the presence of at least two-thirds of the members;
(2) two votes, at least eight days from each other;
(3) a majority of at least two-thirds of the members present at each of the two votes.
The consent of the Head of the Reich is not necessary, if in three immediately following ordinary sessions the same resolution of the Reichstag is passed unchanged. . . .

V.2.c   The 'democratic' male franchise formed part of a deal between the moderates and a section of the Left in the Frankfurt Parliament to permit the 'Little German' solution under the King of Prussia as hereditary German Emperor. Extract translated from the German text in Huber, *Dokumente*, pp. 324 ff.

ARTICLE I

§ 1. Every German of good repute who has completed his twenty-fifth year has the vote.

ARTICLE II

§ 5. Every German entitled to vote who has completed his twenty-fifth year and has belonged for at least three years to a German state is eligible as a deputy of the House of the People.

ARTICLE III

§ 7. In every state, constituencies are to be formed each containing one hundred thousand souls according to the last census. . . .

ARTICLE V

§ 13. The electoral act is public. . . . The vote is exercised in person by voting paper without signature.

§ 14. The election is direct. It takes place by absolute majority of all the votes cast in a constituency. If there is no absolute majority at the election, a second ballot is to take place. If here, too, an absolute majority of the votes is not achieved, a third vote is to be taken on the two candidates who received most votes in the second ballot. . . .

V.3 THE AUSTRIAN CONSTITUTION OF MARCH 1849

Following the example of the King of Prussia in December, 1848, the new Emperor of Austria, Francis Joseph, in March 1849, unilaterally granted a constitution, instead of agreeing it with parliament.

V.3.A

> Extracts from the centralist Austrian constitution of 4th March 1849, weakening Magyar control, are from *Annual Register*, 1848, pp. 318 ff.

. . . Sec. 1. The full enjoyment of political liberty, and the right of domestic exercise of the religious confession, are guaranteed to every one. The enjoyment of civil and political rights is independent of religious confession, but religious confession shall not be allowed to interfere with the political duties of the citizens. . . .

Sec. 2. Every church and religious society, if recognised by law, has the right of a common public exercise of its religion.

Sec. 5. Everybody has the right of a free expression of his opinion, by words, by writing, by print, and by drawings or paintings. The press may not be put under censorship. Supervisory laws shall be published against abuses of the press. . . .

Sec. 7. Austrian citizens have the right to assemble, and to form associations, if the end or the means and the manner of the meeting or association are not opposed to the law, or dangerous to the State.

Sec. 8. Individual liberty is guaranteed.

Sec. 9. The police are bound to liberate persons whom they have taken into custody within forty-eight hours, or to deliver them into the hands of the judge of the district.

Sec. 10. A man's domicile is inviolable.

Sec. 11. The secrecy of correspondence shall not be violated, and letters shall not be seized unless in time of war, or on the strength of a judicial warrant. . . .

CHAPTER II—TREATING OF THE EMPEROR

The Crown of the Empire, and of each single Crown land, is hereditary in the house of Hapsburg-Lorraine. . . .

The Emperor is crowned as Emperor of Austria.

At his coronation the Emperor takes his oath on the Constitution.

The Emperor is august, inviolable, and not answerable; decides on matters of peace and war; receives Ambassadors, and sends them [abroad], and he concludes treaties with foreign Powers.

The Emperor proclaims the laws, and publishes the decrees respecting the same. Each decree must have the counter-signature of a responsible Minister.

The Emperor appoints the Ministers, and he dismisses them; he appoints to all offices in all branches of the Administration; he confers titles, orders, and distinctions. . . .

CHAPTER III—TREATING OF THE CITIZENSHIP OF THE EMPIRE

Sec. 23. For all peoples of the Empire there is but one general Austrian citizenship. . . .

Sec. 24. In no Crown land shall there by any difference between its natives and those of another Crown land, neither in the administration of civil or criminal justice, nor in the ways and manners of justice, nor in the distribution of the public burdens.

The verdicts of the courts of justice of all Austrian Crown lands are equally binding on all.

Sec. 25. No limits shall be put to the right of each citizen to settle wherever he pleases within the confines of the Empire. Emigration is restrained only by the fulfilment of military service.

Sec. 26. Serfdom, no matter of what kind or denomination, is abolished. . . .

Sec. 27. All Austrian citizens are equal before the law and before the courts of justice.

Sec. 28. Public offices are open to all persons qualified for the same. . . .

Sec. 30. Every Austrian citizen has the right to acquire landed property of all kinds in all parts of the Empire, and he is likewise entitled to the practice of any trade or profession which the law permits. . . .

CHAPTER IV—TREATING OF THE IMPERIAL DIET

Sec. 33. The General Austrian Imperial Diet shall consist of two houses—namely, of an Upper House and of a Lower House, to be convoked every year by the Emperor.

Sec. 34. The Imperial Diet assembles at Vienna, but the Emperor has power to summon it to any place.

Sec. 35. The Upper House is formed by deputies, to be chosen by the Crown lands from the members of their respective provincial diets.

Sec. 36. Their number is one-half of the constitutional number of the Lower House.

Sec. 38. The Lower House proceeds from general and direct elections.

The franchise belongs to every Austrian citizen who is of age, who is in the full enjoyment of civil and political rights, and who either pays the annual amount of direct taxes fixed by the electoral law, or who, on account of his personal qualities, possesses the active franchise of a parish of an Austrian Crown land. . . .

Sec. 54. The sittings of the Imperial Diet are public; but each House may resolve itself into a secret committee on the motion of the President or of ten members.

Sec. 58. The arrest and prosecution of a member during the Session can only take place with the express consent of the House to which that member belongs, excepting always a case of seizure *in flagrante.*

Sec. 61. The consent of the Emperor and of both Houses is required for each law. A bill which has been rejected either by the Emperor or by one of the Houses cannot be brought in again in the course of the same Session.

Sec. 62. The Imperial Diet participates in the legislation on the affairs which this constitution designates as affairs of the Empire.

Sec. 64. The Emperor prorogues the Imperial Diet, and he may dissolve it at any time. On the prorogation of the Diet, or on the dissolution of one of the Houses, the sittings of either House must immediately cease. In case of a dissolution of the Imperial Diet, another Diet must be convoked within three months after the dissolution.

CHAPTER V—TREATING OF THE CONSTITUTIONS OF THE COUNTRIES

Sec. 66. The constitution of the Kingdom of Hungary shall so far be maintained that the regulations which do not tally with this constitution lose their effect, and the equality of rights, of all nationalities, and of the languages of the country in all relations of public and civil life, shall be guaranteed by institutions framed for that purpose. These relations are to be regulated by a special statute.

Sec. 67. The Woiwodeship of Serbia has a promise of institutions for the protection of its religion and nationality, emanating from ancient charters of privilege and Imperial declarations of modern times.

Sec. 68. In the kingdoms of Croatia and Slavonia, including the coast, and in the city of Fiume, and its territories, the peculiar institutions of these dominions shall be upheld within the union of those countries with the Empire, as determined by charter of this constitution, but with complete independence of the said countries from the kingdom of Hungary. Deputies from Dalmatia, under the mediation of the Executive Imperial power, will negotiate with the congregation of these kingdoms respecting their annexation and its conditions. The result is to be submitted to the sanction of the Emperor.

Sec. 69. The internal formation and constitution of the Grand Duchy of Transylvania shall be fixed by a new statute for that country, on the principle of its complete independence of the kingdom of Hungary, and of the equality of rights of all the nations which inhabit the country.

Sec. 70. The institution of the military border[3] shall be maintained for the protection of the integrity of the Empire, and, as a component part of the Imperial army, the same shall be placed under the command of the Imperial Executive. The relations of property of the inhabitants of the military border shall have the same alleviations guaranteed by special statute which have been granted to the inhabitants of the other Crown lands.

Sec. 71. The constitution of the kingdom of Lombardy and Venice, and the relations of that Crown land to the Empire, shall be determined by a special statute.

Sec. 72. All the other Crown lands are to have their own special constitutions. The present provincial constitutions (*ständische Verfassungen*) lose their effect.

Sec. 73. The composition of the Diet depends on the interests of the respective countries. The members are chosen by direct elections.

Sec. 75. Every Diet has the right of participating in the legislation on the affairs of its province; it has the right to propose new laws, and to watch over the execution of existing statutes. Each provincial law requires the assent of the Emperor and of the Diet of the province.

CHAPTER VI—TREATING OF THE EXECUTIVE POWER

Sec. 79. The Executive power throughout the Empire, and in all the Crown lands, is one and indivisible. It belongs exclusively to the Emperor, who exercises it by his responsible Ministers, and by their functionaries.

Sec. 83. The Ministers are at the head of the administration of the Empire in general, and of the Crown lands in particular; they publish

[3] Mainly to the north of Bosnia and Serbia.

decrees, and watch over the execution of the laws for the empire and for the provinces.

Sec. 84. The Ministers are entitled, under their own responsibility, to suspend the execution of administrative measures which are opposed to the laws and to the common welfare. . . .

CHAPTER VIII—TREATING OF THE JUDICIAL POWER

Sec. 93. The judicial power shall be exercised by independent courts of justice.

Sec. 94. The administration of justice emanates from the Empire. Patrimonial courts are to be abolished.

Sec. 95. No judge appointed by the State can be suspended in his office, nor can he be dismissed from it, unless it be done by a competent judicial verdict; nor shall it be lawful to remove him from one position to another, or to discharge him with a pension, unless it be done by his express wish and desire.

Sec. 97. Justice shall generally be administered publicly, and by word of mouth, with the exception of cases in which publicity might endanger the public morality. All grave crimes (to be defined by law), political crimes, and cases of libel, are to be decided on by juries.

CHAPTER IX—TREATING OF THE SUPREME COURT OF JUSTICE OF THE EMPIRE

Sec. 100. A supreme court of justice of the Empire shall be instituted to decide on questions between the Empire and the Crown lands, or in matters of litigation of the Crown lands among themselves, unless indeed the subject falls within the province of the legislative Imperial power; and, further, in cases of violation of political rights, and in cases of the impeachment of Ministers and lieutenants of the Emperor, and in cases of conspiracies against the safety of the Monarch or the country; and, lastly, in all cases of treason. . . .

CHAPTER X—TREATING OF THE TAXATION OF THE EMPIRE

Sec. 102. All taxes and rates for the purposes of the Empire, and of the provinces, shall be imposed by laws.

Sec. 103. The expenditure and income of the country must annually be stated in a budget, the same to be fixed by law.

Sec. 104. The national debt is guaranteed by the Empire.

CHAPTER XII—CONTAINING CERTAIN GENERAL REGULATIONS

Sec. 112. For the time being, and until the organic laws required by this constitution shall have been made in a constitutional manner, the necessary decrees will be issued by the Emperor in Council.

Sec. 113. The existing laws and decrees remain in force until the new ones take effect.

Sec. 115. Alterations of this constitution of the Empire may be moved by the first Diet, in the usual way of legislation; but, in future, resolutions purposing such alterations shall not be moved, except in the presence of three-fourths of the number of all the members, and they shall not be allowed to pass without the assent of two-thirds of the members present. . . .

V.4 THE END OF THE WAR IN HUNGARY

The solution for Hungary proposed in the Austrian constitution of 4th March 1849 (see V.3.A, Section 66), was rejected by the Hungarian Parliament, which replied with a declaration of the separation of Hungary from Austria on 14th April 1849. The Hungarian rebellion was finally crushed with Russian help, which the Emperor, Francis Joseph, solicited in April. Russian troops entered Hungary in June. In August, the rebellion was over.

V.4.A Extracts from the Hungarian declaration of separation from Austria are taken from Headley, *Life of Kossuth*, pp. 161 ff.

We, the legally constituted representatives of the Hungarian nation assembled in Diet, do by these presents solemnly proclaim, in maintenance of the inalienable natural rights of Hungary, with all its dependencies, to occupy the position of an independent European State— that the House of Hapsburg-Lorraine, as perjured in the sight of God and man, has forfeited its right to the Hungarian throne. At the same time, we feel ourselves bound in duty to make known the motives and reasons which have impelled us to this decision, that the civilised world may learn we have taken this step not out of overweening confidence in our own wisdom, or out of revolutionary excitement, but that it is an act of the last necessity, adopted to preserve from utter destruction a nation persecuted to the limit of the most enduring patience.

Three hundred years have passed since the Hungarian nation, by free election, placed the House of Austria upon its throne, in accordance with stipulations made on both sides, and ratified by treaty. These three hundred years have been, for the country, a period of uninterrupted suffering.

The Creator has blessed this country with all the elements of wealth and happiness. Its area of 100,000 square miles presents in varied profusion innumerable sources of prosperity. Its population, numbering nearly fifteen millions, feels the glow of youthful strength within its veins and has shown temper and docility which warrant its proving at once the main organ of civilisation in Eastern Europe, and the guardian of that civilisation when attacked. Never was a more grateful task appointed to a reigning dynasty by the dispensation of Providence than that which devolved upon the House of Hapsburg-Lorraine. It would have sufficed to do nothing that could impede the development of the country. Had this been the rule observed, Hungary would now rank amongst the most prosperous nations. It was only necessary that it should not envy the Hungarians the moderate share of constitutional liberty which they timidly maintained during the difficulties of a thousand years with rare fidelity to their sovereigns, and the House of Hapsburg might long have counted this nation amongst the most faithful adherents of the throne.

This dynasty, however, which can at no epoch point to a ruler who based his power on the freedom of the people, adopted a course towards this nation, from father to son, which deserves the appellation of perjury.

Confiding in the justice of an eternal God, we, in the face of the civilised world, in reliance upon the natural rights of the Hungarian nation, and upon the power it has developed to maintain them, further impelled by that sense of duty which urges every nation to defend its existence, do hereby declare and proclaim in the name of the nation legally represented by us the following:

1st. Hungary, with Transylvania, as legally united with it and its dependencies, are hereby declared to constitute a free, independent, sovereign state. The territorial unity of this state is declared to be inviolable, and its territory to be indivisible.

2nd. The House of Hapsburg-Lorraine—having by treachery, perjury, and levying of war against the Hungarian nation, as well as by its outrageous violation of all compacts, in breaking up the integral territory of the kingdom, in the separation of Transylvania, Croatia, Sclavonia, Fiume, and its districts from Hungary—further, by compassing the destruction of the independence of the country by arms, and by calling in the disciplined army of a foreign power, for the purpose of annihilating its nationality, by violation both of the Pragmatic Sanction and of treaties concluded between Austria and Hungary, on which the alliance between the two countries depended—is, as treacherous and perjured, forever excluded from the throne of the united states of Hungary and Transylvania, and all their possessions and dependencies, and is hereby deprived of the style and title, as well as of the armorial bearings belonging to the crown of Hungary, and declared to be banished forever from the united countries and their dependencies and possessions. They are therefore declared to be deposed, degraded, and banished forever from the Hungarian territory.

3rd. The Hungarian nation, in the exercise of its rights and sovereign will, being determined to assume the position of a free and independent state amongst the nations of Europe, declares it to be its intention to establish and maintain friendly and neighbourly relations with those states with which it was formerly united under the same sovereign, as well as to contract alliances with all other nations.

4th. The form of government to be adopted for the future will be fixed by the Diet of the nation.

And this resolution of ours we shall proclaim and make known to all the nations of the civilised world, with the conviction that the Hungarian nation will be received by them amongst the free and independent nations of the world, with the same friendship and free acknowledgement of its rights which the Hungarians proffer to other countries.

We also hereby proclaim and make known to all the inhabitants of the united states of Hungary and Transylvania, and their dependencies, that all authorities, communes, towns, and the civil officers both in the counties and cities, are completely set free and released from all the obligations under which they stood, by oath or otherwise, to the said House of Hapsburg-Lorraine, and that any individual daring to contravene this decree, and by word or deed in any way to aid or abet any one violating it, shall be treated and punished as guilty of high treason. And by the publication of this decree, we hereby bind and oblige all the inhabitants of these counties to obedience to the Government now instituted formally, and endowed with all necessary legal powers. . . .

V.4.B   Extracts from the declaration of the Russian Government on Hungary signed by the Chancellor, Nesselrode, are from *Annual Register*, 1849, pp. 333 f.

St. Petersburg, April 27

. . . The insurrection in Hungary has of late made so much progress that Russia cannot possibly remain inactive. A temporary insufficiency of the Austrian forces, divided as they are on many points, has favoured the progress of the insurgents from the Theiss to the Danube. They occupy almost the whole of Upper Hungary and of Transylvania. Their revolutionary plans have swollen in magnitude in proportion to the success of their arms. The Magyar movement has been adulterated by the presence of Polish emigrants, forming whole corps of the Hungarian army, and by the influence of certain persons, as Bem and Dembinski, who make plans of attack and defence, and it has come to be a general insurrection, especially of Poland. That insurrection was to break out in Galicia first, and in our own provinces afterwards. The intrigues of these insurrectionists undermined Galicia and Cracow; they endeavoured to foil our endeavours and throw off Turkey, to restore tranquillity in the Danubian principalities by encouraging the Moldavians and Wallachians to resistance, and they still keep the vast extent of our frontiers in a perpetual state of excitement and ferment. Such a state of things endangers our dearest interests, and prudence compels us to anticipate the difficulties it prepares for us. The Austrian Government being for the moment unable to oppose a sufficient power to the insurgents, it has formally requested His Majesty the Emperor to assist in the repression of a rebellion which endangers the tranquillity of the two empires. It was but natural that the two Cabinets should understand one another on this point of common interest, and our troops have consequently advanced into Galicia, to co-operate with Austria against the Hungarian rebellion. We trust the Governments that are equally interested in the maintenance of tranquillity will not misunderstand our motives of action. The Emperor is sorry to quit the passive and expectant position which he has hitherto maintained, but still he remains faithful to the spirit of his former declarations, for, in granting to every State the right to arrange its own political constitution according to its own mind, and refraining from interfering with any alterations of their form of government which such States might think proper to make, His Majesty reserved to himself his full liberty of action in case the reaction of revolutions near him should tend to endanger his own safety or the political equilibrium on the frontiers of his empire. Our safety is endangered by what is now being done and prepared in Hungary. This is clearly proved by the insurgents' own plans and endeavours, and any attack of theirs against the existence and the unity of the Austrian monarchy would also be an attack upon those territorial possessions which His Majesty, according to the spirit and the letter of the treaties, deems necessary for the equilibrium of Europe and the safety of his own States. Let it even be granted that passing circumstances might give a short-lived existence to an independent Hungary, it must be clear to every one who is acquainted with the vast powers and resources of Austria that such a State cannot have any hope of duration. But raised on the basis of anarchy, and imbued with that hostile spirit which the Hungarian chiefs have against Russia, there is, nevertheless, a greater danger for us in the movement, at the extension of which we dare not to connive. In protecting his Polish and Danubian provinces from the scourge of a propaganda which means to convulse them, and by granting the assistance which the Austrian Government claims at his hands, the Emperor flatters himself that he acts in his own interest, and also in the interest of European peace and tranquillity.

V.5 BRITAIN AND AUSTRIA

There was considerable sympathy in Britain, particularly among the Whigs, liberals and radicals, for the Italians and the Hungarians in their striving for independence. The punitive measures taken by the Austrians in Hungary after the crushing of the revolt did the Habsburg Empire great harm in Britain. When Austria and Russia put pressure on the Ottoman Porte to surrender Kossuth and other Hungarian refugees who had fled there, Lord Palmerston took successful measures to prevent this.

V.5.A   The extract of Palmerston's letter of 9th September 1849, to Ponsonby, the British Minister in Vienna, is from E. Ashley, *The Life of Henry John Temple, Viscount Palmerston 1846–1865*, I, pp. 139 ff.

. . . The Austrians are really the greatest brutes that ever called themselves by the undeserved name of civilised men. Their atrocities in Galicia, in Italy, in Hungary, in Transylvania are only to be equalled by the proceedings of the Negro race in Africa and Haiti. Their late exploit of flogging forty old people, including two women at Milan, some of the victims being gentlemen, is really too blackguard and disgusting a proceeding. As to working upon their feelings of generosity and gentlemanlikeness that is out of the question, because such feelings exist not in a set of officials who have been trained up in the school of Metternich, and the men in whose minds such inborn feelings have not been crushed by court and office power have been studiously excluded from public affairs, and can only blush in private for the disgrace which such things throw upon their country. But I do hope that *you* will not fail constantly to bear in mind the country and the Government which you represent, and that you will maintain the dignity and honour of England by expressing *openly* and *decidedly* the disgust which such proceedings excite in the public mind in this country; and that you will not allow the Austrians to imagine that the public opinion of England is to be gathered from articles put into the 'Times' by Austrian agents in London, nor from the purchased support of the 'Chronicle', nor from the servile language of Tory lords and ladies in London, nor from the courtly notions of royal dukes and duchesses. I have no great opinion of Schwarzenberg's statesmanlike qualities unless he is very much altered from what he was when I knew him; but, at least he has lived in England, and must know something of English feelings and ideas, and he must be capable of understanding the kind of injury which all these barbarities must do to the character of Austria in public opinion here; and I think that, in spite of his great reliance upon and fondness for Russia, he must see that the good opinion of England is of some value to Austria; if for nothing else, at least to act as a check upon the illwill towards Austria, which he supposes, or affects to suppose, is the great actuating motive of the revolutionary firebrand who now presides at the Foreign Office in Downing Street.

G

You might surely find an opportunity of drawing Schwarzenberg's attention to these matters, which may be made intelligible to him, and which a British ambassador has a right to submit to his consideration. There is another view of the matter which Schwarzenberg, with his personal hatred of the Italians, would not choose to comprehend, but which, nevertheless, is well deserving of attention, and that is the obvious tendency of these barbarous proceedings to perpetuate in the minds of the Italians indelible hatred of Austria; and as the Austrian Government cannot hope to govern Italy always by the sword, such inextinguishable hatred is not an evil altogether to be despised.

The rulers of Austria (I call them not statesmen or stateswomen) have now brought their country to this remarkable condition, that the Emperor holds his various territories at the goodwill and pleasure of three external Powers. He holds Italy just as long as and no longer than France chooses to let him have it. The first quarrel between Austria and France will drive the Austrians out of Lombardy and Venice. He holds Hungary and Galicia just as long as and no longer than Russia chooses to let him have them. The first quarrel with Russia will detach those countries from the Austrian crown. He hold his German provinces by a tenure dependent, in a great degree, upon feelings and opinions which it will be very difficult for him and his ministers either to combine with or to stand out against.

The remedy against these various dangers which are rapidly undermining the Austrian empire would be generous conciliation; but instead of that, the Austrian Government know no method of administration but what consists in flogging, imprisoning, and shooting. The *Austrians* know no argument but force.

V.5.B   The extract of Palmerston's memorandum of 2nd October 1849, is from Ashley, *The Life of Henry John Temple, Viscount Palmerston*, I, pp. 144 ff.

. . . I had a conversation of some length this afternoon with Baron Brunnow [the Russian Minister in London]. His object at first was to show that the best course for England and France to pursue was to remain perfectly quiet, to wait for events, and to trust to the moderation and good feeling of the Emperor to settle the matter amicably with the Sultan, without any injury to the independence of the Porte. In other words, to leave the Emperor time to frighten the Sultan into acquiescence.

I said I agreed with him that the affair is in itself of very slight importance, and that I could not but believe with him that the moderation and good feeling of the two Imperial Governments would lead them to respect the Sultan's repugnance to give up men who have thrown them-

selves on his protection; and that Austria and Russia would be satisfied
with that security which they had a right to ask, and which the Sultan
is ready to afford them, and which would be given by sending into the
interior of Turkey such of the refugees as may have no means of sup-
porting themselves, and by requiring those who are better off to leave
Turkey and come to France or England. With regard to our doing nothing, I said we could not take that course, because the Turkish Government had officially asked us for help in their embarrassment, and we
had determined to address a friendly representation in favour of the
Sultan to the Austrian and Russian Governments. He said he hoped our
representation would be carefully worded, in order that it might not do
harm instead of good. That all men have their faults as well as their
merits. That the fault of his Emperor is that he is very sensitive, and
that anything like the language of menace might prevent him from
doing what he might otherwise be disposed to do. I said that nothing of
that kind would be sent; that we should express our hope, and the
French Government would probably do the same, that the two Emperors
would be satisfied with the removal of danger from their frontiers, and
would not insist on the surrender of men whom they would not know
what to do with when they got them. For it would not be supposed, for
instance, that the Emperor of Russia could take any pleasure in shooting
a cripple like Bem. Brunnow said it would be a pity that such representations should be made by England and France jointly or concurrently; that the joint action of the two would of itself have the appearance of something like menace. I said that this was the unavoidable
result of the fact that the Porte had made application to the two Powers;
but he should remember that this system of duality did not begin with
us; that the two Imperial Governments have been jointly pressing and
threatening at Constantinople, and the Sultan being hard driven by his
two great, strapping neighbours, naturally looked about him to see where
he could find two friends to come and take his part. That the two
Imperial ministers, no doubt from over-zeal, or from a wish to carry
their point by a *coup de main*, and gain credit with their Governments,
had gone probably further than they had been instructed to do, and
had not only held very high and threatening language, but had suspended their diplomatic intercourse, a thing of no real importance, but
meant as a means of intimidation. Brunnow agreed it was a foolish step
to have taken, and repeated a story he had told me before, of how Lord
Aberdeen had suspended his diplomatic intercourse with Aali Pasha
when ambassador in London, because the Turkish Government would
not pay two thousand pounds to Captain Walker for services performed;
and how he, Baron Brunnow, had convinced Lord Aberdeen that he
had done a foolish thing, and persuaded him to resume intercourse with
the Turkish ambassador. I said that the two Imperial Governments were

no doubt entitled to ask for the surrender of their respective subjects, though the Russian demand, being founded upon the events of the Polish war of 1832 [sic], and not upon the Hungarian war of 1849, was somewhat out of date; but that, on the other hand, the Sultan was entitled by his treaties to decline to surrender, and to prefer the other alternatives of either sending the refugees into the interior of his territory, or requiring them to leave Turkey. Brunnow entirely agreed with me in this interpretation of the treaty between Russia and Turkey. He said the treaty of Kainardgi had, like all treaties between Russia and Turkey, been drawn up by the Russian negotiators, and that they had purposely and intentionally left a choice, because it was much more likely that Turks would fly to Russia than that Russians would fly to Turkey; and the Russian Government did not wish to be obliged to give up political refugees to be handed over to the bowstring. With men guilty of ordinary criminal offences the case was different, and the obligation more strict to give such persons up. Brunnow fully and distinctly admitted that the treaty, while it authorised the Emperor to demand surrender, equally authorised the Sultan to decline surrender, and to prefer the sending out of his country. And Brunnow's own opinion seemed to be that the Emperor would, or at least ought to, acquiesce in the Sultan's decision. But it must be borne in mind that his object was avowedly to persuade us to do nothing, and that he professed himself to be without communications from his own Government.

VI

EPILOGUE

THE CONSERVATIVE FORCES were well in control of the European continent once more by the autumn of 1849. However, a number of differences of opinion about the future of Germany still prevailed between the two leading powers there, Prussia and Austria. During 1850, Prussia tried to mobilise the North of Germany under her leadership, whereas Austria was attempting to re-activate the Federal Assembly of the German Confederation. Early in November 1850, troops of both sides clashed briefly on the territory of the Electorate of Hesse, a state included in the Prussian-led 'Union', but whose ruler favoured Austria. An actual war was avoided by Frederick William's abandonment of Prussian initiatives in Germany. Russia played a leading part in forcing Prussia to come to terms with Austria. The German Confederation was restored, the Hessian conflict settled and the way paved hopefully for a peaceful solution of the Schleswig-Holstein question, largely on the basis of the status quo ante 1848. On the extinction of the male line of the Danish royal house, Christian of Glücksburg was to succeed to all the territories of the Danish monarchy, including the Elbe duchies.

VI.1. OLMÜTZ

The convention of Olmütz concluded between Austria and Prussia on 29th November 1850, marked a return to the dualism of the two powers in the German Confederation.

VI.1.A The Olmütz declaration was signed by the Austrian Prime Minister, Prince Schwarzenberg, and by the new Prussian Prime Minister, Otto von Manteuffel, who succeeded to the office on the death of Count Brandenburg. Extracts from Hertslet, *The Map of Europe by Treaty*, II, pp. 1143 ff.

At the confidential Conference which took place yesterday and today between the Undersigned, the following propositions were set forth as possible points for the Settlement of existing Differences, and as means adapted for the prevention of conflicts; and they will be submitted as speedily as possible for the final sanction of the High Governments concerned.

§ 1. The Governments of Austria and Prussia declare that it is their intention to bring about the Final and Definitive Settlement of the Electoral Hessian and Holstein affairs, by the common decision of all the German Governments.

§ 2. In order to render the co-operation of the Governments represented at Frankfurt and of the other German Governments possible, there shall be named, as soon as may be, on the part of the members of the Confederation represented at Frankfurt, as well as on the part of Prussia and her Allies, a Commissioner for each, who will have to agree upon the measures to be taken in common.

§ 3. As it is, however, for the general interest that both in Electoral Hesse and in Holstein, there should be established a legal state of things conformable with the Fundamental Laws of the Confederation, and rendering the fulfilment of the Federal duties possible; as, moreover, Austria has given to the full, in her own name, and in that of the States allied with her, the guarantees for the security of the interests of Prussia required by the latter in regard to the occupation of the Electorate, the two Governments of Austria and Prussia agree, in order to proceed with the discussion of the questions, and without prejudice to the future decision, as follows:

A. In Electoral Hesse, Prussia will oppose no impediment to the action of the Troops called in by the Elector, and, therefore, will issue the necessary orders to the Generals in command there, to allow a thoroughfare by the military roads occupied by Prussia. The two Governments of Austria and Prussia will, in concert with their Allies, call upon His Royal Highness the Elector to give his consent for one battalion of the Troops called in by the Electoral Government, and one Royal Prussian battalion to remain at Cassel, in order to Maintain Tranquillity and Order.

B. After consultation with their Allies, Austria and Prussia will send to Holstein, and that as speedily as possible, joint Commissioners, who shall demand of the Stadtholdership, in the name of the Confederation, the Cessation of Hostilities, the withdrawal of the troops behind the Eyder, and the reduction of the Army to one-third of its now existing strength, threatening common execution in case of refusal. On the other hand, both Governments will endeavour to prevail on the Danish Government not to station in the Duchy of Schleswig more troops than are necessary for the preservation of Tranquillity and Order.

§ 4. Ministerial Conferences will immediately take place at Dresden. The invitation to them will be issued by Austria and Prussia conjointly, and will be so arranged that the Conferences may be opened about the middle of December.

VI.2 THE DANISH SUCCESSION AND THE SCHLESWIG–HOLSTEIN QUESTION

The ethnic issues of the Schleswig-Holstein question were further complicated by the imminent extinction of the male line of the Danish royal house. The European Great Powers eventually agreed that Prince Christian of Glücksburg, the member of a junior branch of the Danish royal house, should be designated heir to all the Danish dominions, including the Duchies of Schleswig and Holstein of which the King of Denmark was Duke.

VI.2.A Extracts from the Treaty of London of 8th May 1852, concluded between Great Britain, Austria, France, Prussia, Russia, and Sweden and Norway, on the one part, and Denmark on the other part, are from Hertslet, *The Map of Europe by Treaty*, II, pp. 1152 ff.

... *Article I.* After having taken into serious consideration the interests of his Monarchy, His Majesty the King of Denmark, with the assent of His Royal Highness the Hereditary Prince, and of his nearest cognates, entitled to the Succession by the Royal Law of Denmark, as well as in concert with His Majesty the Emperor of All the Russias, Head of the elder Branch of the House of Holstein-Gottorp, having declared his wish to regulate the order of Succession in his dominions in such manner that, in default of issue male in a direct line from King Frederick III of Denmark, his Crown should devolve upon His Highness the Prince Christian of Schleswig-Holstein-Sonderbourg-Glücksbourg, and upon the issue of the marriage of that Prince with Her Highness the Princess Louisa of Schleswig-Holstein-Sonderbourg-Glücksbourg, born a Princess of Hesse, by order of Primogeniture from Male to Male; the High Contracting Parties, appreciating the wisdom of the views which have determined the eventual adoption of that arrangement, engage by common consent, in case the contemplated contingency should be realised, to acknowledge in His Highness the Prince Christian of Schleswig-Holstein-Sonderbourg-Glücksbourg, and his issue male in the direct line by his marriage with the said Princess, the Right of Succeeding to the whole of the Dominions now united under the sceptre of His Majesty the King of Denmark.

Article II. The High Contracting Parties, acknowledging as permanent the principle of the Integrity of the Danish Monarchy, engage to take into consideration the further propositions which His Majesty the King of Denmark may deem it expedient to address to them in case (which God forbid) the extinction of the issue male, in the direct line, of His Highness the Prince Christian of Schleswig-Holstein-Sonderbourg-Glücksbourg, by his marriage with Her Highness the Princess Louisa of

Schleswig-Holstein-Sonderbourg-Glücksbourg, born a Princess of Hesse, should become imminent.

Article III. It is expressly understood that the reciprocal Rights and Obligations of His Majesty the King of Denmark, and of the Germanic Confederation, concerning the Duchies of Holstein and Lauenburg, Rights and Obligations established by the Federal Act of 1815, and by the existing Federal Right, shall not be affected by the present Treaty. . . .

FINAL COMMENTS

BEFORE LEAVING THE revolutionary period behind, one might just for a moment try to recapture the exciting atmosphere of those days. For a time, the revolutionaries and those who had come into office thanks to their deeds held some of the strongest powers in Europe at bay. France may have been perennially prone to changes of regime, but the Hohenzollern monarchy in Prussia before 1848 gave the impression of stability. To make the King of Prussia bare his head to the fallen of the barricades was no mean achievement for a revolution. Similarly, the disruption and virtual paralysis of the Habsburg Empire for a time was a dramatic event. For several months in 1848 the Austrian court and the central authorities of the Monarchy were reduced to trying to pacify all those who made demands on them on ideological, ethnic and historical grounds. The centre on which the Empire had so long relied, the city of Vienna, was in the hands of the radicals, mainly Germans, so that at times the flight of the court from the capital of the Empire was the only way to ensure the continued operation of orderly government. Indeed, it may be said that the radicals were stronger in Vienna than in any major city in Europe, as they proved by withstanding a prolonged siege in October. University students in the Academic Legion played a considerable part in the radical movement in Vienna. While ethnic Germans of the Habsburg Empire provided the strongest support for the revolutionary activities in the Austrian capital, Vienna also attracted radical non-Germans, particularly Poles, as did Berlin. The reduction of Vienna involved a considerable military effort on the part of the authorities. The Hungarian insurrection was not, in the end, finally mastered without foreign aid. Fighting in Italy was prolonged, though here not only revolutionary forces, but established states, like Sardinia, were involved. Even without Sardinian support, the republics established by more radical forces were only subdued after a prolonged struggle. In the summer of 1849, risings in several German states had to be crushed with outside—largely Prussian—help.

For a time emperors, kings and grand-dukes were forced to flee from the revolutionaries and the lives of their ministers were not safe, as is shown by the murders of the Austrian minister of war, Count Latour, in October and of the Papal minister Pellegrino Rossi in November

1848. But in the end it was the revolutionaries who had to fight for their lives and their liberty. We have seen how the established powers one after another rose to the challenge and reasserted their authority. Are there deeper reasons for this change of fortune?

Perhaps the first factor to be noted is that the original revolutionary mood cannot last. There are several reasons for this. For a time the abnormality of uprisings may provide a welcome relief from the drabness of everyday life, though casualties soon add a sombre note. Still, a strong enthusiasm and a feeling of togetherness are generated which for a certain period make men devote their attention more to the affairs of the community than to their own individual concerns. Sooner or later, the realities of individual livelihood have to be faced. This sets one limit to the duration of revolutionary preparedness. If the insurgents take over the Government on the basis of some permanence, like the Communists in Russia in 1917, they will at some stage be accused of being too conservative. Unless the revolution is at once crushed without the necessity for concessions, the authorities have to go some way to meet the demands which have been made. This success of the rising will in itself at once weaken the revolutionary impulse. Not all the demands will normally be fulfilled and indeed cannot be, for many of them, for instance in 1848, were vague, ill-conceived or mutually contradictory. The closer the opposition came to their goal of power, the more the divergences in their views became exposed. While an opposition may indulge in disagreements and may even be helped by being able to draw on a wide range of support at a time of revolution, a government must have a single policy. In France, Germany, Italy and the Habsburg Monarchy, radicals and moderate liberals found difficulty in collaborating after the revolution. Certainly in France and Germany, the coalition between them came to an end within the first few weeks and months. In Germany, the moderate liberals won the race for government office, in France the radicals were soon eliminated after first participating in a coalition. In Italy, both groups were influential at different times and in different places and no clear victory was achieved by either in 1848 and 1849. In Austria, the radicals on the whole remained in opposition, while the moderate liberals provided some ministers. The position is complicated by the difficulty of classifying standpoints at a time of constant change and fluctuation, particularly in the case of Alexander Bach, who for a time in the late spring and early summer of 1848 flirted with the radicals, thereafter to take office and to move increasingly to the Right. It was only in Hungary that the radicals eventually predominated, thanks to the leadership given by Louis Kossuth and to the exacerbation of the conflict.

Was the failure of the radicals to dominate the Government, except in Hungary, due simply to coincidence and perhaps to intrigue, as some of them felt then and afterwards? There is likely to have been some general reason not connected with fortuitous circumstances, as they did not even succeed in France, where they did not have to contend with possibly or allegedly unreliable rulers and where the writ of the conservative powers did not run even after 1849. It may be that the European radicals could make or mar whatever reforms were put in hand, initially at any rate, as a result of the revolution they had made. Historians are not likely to agree on their interpretation of the radicals, or on the extent of their responsibility, as their own political views and assumptions are involved. All the present writer can do is to put forward his own interpretation, in the knowledge that it will be challenged.

One of the reasons why the radicals failed in 1848 was that they did not generally possess a majority in the regions involved. What they were trying to do was (in the hackneyed phrase of school history essays) to be 'ahead of their time'. In Germany and Austria, they did not carry most people with them in their republican views. In France, the moderate republicans were not sufficiently advanced for them. In Italy, if the eventual triumph of monarchism over republicanism in the national movement is any indication, the country was not yet ready for the abandonment of monarchy. Among Poles radicalism was strong, because their oppressors were identified with the monarchical principle. In Hungary, there was support for Kossuth's radicalism at the height of the struggle, but we may note that on the whole the Magyars were quite content to serve under the Habsburgs after the *Ausgleich* of 1867, when their interests were secured. The rejection of republicanism and the clinging to monarchy were part of a popular refusal to move too far too quickly. Rapid change does not usually take place in response to popular opinion, but is enforced by the authorities, from the enlightened despots in the eighteenth century to the communists in the twentieth. Certainly public opinion in Europe was not ready for major political, social, economic and religious changes in 1848. Even in France, radical demands are heard mainly from the cities, particularly from Paris. The majority of the population, still in rural districts, was much more conservative. Mediatisation was advocated in Germany not only by the radicals but by many moderate liberals. Yet opposition to the dissolution of smaller states came not only from the princes, but also from their peoples. Particularism was deeply ingrained in German life and could not so easily be eradicated. In general, the radicals were too far off centre to be representative of a major segment of public opinion. In countries in which the greater part of the people still held religious beliefs or were at any rate regular churchgoers, the rejection of these beliefs and traditions by the radicals was bound to separate them from the masses. This leads to the question of personalities, an intensely subjective topic.

Those prominent in the radical movement, Louis Blanc in France, Arnold Ruge and Julius Fröbel in Germany, Mazzini and Manin in Italy, Louis Kossuth in Hungary, were highly educated men, some of them with private means. The leader of the Left in the Frankfurt Parliament, Robert Blum, who was executed in Vienna, came from a somewhat humbler background, which accounted for some of his difficulties in the assembly. Stephan Born, too, one of the chief organisers of the workers' movement in Germany in 1848, worked his way up the social scale. But in general the leaders of the radical movement, Ferdinand Lassalle, Karl Marx and Friedrich Engels included, came from the bourgeois class—much despised by them—and benefited from its superior wealth. They never had to live on a pittance or knew what long-term unemployment or social upheaval meant. Many of them were the 'terribles simplificateurs' who were liable to do great harm by propounding radical remedies for complex problems and by advocating force in the last resort to achieve their aims, even though the pursuit of them was ultimately hopeless and did not stand any chance of success in the short run. They were arrogant, if this is the correct term to describe men who believed they were the only ones who knew the answers to the problems of the day, and they were undeterred by the rejection of their views by the vast majority. The present writer has formed the impression that some of them—like the German philosopher Arnold Ruge—were frivolous in their revolutionary activities, treating losses of life lightheartedly and regarding revolution as an exciting adventure, in the hope that they would if necessary be able to flee to safer parts, such as Switzerland, Britain or the United States of America, taking their money with them. They did not sufficienty appreciate the far greater problems of the humble folk who followed their call and who did not have the same resources and connections to make good their escape. In spite of their perseverance, devotion to the cause and courage, the leaders of the radical movement in 1848 were often not practical men, but dilettantes. But if they did not succeed then, they blazed the trail for their more fortunate successors, who forged and led great mass movements. They were right in the long term, but in the short term they for a time destroyed constitutionalism and the tender beginnings of representative government by using force when they could not gain their ends by persuasion. It was they who made the task of moderate liberal governments impossible in Germany and Austria.

This is not to imply that the moderate liberals made the most of their opportunity. Some opportunities do not recur so easily and in Germany they did not have another chance until 1918, though thanks to Cavour the liberals were able to establish some form of parliamentary control in Italy. The German moderate liberals have often been charged with being impractical, the very criticism that the present writer makes of the radicals. Considering the difficulties of their position, between the princes and the radicals, the liberal ministers did not do badly. They very quickly adapted themselves to their new situations and duties. They failed in the 1848 period because of the complex relationship between their liberalism and the German national movement, though not in the way often suggested.

It has been asserted that the German liberals sacrificed their constitutionalism to nationalism in the long run, that even in 1848 their liberalism was only skin-deep and that they propagated an unbounded nationalism providing a foretaste of the Nazis. This seems wide of the mark. Rather it may be suggested, that not all the liberals in all the different German states were prepared to sacrifice their particularist interests on the altar of German unity and that erstwhile members of the opposition considerably strengthened the individual states whose governments they entered. There was indeed some danger that states which had developed parliamentary government would be more difficult to fit into a united Germany than the pre-1848 regimes. The liberal ministers were representative of public opinion in their states and in many ways Germany was not ready for unity in 1848. What they did not realise sufficiently was that they had a common interest in the maintenance of constitutional government and that they should have established some co-operation, even if they did not want to end their particularism completely. Also prominent personalities among the Rhenish liberals did not see eye to eye. Already in 1848 liberalism showed one of its great defects from the point of view of political organisation, its individualism.

There was no necessary contradiction between liberalism and nationalism. The liberals in Germany were no more and no less nationalistic than in other countries. The German radicals were much more intolerant in their attitude to the interests of other nationalities, for instance towards the Danes over Schleswig-Holstein.

It has been held that the liberals were doomed to political failure because they were too much the party of capital and of the bourgeoisie. But who else could have provided the ability and leisure for political leadership in European countries before the spread of popular education and in the midst of intensive industrialisation? The radicals in 1848 were hardly better placed socially in this respect. The initially rather limited composition of the leadership did not necessarily prejudice an eventual widening of the social base. Indeed the combined effects of increasing industrialisation and of the 1848 revolutions was that change was bound to be intensified in the long run.

The revolution was not simply a failure and not all the institutions set up following it vanished. In Prussia, for instance, many of the stipulations of the granted (*oktroyierte*) constitution of December 1848 were whittled away, but the chamber continued to function. This was shown in the constitutional crisis of the early 1860s, which Bismarck was called to solve. Great social reforms, like the liberation of the peasants in Austria, were not undone. Even if there was an attempt at first to establish a perhaps excessively rigid stability after the disorders, gradually government had to become more responsive to public opinion, and particularly to its constitutional and national demands. It is because of this remedial action that nothing like the 1848 revolutions occurred again in Europe until well into the First World War. By then, many of the aims of 1848, both constitutional and national, had been realised. How was the hold of the conservative powers, which seemed to be so strong in 1850, loosened?

The solvent was diplomatic. It was the Eastern question, leading to the Crimean War, which broke up the alliance of Austria and Russia, though this had apparently been cemented even further by the crushing of the Hungarian rebellion. *Realpolitik*, a policy promoting the real interests of the country, in the 1850s replaced legitimism and the ideological co-operation of the three Eastern powers. Even Nicholas I may have been a partial convert to *Realpolitik*, perhaps after witnessing the events of 1848, which revealed possibilities of change not before suspected. The focusing on the interests of nationalities, particularly German, Italian and Slav, had created a new climate of opinion against which not even conservative governments could insulate themselves. With the help of the Emperor Napoleon III—whose rise was another consequence of 1848—the first steps towards Italian unification were taken in 1859, which in turn opened the way for moves towards a German national state in the 1860s under Bismarck. Both Italian and German unification owe much to the dress rehearsal of 1848.

In the meantime, a hard fate lay in store for many of the participants in the attempts at a second revolution. The cases which attracted the most attention in Europe, particularly in Britain, were some of those resulting from the punitive measures taken after the crushing of the Hungarian rising. In Germany, the great epic was the freeing of the Bonn professor Gottfried Kinkel from the penitentiary by Carl Schurz. The latter was one of the many political refugees from Germany after 1848, became a general in the Union army during the American Civil War, a U.S. senator and Secretary for the Interior. Others were not so lucky and spent years in prison, to be gradually freed as conditions were relaxed, particularly from about 1858 onwards. The exodus of refugees was an important consequence of 1848, both for the countries to which they went and for those from which they came. The immigrants contributed something to the cultural life of the countries which received them, including the United States, Britain and Switzerland. When they were allowed to return to the lands of their origin, those who took advantage of the opportunity did so enriched by the experience they had received abroad, like Garibaldi when he returned to Italy, and Ludwig Bamberger, who became a liberal member of the German Reichstag. Perhaps the most amazing story was that of Julius Fröbel, who narrowly escaped execution in Vienna in November 1848.[1] Fröbel fled to the United States in 1849, and on his return to Europe in the early 1860s worked as a propagandist for the 'Great German' plans of the Habsburg Monarchy, only to accept a consulate from Bismarck in the 1870s. One of Bismarck's closest confidants in office was Lothar Bucher, who had belonged to the Extreme Left in 1848, had afterwards been sentenced to prison and was for a decade a refugee in London. The co-architect of the Dual Alliance of 1879, the Hungarian Count Andrassy, had fought against the Austrians in 1848 and had spent years in exile. While the second revolutions initially led to an exacerbation of divisions, eventually even the former radicals contributed something to the further development of their countries, in co-operation with men who had come from the conservative camp. The moderate liberals were able to play a part again even earlier, in Germany for instance from 1858, during the 'New Era' of the Prince Regent—later King William I—of Prussia.

In this way, the revolutions of 1848 remained interwoven with later history. As some of the ideas of the revolutionary period were realised or resisted, so interpretations changed. Different factors were given prominence and often the struggles of the past were seen from the point of view of the conflicts of the present. Perhaps the greatest disservice done to history by this topical interest has been the tendency to view the events of 1848 and 1849 as a bilateral affair, as a fight between 'progress' and 'reaction'. With the lengthening of the perspective, there is now a greater readiness among historians to look at matters afresh, with some detachment.

There is still plenty of work to be done on this period. The study of each country has become highly specialised. That has perhaps tended to obscure the connections between the movements and events in the various countries. What contacts were there between the different radicals and, indeed, between the moderate liberals of various countries? How did they influence each other? Perhaps more is known about the circle of Marx and Engels than about any other radical group. But Marx and Engels were not central figures in 1848.

Of the main movements, the moderate liberals and the Catholic groups have probably been studied most closely. More knowledge is needed about what the different radical groups were trying to achieve, particularly about the relative weight of the political and economic-social parts of their programme. As to the conservatives, as the past recedes and the historian is less emotionally involved, it becomes easier

[1] See document IV. 4. D.

to judge them fairly. In the period from about 1870 to 1933, and to some extent still later, all those who opposed constitutionalism, democracy and national unification in Europe were simply written off as rather odd. Perhaps the fears of conservative governments were not all unjustified, even if their actions did not necessarily help to avert the developments they feared.

Then there are particular problems which need investigating further. We know something of the composition of, for example, the crowds of demonstrators in Berlin on 18th March, from the occupations of those that fell. But much more could be done on this aspect for each country concerned, along the lines of G. Rudé's *The crowd in the French Revolution*.[2] Where the material is scattered, as in the case of Germany, which in 1848 had nearly forty states, prolonged and patient research is needed to establish necessary details, such as voting participation and election results in the constituencies. For all the countries concerned, a systematic attempt is still needed to assemble the relevant source materials, including the private papers of groups such as the parliamentarians, and the correspondence of individuals. It seems likely that in the years to come the revolutionary period 1848–49 will continue to engage the attention of historians.

[2] Oxford, 1959.

BIBLIOGRAPHY

The editor thanks Mr. T. W. Riley for his assistance with the bibliography.

I—GENERAL

(a) Primary Sources in English

Annual Register for 1848, 1849 & seq., London.

HERTSLET, E. *Map of Europe by Treaty*. Vol. II, London, 1875.

The Times, London.

(b) General Works Covering the Revolutions of 1848

(i) *Books*

ASHLEY, E. *The Life of Henry John Temple, Viscount Palmerston*. Vol. I, London, 1876.

BELL, H. C. F. *Lord Palmerston*. (2 vol.). London, 1936.

BRINTON, C. *The Anatomy of Revolution*. New York, 1965.

BRUUN, G. *Revolution and Reaction*. Princeton, N.J., 1958.

BURY, J. P. *The Zenith of European Power, 1830–1870*. The New Cambridge Modern History. Vol. X, Cambridge, 1960.

CLAPHAM, J. H. *The Economic Development of France and Germany 1815–1914*. Cambridge, 1921.

COMITE FRANCAIS DES SCIENCES HISTORIQUES, *Congrès Historique du. Centenaire de la Révolution de 1848*. Paris, 1948.

DROZ, J., *Europe between Revolutions 1815–1848*. Trans., New York, 1967.

DROZ, J., L. GENT & J. VIDALENC. *L'Epoque Contemporaine. I: Réstaurations et Révolutions 1815–1871*. Paris. 1953.

EYCK, F. *The Prince Consort*. London, 1959.

FETJO, F. ed. *Opening of an Era, 1848. An Historical Symposium*. London, 1949.

GOOCH, G. P. *The Later Correspondence of Ld. John Russell, 1840–78*. London, 1925.

HEARDER, H. *Europe in the Nineteenth Century, 1830–1880*. London, 1966.

HOBSBAWM, E. J. *The Age of Revolution, 1789–1848*. New York, 1962.

LANGER, W. L. *Political and Social Upheaval, 1832–1852*. New York, 1969.

LASKI, H. J. *The Communist Manifesto: Socialist Landmark*. London, 1948.

MARX, K. & ENGELS, F. *The Communist Manifesto*. Toronto, n.d.

POSTGATE, R. W., *Story of a Year: 1848*. New York, 1956.

— ed. *Revolution from 1789 to 1906*. London, 1920.

ROBERTSON, P. *Revolutions of 1848: a Social History*. Princeton, 1952.

RUGGIERO, G. de. *The History of European Liberalism*. Trans. London, 1927.

STERN, A. *Geschichte Europas seit den Verträgen von 1815 bis zum Frankfurter Frieden von 1871.* vol. VII, Stuttgart, 1916.

WEILL, G. *L'Eveil des Nationalités et le Mouvement Libéral, 1815–1848.* Paris, 1930.

WHITRIDGE, A. *Men in Crisis, the Revolution of 1848.* New York, 1949.

WOODCOCK, G. ed. *A Hundred Years of Revolution: 1848 and After.* London, 1948.

WOODWARD, E. L. *Three Studies in European Conservatism: Metternich, Guizot, the Catholic Church in the Nineteenth Century.* London, 1929.

(ii) *Articles*

EYCK, E. 'Freiheit und Demokratie 1848–1948'. *Convegno di Scienze Morali Storiche e Filologiche. 4–10 Ottobre, 1948.* Rome: Accademia Nazionale (1949), pp. 23–95.

KOHN, H. 'The End of 1848'. *Current History* (May, 1949). Vol. 16, pp. 276–80.

NAMIER, L. B. '1848: the Revolution of the Intellectuals'. Originally in *Proceedings of the British Academy,* 30, (1944), pp. 161–282.

— 'Nationality and Liberty'. *Convegno di Science Morali Storiche e Filologiche. 4–10 Ottobre, 1948.* Rome: Accademia Nazionale (1949), pp. 162–184.

ROTHFELS, H. '1848: One Hundred Years After'. *Journal of Modern History,* XX, (December, 1948), no. 4, pp. 291–319.

II—FRANCE

(a) *General*

(i) *Books*

BOON, H. N. *Rêve et Realité dans l'oeuvre Economique et Sociale de Napoléon III.* The Hague, 1936.

CHEETHAM, F. H. *Louis Napoleon and the Genesis of the Second Empire.* New York, 1909.

DAUMARD, A. *La Bourgeoisie Parisienne de 1815 à 1848.* Paris, 1963.

DELAHODDE, L. *History of the Secret Societies and of the Republican Party of France from 1830 to 1848.* Philadelphia, 1856.

ELTON, G. *The Revolutionary Idea in France, 1789–1871.* London, 1931.

GUEDELLA, P. *The Second Empire: Bonapartism, the Prince, the President, the Emperor.* New York, 1922.

HELIE, F.-A. *Les Constitutions de la France.* Paris, 1880.

HERZEN, A. *My Past and Thoughts.* Translated by Constance Garnett. London, 1924–27.

HUGO, V. M. *Napoleon le petit. Présentation et nôtes de Francois Herbolt.* Paris, 1964.

MICHEL, H. *L'Idée de l'état: Essai sur l'Histoire des Théories Sociales et Politiques en France depuis la Révolution.* Paris, 1896.

MONTAGNE, P. *Le Compartement politique de l'armée à Lyons sous la monarchie de juillet et la seconde république.* Paris, 1966.

NAPOLÉON III. *Oeuvres de Napoléon III.* Paris, 1869.

OLLIVIER, E. *Journal 1846–1869.* Texte choisi et annoté par Théodore Zeldin et Anne Troisier de Diaz, Lief de Ramond Dumay. Paris, 1961.

SEIGNOBOS, C. *La Révolution de 1848 et l'Empire.* Paris, 1920–22.

SENIOR, N. W. *Journals kept in France and Italy from 1848 to 1852.* London, 1871.

SIMPSON, F. A. *Louis Napoleon and the Recovery of France, 1848–1856.* New York, 1951.

— *The Rise of Louis Napoleon.* New York, 1925.

SOLTAU, R. *French Political Thought in the Nineteenth Century.* New Haven, 1932.

STEIN, L. von. *Geschichte der Sozialen Bewegung in Frankreich von 1789 bis auf Unsere Tage.* Leipzig, 1850.

THIRRIA, H. *Napoléon III avant l'Empire.* Paris, 1895.

TOCQUEVILLE, A. de. *The Recollections of Alexis de Tocqueville.* New York, 1949.

WEILL, G. *Histoire du Parti Républicain en France de 1814 à 1870.* Paris, 1928.

(ii) *Articles*

AMANN, P. 'Revolution: a Redefinition'. *Political Science Quarterly,* 77, (March, 1962), pp. 36–53.

BARRY, J. '1848 Again?' *Horizon,* (Spring, 1969), pp. 66–83.

DANSETTE, A. 'Deuxième Republique et Second Empire', *Connaissance de l'Histoire.* Paris (1942).

GASS, O. 'Democracy and Revolution: a Commentary on Some Recent Publications'. *Commentary,* 29, (January, 1960), pp. 69–73.

THOMSON, D. 'Ideal of Fraternité (1789–1849)'. *Fortnightly,* 177, (June, 1952), pp. 415–21.

(b) *Revolutions of 1848*

(i) *Books*

D'ALMERAS, H. *La Vie Parisienne sous la Republique de 1848.* Paris, n.d.

D'ALTON-SHEE, E. Comte. *Souvenirs de 1847 et de 1848.* Paris, 1879.

BASTIDE, P. *Doctrines et Institutions Politiques de la Seconde Republique.* Paris, 1945.

BLANC, L. *Organisation du Travail.* Paris, 1848.

— *Pages d'Histoire de la Révolution de Février, 1848.* Paris, 1850.

BOURGIN, G. *1848. Naissance et Mort d'une Révolution.* Paris 1948.

BOUTEILLER, P. *La Révolution Française de 1848 vue par les Hongrois.* Paris, 1949.

CALMAN, A. R. *Ledru—Rollin and the Second French Republic.* New York, 1922.

CAMP, M. DU. *Souvenirs de l'Année 1848.* Paris, 1848.

CASSOU, J. *Quarante-huit*. Paris, 1939.

CAUSSIDIERE, M. *Memoirs*. Paris, 1849.

CORBON, A. *Le Secrèt du Peuple de Paris*. Paris, 1863.

CREMIEUX, A. *La Révolution de Février*. Paris, 1912.

DAUTRY, J. *Histoire de la Révolution de 1848 en France*. Paris, 1948.

DELVAU, A. *Les Murailles Révolutionnaires*. Paris, 1852.

DOLLEANS, E. & PUECH, J. L. *Proudhon et la Révolution de 1848*. Paris, 1948.

DOMMANGET, M. *Un Drâme Politique en 1848*. Paris, 1948.

DREYFUS, F. *L'Assistance sous la Seconde République, 1848–1851*. Paris, 1907.

DROZ, H. A. *Lamartine und die Revolution von 1848*. Zurich, 1919.

DUVEAU, G. *1848: The Making of a Revolution*, New York, 1968.

GARGAN, E. T. *Alexis de Tocqueville: The Critical Years 1848–1851*. Washington, D.C., 1955.

GARNIER-PAGES, L. *Histoire de la Révolution de 1848*. Paris, 1860–71.

GRANT, E. M. *Victor Hugo during the Second Republic*. Northampton, 1935.

GUILLEMIN, H. *Lamartine en 1848*. Paris, 1948.

— *Le Tragédie de Quarante-Huit*. Geneva, 1948.

IBOS, P. E. M. *Le Général Cavaignac, un Dictateur Républicain*. Paris, 1930.

KELLER, P. *Louis Blanc und die Revolution von 1848*. Zürich, 1926.

LAGORCE, P. F. G. de. *Histoire de la Seconde République Française*. Paris, 1925.

LAMARTINE, A. M. L. de. *History of the French Revolution of 1848*. Trans. London, 1875.

LUNA, F. de. *The French Republic under Cavaignac, 1848*. Princeton, 1969.

MARRIOT, J. A. R. *The French Revolution of 1848 in its Economic Aspect*. (2 vol.) Oxford, 1913.

MARX, K. *The Class Struggles in France, 1848–1850*. New York, 1852.

— *The Eighteenth Brumaire of Louis Bonaparte*. New York, 1935.

MCKAY, D. M. *The National Workshops*. Cambridge, Massachusetts, 1948.

MOULIN, C. *1848, le Livre du Centenaire*. Paris, 1948.

NORMANBY, C. H. D. *A Year of Revolution, from a Journal kept in Paris in 1848*. London, 1857.

PROUDHON, P. J. *Les Confessions d'un Révolutionnaire*. Paris, 1851.

SAND, G. *Souvenirs de 1848*. Paris, 1882.

SCHMIDT, C. *Les Journées de Juin 1848*. Paris, 1926.

STERN, D. *Histoire de la Révolution de 1848*. Paris, 1862.

WASSERMANN, S. *Les Clubs de Barbes et de Blanqui en 1848*. Paris, 1913.

(ii) *Articles*

AMANN, P. 'Huber Enigma: Revolutionary or Police-Spy'. *Int. Review of Social History*, 12, (1967), no. 2, pp. 190–203.

— 'Changing Outlines of 1848'. *American Historical Review*, 68, (July, 1963), pp. 938–53.

BENOIST, C. 'L'Homme de 1848'. *Revue des Deux Mondes*, 1913.
FISHMAN, W. J. 'Louis Auguste Blanqui; Stormbird of Revolution', *History Today*, 14, (June, 1964), pp. 408–17.
KLEIN, R. J. 'Baudelaire and Revolution: Some Notes', *Yale French Studies*, no. 39, (1967), pp. 85–97.
MONIN, G. 'George Sand et la République de Février, 1848'. *Révolution Française*, Vol. 37, (1899).
ZELDIN, T. 'Government Policy in the French General Election of 1849'. *English Historical Review*, 74, (April, 1959), pp. 240–48.

III—GERMANY (INCL. SCHLESWIG-HOLSTEIN)

(a) *General*

Books
BAILLEU, P. & SCHUSTER, G. ed. *Aus dem literarischen Nachlass der Kaiserin Augusta*, I, Berlin, 1912.
BAMBERGER, L. *Gesammelte Schriften*. (5 vol.). Berlin, 1897–8.
— *Erinnerungen*. ed. P. Nathan, Berlin, 1899.
BAUER, B. *Vollständige Geschichte der Partheikämpfe in Deutschland der Jahre 1842–1846*. (3 vol.). Charlottenburg, 1847.
BERGSTRÄSSER, L. *Geschichte der politischen Parteien in Deutschland*. Munich, 1955.
BERLIN, I. *Karl Marx*. New York, 1939.
BISMARCK, O. von. *Gedanken und Erinnerungen*, I. Stuttgart, 1915.
BORN, S. ed. *Erinnerungen von J. Temme*. Leipzig, 1893.
BRANDES, G. *Young Germany*. London, 1903.
CARR, W. *A History of Germany, 1815–1945*. London, 1969.
— *Schleswig-Holstein 1815–1848: A Study in National Conflict*. Manchester, 1963.
EYCK, E. *Bismarck*. (3 vol.). Zürich, 1941–44.
— *Bismarck and the German Empire*, London, 1950.
FLENLEY, R. *Modern German History*. London, 1953.
FONTANE, T. *Von Zwanzig bis Dreissig*. Berlin, 1925.
FREDERICK WILLIAM IV. *Leben und Wirken Sr. Majestät Friedrich Wilhelm des Vierten, Königes von Preussen*, I. Leipzig, 1855.
FREDERICK III. German Emperor. *Tagebücher von 1848–1866, Mit einer Einleitung und Ergänzungen*. ed. H. O. Meisner, Leipzig, 1929.
FRÖBEL, J. *Ein Lebenslauf*. (2 vol.). Stuttgart, 1890–1.
GERLACH, L. von. *Denkwürdigkeiten aus dem Leben Leopold von Gerlachs*, I. Berlin, 1891.
GEBHARDT, B. *Handbuch der deutschen Geschichte*, Vol. III. Stuttgart, 1959.
HAMEROW, T. S. *Restoration, Revolution, Reaction: Economics and Politics in Restoration Germany, 1815–1871*. Princeton, 1958.
HANSEN, J. *Gustav von Mevissen*. (2 vol.). Berlin, 1906.
HAWGOOD, J. A. *The Evolution of Modern Germany*. London, 1953.

HENDERSON, W. O. *The Zollverein*. London, 1939.

HOOK, S. *From Hegel to Marx*. New York, 1935.

HUBER, E. R. *Deutsche Verfassungsgeschichte seit 1789*, Vol. II. Stuttgart, 1960.

— *Dokumente zur deutschen Verfassungsgeschichte*, Vol. I. Stuttgart, 1961.

KLÖTZER, W. ed. *Clotilde Koch-Gontard an ihre Freunde; Briefe und Erinnerungen aus der Zeit der deutschen Einheitsbewegung 1843–1869*. Frankfurt-on-Main, 1969.

KRIEGER, L. *The German Idea of Freedom, History of a Political Tradition*. Boston, 1957.

LEGGE, J. G. *Rhyme and Revolution in Germany: A Study in German History, Life, Literature and Character, 1813–50*. London, 1918.

MANN, G. *The History of Germany since 1789*. Trans. London, 1968.

MARCUSE, H. *Reason and Revolution: Hegel and the Rise of Social Theory*. New York, 1941.

MEINECKE, F. *Weltbürgertum und Nationalstaat. Studien zur Genesis des Deutschen Nationalstaates*. Munich, 1908.

MOMMSEN, W. *Deutsche Parteiprogramme*. Munich, 1960.

PAGENSTECHER, C. H. *Lebenserinnerungen*. (3 vol.). Leipzig, 1913.

PASSANT, E. J. *A Short History of Germany, 1815–1945*. Cambridge, 1959.

PFLANZE, O. *Bismarck and the Development of Germany*, Vol. I. Princeton, New Jersey, 1963.

PINSON, K. S. & EPSTEIN, K. *Modern Germany: Its History and Civilization*. New York, 1966.

PROSS, H. ed. *Dokumente zur deutschen Politik, 1806–1870*. Frankfurt, 1963.

RAMM, A. *Germany, 1789–1919*. London, 1967.

ROHR, D. G. *The Origins of Social Liberalism in Germany*. Chicago, 1964.

SCHNABEL, F. *Deutsche Geschichte im Neunzehnten Jahrhundert*. (4 vol). Freiburg-im-Breisgau, 1948–51.

SRBIK, H. RITTER von. *Deutsche Einheit. Idee und Wirklichkeit vom Heiligen Reich bis Königgrätz*. (4 vol.). Munich, 1935–42.

STEEFEL, L. D. *The Schleswig-Holstein Question*. Cambridge, U.S.A., 1932.

THOMAS, R. *Liberalism, Nationalism, and the German Intellectuals, 1822–47*. Cambridge, 1951.

TREITSCHKE, H. von. *German History in the Nineteenth Century*. (7 vol.). Trans. London, 1915–19.

VITZTHUM VON ECKSTÄDT, E. K. *Berlin und Wien in den Jahren 1845–1852*. Stuttgart, 1886.

WENTZCKE, P. & KLÖTZER, W. *Der Deutsche Liberalismus im Vormärz: Heinrich von Gagern, Briefe und Reden, 1815–1848*. Göttingen, 1959.

WOLFF, W. *Das Elend und der Aufruhr in Schlesien*. 1844, reprinted in Berlin, 1909.

(ii) *Articles*

KOBYLINSKI, H. 'Die französische Revolution als Problem in Deutschland, 1840–48', *Historische Studien.* Heft 237, 1933.

(b) *Revolutions of 1848–49*

(i) *Books*

BASSERMANN, F. D. *Denkwürdigkeiten.* Frankfurt-on-Main, 1926.

BECKER, B. *Die Reaction in Deutschland gegen die Revolution von 1848.* Vienna, 1869.

BIEDERMANN, K. *Erinnerungen aus der Paulskirche.* Leipzig, 1849.

BLUM, H. *Die deutsche Revolution, 1848–1849.* Leipzig, 1897.

BORN, S. *Erinnerungen eines Achtundvierzigers.* Leipzig, 1898.

BRANDENBURG, E. *Die deutsche Revolution 1848.* Leipzig, 1919.

BUSCH, W. *Die Berliner Märztage von 1848.* Munich, 1899.

DAHLINGER, C. W. *The German Revolution of 1849.* New York, 1903.

DROZ, J. *Les Révolutions allemandes de 1848.* Paris, 1957.

ENGELS, F. *Germany: Revolution and Counter-Revolution.* New York, 1933.

EYCK, F. *The Frankfurt Parliament, 1848–49.* London, 1968.

FREDERICK WILLIAM IV. *Briefwechsel zwischen König Friedrich Wilhelm IV und dem Reichsverweser Erzherzog Johann von Österreich.* ed. G. Küntzel. Frankfurt, 1924.

— *Briefwechsel mit L. Camphausen (1848–1850).* ed E. Brandenburg. Berlin, 1906.

FREYTAG, G. *Karl Mathy: Geschichte seines Lebens.* Leipzig, 1870.

Gegenwart, Die. Eine encyklopädische Darstellung der neuesten Zeitgeschichte für all Stände, I et seq. Leipzig: F. A. Brockhaus, 1848 ff.

GNEIST, R. *Berlinder Zustände: Skizzen aus der Zeit vom 18. März 1848 bis 18. März 1849.* Berlin, 1849.

HAENCHEN, K. ed. *Revolutionsbriefe 1848. Ungedrucktes aus dem Nachlass von König Friedrich Wilhelm IV von Preussen.* Leipzig, 1930.

HAYM, R. *Die deutsche Nationalversammlung . . . Ein Bericht aus der Partei des rechten Centrum.* (3 vol.). Frankfurt-on-Main, 1848–50.

— *Reden und Redner des ersten Preussischen Vereinigten Landtags.* Berlin, 1847.

HEUSS, T. *1848, Werk und Erbe.* Stuttgart, 1948.

HJELHOLT, H. *British Mediation in the Danish–German Conflict 1848–1850.* Copenhagen, 1965.

HÜBNER, R. ed *Aktenstücke und Aufzeichnungen zur Geschichte der Frankfurter Nationalversammlung aus dem Nachlass von J. G. Droysen.* Stuttgart, 1924.

HOCK, W. *Liberales Denken im Zeitalter der Paulskirche, Droysen und die Frankfurter Mitte.* Münster, 1957.

HOHLFELD, J. *Die deutsche Revolution 1848–49.* Leipzig, 1948.

JUCHO, F. ed. *Verhandlungen des deutschen Parlaments.* Officielle Ausgabe. Frankfurt-on-Main, 1848.

JÜRGENS, K. *Zur Geschichte des deutschen Verfassungswerkes 1848-49.* (3 vol.). Brunswick, 1850, and Hanover, 1857.

KLEIN, T. ed. *1848, der Vorkampf deutscher Einheit und Freiheit.* Leipzig, 1914.

LÜDERS, G. *Die demokratische Bewegung in Berlin im October 1848.*

LUDERS, G. *Die demokratische Bewegung in Berlin im October 1848.* Berlin, 1909.

MEINECKE, F. *Radowitz und die deutsche Revolution.* Berlin, 1913.

MOMMSEN, W. *Grösse und Versagen des deutschen Bürgertums.* Stuttgart, 1949.

NOYES, P. H. *Organization and Revolution: Working-class Associations in the German Revolution of 1848-49.* Princeton, 1966.

PAUR, T. *Briefe aus der Paulskirche.* Mitteilungen aus dem Literatur-Archive in Berlin, Neue Folge 16, 1919.

QUARK, M. *Die erste deutsche Arbeiterbewegung: Geschichte der Arbeiter-verbrüderung 1848-49.* Leipzig, 1924.

RADOWITZ, J. M. von. *Nachgelassene Briefe und Aufzeichnungen zur Geschichte der Jahre 1848-1853.* ed. Walter Möring. Stuttgart, 1922.

— *Deutschland und Friedrich Wilhelm IV.* Hamburg, 1848.

REPGEN, K. *Märzbewegung und Maiwahlen . . . 1848 im Rheinland.* Bonn, 1955.

ROTH, P. & MERCK, H. *Quellensammlung zum deutschen öffentlichen Recht seit 1848.* Erlangen, 1850-52.

SCHILFERT, G. *Sieg und Niederlage des demokratischen Wahlrechts in der deutschen Revolution, 1848-49.* Berlin, 1952.

SCHURZ, C. *The Reminiscences of Carl Schurz.* New York, 1906.

SPRINGER, R. *Berlins Strassen, Kneipen und Klubs im Jahre 1848.* Berlin, 1850.

STADELMANN, R. *Soziale und Politische Geschichte der Revolution von 1848.* Munich, 1948.

STRUVE, G. *Geschichte der drei Volkserhebungen in Baden.* Bern, 1849.

UNRUH, H. V. von. *Erinnerungen,* ed. H. V. Poschinger, Berlin, 1895.

VALENTIN, V. *Geschichte der deutschen Revolution 1848-49.* (2 vol.). Berlin, 1930-31.

WIGARD, F. ed. *Stenographischer Bericht über die Verhandlungen der deutschen constituirenden Nationalversammlung.* (9 vol.). Frankfurt-on-Main, 1848-49.

WICHMANN, W. *Denkwürdigkeiten aus der Paulskirche.* Hanover, 1888.

ZIMMERMANN, W. *Die Deutsche Revolution.* Karlsruhe, 1851.

(ii) *Articles*

COUPE, W. A. 'German Cartoons and the Revolution of 1848'. *Comparative Studies in Society and History,* 9, (January, 1967), pp. 137-67.

HAMEROW, J. S. 'The Elections to the Frankfurt Parliament'. *Journal of Modern History,* 33, (March, 1961), pp. 15-32.

O'BOYLE, L. 'The Democratic Left in Germany, 1848'. *Journal of Modern History,* 33, (December, 1961), pp. 374-383.

WEBER, F. G. 'Palmerston and Prussian Liberalism, 1848'. *Journal of Modern History*, 35, (June, 1963), pp. 125–136.

IV—ITALY

(a) *General*

ALBRECHT-CARRIÉ, R. *Italy from Napoleon to Mussolini*. New York, 1950.
D'AZEGLIO, M. *L'Italie de 1847 à 1865: Correspondence Politique*. Paris, 1867.
BERKELEY, G. F. H. *Italy in the Making*. (3 vol.). New York, 1932–40.
FARINA, G. La, *Storia d'Italia dal 1815 al 1850*. (6 vol.). Turin, 1850–51.
FARINI, L. C. *The Roman State from 1815 to 1850*. (4 vol.). Trans. by W. E. Gladstone. London, 1851–54.
GARIBALDI, G. *Autobiography*. (3 vol.). London, 1889.
KING, B. *A History of Italian Unity*. (2 vol.). London, 1899.
— *The Life of Mazzini*. New York, 1929.
MACK SMITH, D. *Garibaldi: a Great Life in Brief*. New York, 1956.
— *Modern Sicily after 1713*. London, 1968.
— ed. *The Making of Italy, 1796–1870*. New York, 1968.
MARTINENGO-CESARESCO, E. *The Liberation of Italy 1815–1870*. London, 1920.
MAZZINI, G. *Life and Writings of Guiseppe Mazzini*. (6 vol). London, 1864–1870.
RICHARDS, E. F. *Mazzini's Letters to an English Family, 1844–1854*. London, 1920.
SILONE, I. *Mazzini*. New York, 1939.
THAYER, W. R. *Dawn of Italian Independence*. (2 vol.). Boston, 1892.
VIDAL, C. *Charles-Albert et le risorgimento italien*. Paris, 1927.
WICKS, M. C. *The Italian Exiles in London, 1816–1848*. Manchester, 1937.
WHYTE, A. J. B. *The Early Life and Letters of Cavour, 1810–1848*. Oxford, 1925.
— *The Political Life and Letters of Cavour, 1848–1861*. London, 1930.
— *The Evolution of Modern Italy*. London, 1944.

(b) *Revolutions of 1848–49*

(i) *Books*

D'AZEGLIO, M. *Austrian Assassinations in Lombardy*. London, 1848.
BELLUZZI, R. *La Retirata di Garibaldi da Roma nel 1849*. Rome, 1899.
CATTANEO, C. *L'Insurrection de Milan en 1848*. Paris, 1848.
CIASCA, R. *L'origine del 'Programma per l'opinione nazionale italiana' del 1847–1848*. Milan, 1916.
DANDOLO, E. *The Italian Volunteers and the Lombard Rifle Brigade*. London, 1851.
DEMARCO, D. *Una rivoluzione sociale: la repubblica romana del 1849*. Naples, 1944.

FARINA, G. La. *Istoria documentata della rivoluzione siciliana 1848–49*. (2 vol.). Turin, 1860–61.

FERRARI, A. *L'Italia durante la rivoluzione 1848–1849*. Rome, 1935.

FERRERO, G. M. *Journal d'un officier de la Brigade de la Savoie sur la Campagne de Lombardie*. Turin, 1848.

Il Primo passo verso l'unita d'Italia 1848–1849. Rome, 1948.

JOHNSTON, R. M. *The Roman Theocracy and the Republic 1846–1849*. London, 1901.

LAFORGE, A. de *Histoire de la république de Venise sous Manin*. (2 vol.). Paris, 1853.

MANIN, D. *Documents et pièces authentiques laissés par Daniel Manin*. ed. F. Planat de la Faye. (2 vol.). Paris, 1860.

MARCHETTI, L. *Il governo provisorio della Lombardia*. Milan, 1948.

OTT, W. M. *Military Events in Italy 1848–1849*. Trans. by Lord Ellesmere. London, 1851.

PRATO, G. *Fatti e dottrine alle vigilia del 1848*. Turin, 1921.

SPADA, G. *Storia della rivoluzione di Roma*. (3 vol.). Florence, 1868–69.

TAYLOR, A. J. P. *The Italian Problem in European Diplomacy, 1847–1849*. Manchester, 1934.

TREVELYAN, G. M. *Manin and the Venetian Revolution of 1848*. London, 1923.

— *Garibaldi's Defence of the Roman Republic*. London, 1907.

(ii) *Articles*

SMITH, H. M. 'Piedmont and Prussia: the Influence of the Campaigns of 1848–1849 on the Constitutional Development of Italy'. *American Historical Review*, 55, (April, 1950), pp. 479–502.

V—HABSBURG EMPIRE (ALSO SLAV QUESTION)

(a) *Empire* (except dealing specifically with Bohemia–Moravia and Hungary)

(i) *Books*

AUERBACH, B. *A Narrative of Events in Vienna from Latour to Windischgrätz*. Trans. London, 1849.

BIBL, V. *Metternich, der Dämon Österreichs*. Leipzig, 1936.

— *Die Niederösterreichischen Stände im Vormärz*. Vienna, 1911.

BLUM, J. *Noble Landowners and Agriculture in Austria 1815–1848*. Baltimore, 1948.

BURIAN, P. *Die Nationalitäten in 'Cisleithanien' und das Wahlrecht der Märzrevolution 1848–49*. Graz, 1962.

CHARMATZ, R. *Österreichische innere Geschichte von 1848 bis 1895*. (3 vol.). Leipzig. 1918.

ENDRES, R. *Revolution in Österreich 1848*. Vienna, 1947.

FISCHEL, A. ed. *Materialien zur Sprachenfrage in Österreich*. Brünn, 1902.

FISCHER, E. *Österreich 1848. Probleme der demokratischen Revolution in Österreich*. Vienna, 1946.

FRIEDJUNG, H. *Österreich von 1848 bis 1860.* (2 vol.). Stuttgart, 1908–12.

FÜSTER, A. *Memorien vom März 1848 bis Juli, 1849.* (2 vol.). Frankfurt, 1850.

GEIST-LANYI, P. *Das Nationalitätenproblem auf dem Reichstag zu Kremsier 1848–49.* Munich, 1920.

GOLDMARK, J. *Pilgrims of '48: One Man's Part in the Austrian Revolution of 1848 and a Family Migration to America.* New Haven, 1930.

HANTSCH, H. *Geschichte Österreichs,* Vol. II: *1648–1918.* Graz, 1953.

HARTIG, Graf F. von. *Genesis: or Details of the Late Austrian Revolution, by an Officer of State.* London, 1853.

HELFERT, J. A. von. *Aufzeichnungen und Erinnerungen aus jungen Jahren: im Wiener konstituierenden Reichstag Juli bis Oktober 1848.* Vienna, 1904.

— *Die Wiener Journalistik im Jahre 1848.* Vienna, 1928.

HELLER, E. *Mitteleuropas Vorkämpfer Fürst Felix zu Schwarzenberg.* Vienna, 1933.

JELAVICH, C. & JELAVICH, B. *The Habsburg Monarchy: Toward a Multinational Empire or National States.* New York, 1959.

KANN, R. A. *The Habsburg Monarchy, A Study in Integration and Disintegration.* New York, 1957.

— *The Multinational Empire: Nationalism and National Reform in the Habsburg Monarchy 1848–1918.* (2 vol.). New York, 1950.

KISZLING, R. *Die Revolution im Kaisertum Österreich, 1848–49* (2 vol.). Vienna, 1948.

KOHN, H. *The Habsburg Empire, 1804–1918.* Princeton, 1961.

LADES, H. *Die Nationalitätenfrage im Karpatenraum 1848/49.* Vienna, 1941.

METTERNICH-WINNEBURG, C. W. N. L. *Fürst von. Mémoires, Documents et Ecrits divers.* ed. R. von Metternich. Paris, 1880–84.

MÜLLER, P. *Feldmarschall Fürst Windischgrätz: Revolution und Gegenrevolution in Österreich.* Vienna, 1934.

NOVOTNY, A. *1848, Österreichs Ringen um Freiheit und Völkerfrieden vor hundert Jahren.* Graz, 1948.

PILLERSDORF, Baron F. von. *Austria in 1848 and 1849.* London, 1850.

RATH, R. J. *The Viennese Revolution of 1848.* Austin, Texas, 1957.

REDLICH, J. *Emperor Francis Joseph of Austria.* Trans. New York, 1929.

RESCHAUER, H. & SMETS, M. *Das Jahr 1848: Geschichte der Wiener Revolution.* (2 vol.). Vienna, 1872.

SCHWARZENBERG, A. *Prince Felix zu Schwarzenberg, Prime Minister of Austria 1848–1852.* New York, 1946.

SPRINGER, A. *Geschichte Österreichs,* Vol. II. Leipzig, 1865.

SRBIK, H. Ritter von. *Metternich, der Staatsmann und der Mensch.* (3 vol.). Munich, 1925–54.

STILES, W. H. *Austria in 1848–49.* (2 vol.). New York, 1852.

TAYLOR, A. J. P. *The Habsburg Monarchy, 1809–1918.* London, 1948.

UHLIRZ, K. *Handbuch der Geschichte Österreich-Ungarns.* Graz, 1963.

ZENKER, E. V. *Die Wiener Revolution 1848 in ihren sozialen Voraussetzungen und Beziehungen.* Vienna, 1897.

196 THE REVOLUTIONS OF 1848–49

(ii) *Articles*

EDWARDS, J. 'Vienna'. *History Today*, 10, (October, 1960), pp. 668–77.

HAFNER, S. 'Das austro-slawische Konzept in der ersten Hälfte des 19. Jahrhunderts'. *Österreichische Osthefte*. Vienna, (1963), pp. 435–44.

LUTZ, R. Jr. 'Fathers and Sons in the Vienna Revolution'. *Journal of Central European Affairs*, 22, (July, 1962), pp. 161–73.

MOLISCH, P. 'Die Wiener Akademische Legion und ihr Anteil an den Verfassungskämpfen des Jahres 1848'. *Archiv für österreichische Geschichte*, (1924).

SCHROEDER, P. 'Metternich Studies since 1825'. *Journal of Modern History*, (September, 1961), pp. 237–260.

(b) *Bohemia and Moravia (including the Slav Question)*

(i) *Books*

BRAUNER, F. A. *Von der Robot und deren Ablösung*. Prague, 1848.

ERNST, W. *Gefängniserlebnisse von Prager Studenten 1848–54*. Vienna, 1913.

KOPP, F. *Die Ereignisse der Pfingstwoche des Jahres 1848 in Prag und in dessen nächster Umgebung*. Prague, 1848.

KOHN, H. *Pan-Slavism: Its History and Ideology*, 2nd ed. New York, 1960.

PALACKÝ, F. ed. *Gedenkblätter*. Prague, 1874.

PECH, S. Z. *The Czech Revolution of 1848*. North Carolina, 1969.

SCHOPF, F. J. ed. *Wahre und ausführliche Darstellung der am 11. März 1848 . . . in Prag begonnenn Volks-Bewegung*. Leitmeritz, 1848.

SETON-WATSON, R. W. *A History of the Czechs and Slovaks*. London, 1943.

SIEBER, E. K. *Ludwig von Löhner: Ein Vorkämpfer des Deutschtums in Böhmen, Mähren, und Schlesien . . . 1848–49*. Munich, 1965.

UDALZOW, I. I. *Aufzeichnungen über die Geschichte des nationalen und politischen Kampfes in Böhmen im Jahre 1848*. Trans. from Russian. Berlin, 1953.

WERNER, A. *Die Studenten-Legionen der Prager Universität vom 30 jährigen Krieg bis 1848*. Prague, 1934.

(ii) *Articles*

BATOWSKIE, H. 'The Poles and Their Fellow Slavs, 1848–49'. *Slavonic and East European Review*, XXVII, (1948–49), pp. 404–13.

BENEŠ, V. L. 'Bakunin and Palacký's Concept of Austroslavism'. *Indiana Slavic Studies*, II, (1958), pp. 79–111.

BOHMANN, A. 'Bevölkerungsbewegungen in Böhmen bis zur Mitte des 19. Jahrhunderts'. *Zeitschrift für Ostforschung*, XIV, (1965), pp. 249–65.

KLÍMA, A. 'Ein Beitrag zur Agrarfrage in der Revolution von 1848 in Böhmen'. *Studien zur Geschichte der österreich-ungarischen Monarchie*, Budapest, (1961), pp. 15–26.

KOŘALKA, J. 'Das Nationalitätenproblem in den böhmischen Ländern 1848–1918'. *Österreichische Osthefte*, V, (1963), pp. 1–12.

MENCIK, F. 'Ein Prager Polizist über die Junitage 1848'. *Mitteilungen des Vereins für Geschichte der Deutschen in Böhmen*, LIV, (1916), pp. 320–45.

NOVOTNÝ, M. 'Die Opfer der Prager Pfingsten'. *Vierteljahrschrift für die praktische Heilkunde*, IV, (1848), pp. 141–54.

ODLOŽILÍK, O. 'The Slavic Congress of 1848'. *Polish Review*, IV, (1959), pp. 3–15.

PECH, S. Z. 'The June Uprising in Prague in 1848'. *The East European Quarterly*, I, (June, 1968), pp. 341–70.

WARD, D. 'Windischgrätz and the Bohemian Revolt, 1848'. *History Today*, 19, (September, 1969), pp. 625–33.

(c) *Kingdom of Hungary*

(i) *Books*

GÖRGEI, A. *My Life and Acts in Hungary in the Years 1848–49.* (2 vol.). London, 1852.

HEADLEY, P. C. *The Life of Kossuth.* Auburn, 1852.

HORVATH, M. *Geschichte des Unabhängigkeitskrieges 1848–1849* (3 vol.). Budapest.

IRANYI, D. & CHASSIN, C. L. *Histoire politique de la révolution de Hongroie 1847–1849.* Paris, 1859.

KERCHNAWE, H. *Feldmarschall Fürst Windischgrätz und die Russenhilfe 1848.* Innsbruck, 1930.

KLAPKA, G. *Memoirs of the War of Independence.* London, 1850.

KMETY, G. *A Refutation of some of the Principal Misstatements in Görgei's 'Life and Actions in Hungary in the Years 1848–1849'.* London, n.d.

KOSARY, D. G. *History of Hungary.* Cleveland, 1941.

KOSSUTH, L. *Die Katastrophe in Ungarn.* Leipzig, 1849.

MACARTNEY, C. A. *Hungary, a Short History.* Edinburgh, 1962.

PULSZKY, F. *Meine Zeit, mein Leben.* Pressburg, 1881.

SCHLESINGER, M. *The War in Hungary, 1848–1849.* Trans. London, 1851.

SCHÜTTE, A. *Ungarn und der ungarische Unabängikeitskrieg.* (2 vol.). Dresden, 1850.

SINOR, S. *History of Hungary.* New York, 1959.

SPROXTON, C. *Palmerston and the Hungarian Revolution.* Cambridge, 1930.

SZEMERE, B. *Hungary from 1848–1860.* London, 1860.

TELEKI, L. *De l'Intervention russe.* Paris, 1849.

WALTER, F. *Magyarische Rebellenbriefe 1848.* Munich, 1964.

WIESNER, A. C. *Ungarns Fall und Görgeys Verrath.* Zürich, 1849.

ZAREK, O. *Kossuth.* Trans. London, 1932.

(ii) *Articles*

GORDON, M. 'Louis Kossuth'. *Contemporary Review*, 182, (September, 1952), pp. 175–78.

JANOSSY, D. V. 'Die russische Intervention in Ungarn im Jahre 1849'. *Jahrbuch des Wiener ungarischen historischen Institutes*, Budapest, 1931.

SZILASSY, S. 'America and the Hungarian Revolution of 1848–49'. *Slavonic and East European Review*, 44, (January, 1966), pp. 180–96.

INDEX